quick
&
easy

quick
&
easy

Bath · New York · Singapore · Hong Kong · Cologne · Delhi · Melbourne

This edition published by Parragon in 2009

Parragon Publishing
Queen Street House
4 Queen Street
Bath BA1 1HE, UK

Copyright © Parragon Books Ltd 2009
Designed by Terry Jeavons & Company
Additional text written by Linda Doeser

ISBN 978-1-4075-4708-4

Printed in Indonesia

Notes for the Reader

This book uses both imperial, metric, and U.S. cup measurements. Follow the same units of measurement throughout; do not mix imperial and metric. All spoon measurements are level: teaspoons are assumed to be 5 ml, and tablespoons are assumed to be 15 ml. Unless otherwise stated, milk is assumed to be whole, eggs and individual vegetables are medium, and pepper is freshly ground black pepper.

The times given are an approximate guide only. Preparation times differ according to the techniques used by different people and the cooking times may also vary from those given. Optional ingredients, variations, or serving suggestions have not been included in the calculations.

Recipes using raw or very lightly cooked eggs should be avoided by infants, the elderly, pregnant women, convalescents, and anyone with a chronic condition. Pregnant and breastfeeding women are advised to avoid eating peanuts and peanut products. People with nut allergies should be aware that some of the ready-made ingredients used in the recipes in this book may contain nuts. Always check the packaging before use.

contents

introduction 6

soups, salads & snacks 12

chicken 130

meat 248

fish & seafood 366

vegetarian 484

sweet treats 602

index 716

introduction

With the ever-increasing pace of modern life, finding time to feed the family without relying too heavily on takeout or convenience foods can be a daily struggle. But help is at hand in this mouthwatering collection of quick and easy recipes, guaranteed to provide you with inspiration for every meal and occasion. With step-by-step instructions, they are certainly easy to follow and, although they are inspired by delicious dishes from around the world, the ingredients are widely available. All of them can be prepared and cooked within an hour and many take far less time, some only minutes.

Some ingredients are the ideal choice for the busy cook—pasta, noodles, fish fillets, diced chicken breasts, and steaks, for example, require little preparation and cook very rapidly. You may need to spend more time preparing others but this is often counterbalanced by the speed with which they can then be

cooked. Some cooking techniques are also particularly rapid—stir-frying could legitimately be called the original fast food and both pan-frying and broiling are quick cooking methods.

There is no doubt that fresh ingredients have the most flavor, the best texture, and high nutritional levels. However, there are shortcuts that will make cooking easier and quicker without detracting from the quality of the finished dish. In this book, any recipes that include a tomato sauce, for example, will almost always suggest using canned chopped tomatoes. Peeling and chopping fresh tomatoes isn't difficult but it's not really worth the effort, especially if they have been picked before they are fully ripe and are neither sweet nor colorful. Similarly, there is no great virtue in soaking dried beans and then boiling them for hours when you can simply open a can, drain and rinse the beans, and add them straight to the dish you are preparing. Also, while homemade stock may be delicious, particularly for making soup, it does take lots of time to make. It is therefore perfectly acceptable to use bouillon cubes, bouillon powder, or store-bought fresh stock. Make sure to buy a high-quality brand for maximum flavor and check the sodium content on the label first because some brands are very salty.

All the recipes in this book clearly describe how the ingredients should be prepared—finely chopped, thickly sliced, diced into cubes, cut into strips, and so on—and it is a matter of personal choice whether you buy them already prepared or do the work yourself. Nowadays, most supermarkets stock a wide variety of prepared ingredients, such as chopped onions, diced carrots, and sliced mushrooms. These ingredients undoubtedly save time, but will usually be more expensive and it is worth remembering that the cut surfaces of vegetables quickly begin to lose some of their vitamins. However, there are some shortcuts you can take that aren't necessarily costly. For example, most home cooks are far from enthusiastic about scaling, cleaning, and filleting whole fish because this can be fussy work and time-consuming, so you may prefer to ask your fish supplier to do this for you.

Some of the recipes in this book involve marinating ingredients. This does admittedly take time, sometimes hours, but resist the temptation to skip this stage. Marinating adds flavor to all kinds of ingredients and also helps to tenderize meat. If you're well organized, you can mix the marinade and pour it over the chicken or meat the night before or in the morning, then cover the dish and let marinate in the refrigerator. Remember to remove it from the refrigerator about 30 minutes before you're ready to cook to bring it back to room temperature. However, do not leave fish to marinate in an acid mixture—one containing citrus juice, wine, or vinegar—for more than 1 hour, because, after this time, the delicate flesh reacts almost as if it has been cooked and the texture will change. In fact, 30 minutes marinating time is sufficient for most fish and shellfish and if, like most of us, you are not a well-organized cook, even meat and poultry will benefit from this brief time marinating.

Additional time may be required for cooling and chilling times, so always read the recipe in advance so you can factor this into your plans. You can try to speed up cooling by putting the dish in a cool place, but do not put hot food into the refrigerator because it will affect the thermostat and could cause other food to spoil.

soups, salads & snacks

Soup is undoubtedly one of the easiest dishes to cook at home. It is always welcome and comforting and does not involve hours of stirring, straining, and toiling over a hot stove. In fact, most recipes take no more than 30 minutes and are almost impossible to get wrong. Substantial soups are great for easy lunches when served with crusty bread, and more delicate broths make fantastic appetizers for both family suppers and for entertaining friends. For best results, make sure you use a good-quality stock, whether a store-bought fresh stock from the chiller cabinet or one mixed from bouillon cubes or powder.

Salads are wonderfully versatile and may be served as a light main course, a side dish, or an appetizer. They may be wholly vegetarian or feature meat, chicken, fish, or shellfish. The easiest and quickest salads to assemble are made from raw vegetables and fruit and may also contain other ingredients, such as nuts or cheese. A small amount of cooking is required for a number of familiar favorites, such as pasta and potato salads, and you will need to allow time for cooling. Of course, there are also time-saving salads designed to be served warm.

Homemade canapés, snacks, and dips add that special extra touch when you are entertaining. Although they look impressive and are much

tastier than their packaged equivalents, they require very little effort in the kitchen. Delightful hot snacks can be prepared in advance and cooked in minutes, while you can make dips and prepare vegetable crudités—store them in plastic bags in the refrigerator—well before the party begins.

vegetable & bean soup

ingredients

SERVES 4–6

8 oz/225 g fresh fava beans

2 tbsp olive oil

2 large garlic cloves, crushed

1 large onion, finely chopped

1 celery stalk, finely chopped

1 carrot, peeled and chopped

6 oz/175 g firm new potatoes,
    diced

3¾ cups vegetable stock

2 beefsteak tomatoes, peeled,
    seeded, and chopped

salt and pepper

1 large bunch of fresh basil,
    tied with kitchen string

7 oz/200 g zucchini, diced

7 oz/200 g green beans,
    trimmed and chopped

2 oz/55 g dried vermicelli,
    broken into pieces, or
    small pasta shapes

pesto sauce

3½ oz/100 g fresh basil leaves

2 large garlic cloves

1½ tbsp pine nuts

scant ¼ cup fruity extra virgin
    olive oil

½ cup finely grated Parmesan
    cheese

method

1 If the fava beans are very young and tender, they can be used as they are. If they are older, use a small, sharp knife to slit the gray skins, then "pop" out the green beans.

2 Heat the olive oil in a large, heavy-bottom pan over medium heat. Add the garlic, onion, celery, and carrot and sauté for 5–8 minutes, or until the onion is soft, but not brown.

3 Add the potatoes, stock, and tomatoes, and season to taste with salt and pepper. Bring the stock to a boil, skimming the surface if necessary, then add the basil. Reduce the heat and cover the pan. Let simmer for 15 minutes, or until the potatoes are tender.

4 Meanwhile, make the pesto sauce. Put the basil, garlic, and pine nuts in a food processor or blender and blend until a thick paste forms. Add the extra virgin olive oil and blend again. Transfer to a bowl and stir in the cheese, then cover and chill until required.

5 When the potatoes are tender, stir the fava beans, zucchini, green beans, and vermicelli into the soup and continue simmering for 10 minutes, or until the vegetables are tender and the pasta is cooked. Taste, and adjust the seasoning if necessary. Remove and discard the bunch of basil.

6 Ladle the soup into bowls and add a spoonful of pesto sauce to each bowl.

brown lentil & pasta soup

ingredients
SERVES 4

4 strips lean bacon, cut into
  small squares
1 onion, chopped
2 garlic cloves, crushed
2 celery stalks, chopped
1¾ oz/50 g farfalline or
  spaghetti, broken into
  small pieces
14 oz/400 g canned brown
  lentils, drained
5 cups hot vegetable stock
2 tbsp chopped fresh mint
fresh mint sprigs, to garnish

method

1 Place the bacon in a large skillet together with the onion, garlic, and celery. Dry fry for 4–5 minutes, stirring, until the onion is tender and the bacon is just beginning to brown.

2 Add the pasta to the skillet and cook, stirring, for 1 minute to coat the pasta in the fat.

3 Add the lentils and the stock, and bring to a boil. Reduce the heat and let simmer for 12–15 minutes, or until the pasta is tender but still firm to the bite.

4 Remove the skillet from the heat and stir in the chopped fresh mint. Transfer the soup to warmed soup bowls, garnish with fresh mint sprigs, and serve immediately.

watercress soup

ingredients

SERVES 4

2 bunches of watercress
(approx 7 oz/200 g),
thoroughly cleaned

3 tbsp butter

2 onions, chopped

8 oz/225 g potatoes, peeled
and roughly chopped

5 cups vegetable stock or
water

salt and pepper

whole nutmeg, for grating
(optional)

1/2 cup plain yogurt or, or sour
cream

method

1 Remove the leaves from the stalks of the watercress and keep on one side. Roughly chop the stalks.

2 Melt the butter in a large saucepan over medium heat, add the onions, and cook for 4–5 minutes, until soft. Do not brown.

3 Add the potatoes to the saucepan and mix well with the onion. Add the watercress stalks and the stock. Bring to a boil, then reduce the heat, cover, and simmer for 15–20 minutes, until the potato is soft.

4 Add the watercress leaves and stir in to heat through. Remove from the heat and use a handheld stick blender to process the soup until smooth. Alternatively, pour the soup into a blender, process until smooth, and return to the rinsed-out saucepan. Reheat and season with salt and pepper to taste, adding a good grating of nutmeg, if using.

5 Serve in warmed bowls with the yogurt spooned on top.

leek & potato soup

ingredients
SERVES 4

1/4 cup butter

1 onion, chopped

3 leeks, sliced

8 oz/225 g potatoes, peeled
    and cut into 3/4-inch/2-cm
    cubes

3 1/2 cups vegetable stock

salt and pepper

2/3 cup light cream (optional)

2 tbsp snipped fresh chives,
    to garnish

method

1 Melt the butter in a large saucepan over medium heat, add the prepared vegetables, and sauté gently for 2–3 minutes, until soft but not brown. Pour in the stock, bring to a boil, then reduce the heat and simmer, covered, for 15 minutes.

2 Remove from the heat and blend the soup in the saucepan using a handheld stick blender if you have one. Otherwise, pour into a blender, process until smooth, and return to the rinsed-out saucepan.

3 Reheat the soup, season with salt and pepper to taste, and serve in warmed bowls, swirled with the cream, if using, and garnished with chives.

potato & pesto soup

ingredients

SERVES 4

3 slices rindless, smoked, fatty
    bacon or pancetta

1 lb/450 g mealy potatoes

1 lb/450 g onions

2 tbsp butter

2½ cups chicken stock

2½ cups milk

3½ oz/100 g dried
    conchigliette

⅔ cup heavy cream

chopped fresh parsley

salt and pepper

garlic bread and Parmesan
    cheese shavings, to serve

pesto sauce

2 oz/55 g finely chopped fresh
    parsley

2 garlic cloves, crushed

½ cup pine nuts, crushed

2 tbsp chopped fresh basil
    leaves

½ cup freshly grated
    Parmesan cheese

white pepper

⅔ cup olive oil

method

1 To make the pesto sauce, put all of the ingredients in a blender or food processor and process for 2 minutes, or blend by hand using a pestle and mortar.

2 Finely chop the bacon, potatoes, and onions. Cook the bacon in a large pan over medium heat for 4 minutes. Add the butter, potatoes, and onions, and cook for 12 minutes, stirring constantly.

3 Add the stock and milk to the pan, bring to a boil, and simmer for 10 minutes. Add the conchigliette and simmer for an additional 10–12 minutes.

4 Blend in the cream and simmer for 5 minutes. Add the chopped parsley, salt and pepper to taste, and 2 tablespoons of the pesto sauce. Transfer the soup to individual serving bowls and serve with Parmesan cheese and fresh garlic bread.

fava bean & mint soup

ingredients

SERVES 4

2 tbsp olive oil

1 red onion, chopped

2 garlic cloves, crushed

2²/₃ cups diced potatoes

3 cups fava beans, thawed if
   frozen

3³/₄ cups vegetable stock

2 tbsp freshly chopped mint

plain yogurt and fresh mint
   sprigs, to garnish

method

1 Heat the olive oil in a large pan. Add the onion and garlic and sauté for 2–3 minutes, until softened. Add the potatoes and cook, stirring constantly, for 5 minutes.

2 Stir in the beans and the stock. Cover and simmer gently for 30 minutes, or until the beans and potatoes are tender.

3 Remove a few vegetables with a slotted spoon and set aside. Place the remainder of the soup in a food processor or blender and process to a smooth puree.

4 Return the soup to a clean pan and add the reserved vegetables and chopped mint. Stir thoroughly and heat through gently.

5 Ladle the soup into individual serving bowls. Garnish with swirls of plain yogurt and sprigs of fresh mint and serve immediately.

yogurt & tomato soup

ingredients

SERVES 4

4 large tomatoes

2 tbsp olive oil

1 onion, chopped roughly

1 garlic clove, chopped

1¼ cups vegetable stock

2 oil-packed sun-dried
    tomatoes, chopped

1 tsp chopped fresh thyme

½ tsp ground cinnamon

salt and pepper

1¼ cups strained plain yogurt

method

1 Coarsely grate the tomatoes into a bowl, discarding their skins left in your hand. Heat the oil in a saucepan, add the onion and garlic, and fry for 5 minutes, until softened. Add the tomatoes and cook gently for an additional 5 minutes.

2 Add the stock, sun-dried tomatoes, thyme, cinnamon, and salt and pepper, bring to a boil, then simmer for 10 minutes.

3 Allow the soup to cool slightly then process in a food processor, stick blender, or with a handheld blender. Add the yogurt and mix. Season with salt and pepper.

4 If serving hot, reheat the soup gently. (Do not boil or the soup will curdle.) If serving cold, cool and then chill in the refrigerator for 3–4 hours.

corn, potato & cheese soup

ingredients

SERVES 4

4 tbsp butter

2 shallots, finely chopped

8 oz/225 g potatoes, diced

4 tbsp all-purpose flour

2 tbsp dry white wine

1¼ cups milk

11½ oz/325 g canned corn
   kernels, drained

generous ¾ cup grated Swiss
   cheese or cheddar cheese

8–10 fresh sage leaves,
   chopped

generous 1¾ cups heavy
   cream

fresh sage sprigs, to garnish

croutons

2–3 slices of day-old white
   bread

2 tbsp olive oil

method

1 To make the croutons, cut the crusts off the bread slices, then cut the remaining bread into ¼-inch/5-mm squares. Heat the olive oil in a heavy-bottom skillet and add the bread cubes. Cook, tossing and stirring constantly, until evenly colored. Drain the croutons thoroughly on paper towels and reserve.

2 Melt the butter in a large, heavy-bottom pan. Add the shallots and cook over low heat, stirring occasionally, for 5 minutes, or until softened. Add the potatoes and cook, stirring, for 2 minutes.

3 Sprinkle in the flour and cook, stirring, for 1 minute. Remove the pan from the heat and stir in the white wine, then gradually stir in the milk. Return the pan to the heat and bring to a boil stirring constantly, then reduce the heat and simmer.

4 Stir in the corn kernels, cheese, chopped sage, and cream and heat through gently until the cheese has just melted. Ladle the soup into warmed bowls, scatter over the croutons, garnish with fresh sage sprigs, and serve.

vegetable & noodle soup

ingredients

SERVES 4

2 tbsp vegetable or peanut oil

1 onion, sliced

2 garlic cloves, chopped finely

1 large carrot, cut into thin
   sticks

1 zucchini, cut into thin sticks

4 oz/115 g broccoli, cut into
   florets

4 cups vegetable stock

$1^3/_4$ cups coconut milk

3–4 tbsp Thai soy sauce

2 tbsp Thai red curry paste

2 oz/55 g wide rice noodles

$^3/_4$ cup mung or soy bean
   sprouts

4 tbsp chopped fresh cilantro

method

1 Heat the oil in a wok or large skillet and stir-fry the onion and garlic for 2–3 minutes. Add the carrot, zucchini, and broccoli and stir-fry for 3–4 minutes, until just tender.

2 Pour in the stock and coconut milk and bring to a boil. Add the soy sauce, curry paste, and noodles, and let simmer for 2–3 minutes, until the noodles have swelled. Stir in the bean sprouts and cilantro and serve immediately.

hot-&-sour soup

ingredients

SERVES 4

6 dried shiitake mushrooms

4 oz/115 g rice vermicelli
  noodles

4 small fresh green chiles,
  seeded and chopped

6 tbsp rice wine vinegar

3½ cups vegetable stock

2 lemongrass stalks, snapped
  in half

4 oz/115 g canned water
  chestnuts, drained, rinsed,
  and halved

6 tbsp Thai soy sauce

juice of 1 lime

1 tbsp jaggery or light brown
  sugar

3 scallions, chopped,
  to garnish

method

1 Place the dried mushrooms in a bowl and pour in enough hot water to cover. Set aside to soak for 1 hour. Place the noodles in another bowl and pour in enough hot water to cover. Set aside to soak for 10 minutes. Combine the chiles and rice wine vinegar in a third bowl and set aside.

2 Drain the mushrooms and noodles. Bring the stock to a boil in a large pan. Add the mushrooms, noodles, lemongrass, water chestnuts, soy sauce, lime juice, and sugar, and bring to a boil.

3 Stir in the chile and vinegar mixture and cook for 1–2 minutes. Remove and discard the lemongrass. Ladle the soup into warmed bowls and serve hot, garnished with the scallions.

chicken & pasta broth

ingredients

SERVES 6

12 oz/350 g boneless chicken
   breasts

2 tbsp corn oil

1 onion, diced

2 cups carrots, diced

9 oz/250 g cauliflower florets

3½ cups chicken stock

2 tsp dried mixed herbs

4½ oz/125 g dried small pasta
   shapes

salt and pepper

freshly grated Parmesan
   cheese, for sprinkling
   (optional)

crusty bread, to serve

method

1 Using a sharp knife, finely dice the chicken, discarding any skin.

2 Heat the corn oil in a large pan and quickly cook the chicken, onion, carrots, and cauliflower until they are lightly colored.

3 Stir in the stock and dried mixed herbs and bring to a boil.

4 Add the pasta shapes to the pan and return to a boil. Cover the pan and let the broth simmer for 10 minutes, stirring occasionally to prevent the pasta from sticking together.

5 Season the broth with salt and pepper to taste and sprinkle with grated Parmesan cheese, if using. Serve with fresh crusty bread.

chicken & broccoli soup

ingredients
SERVES 4–6
8 oz/225 g head broccoli

salt and pepper

4 tbsp unsalted butter

1 onion, chopped

1$^1/_3$ cups basmati rice

8 oz/225 g skinless, boneless
   chicken breast, cut into
   thin slivers

$^1/_4$ cup all-purpose whole
   wheat flour

1$^1/_4$ cups milk

2 cups chicken stock

generous $^1/_3$ cup corn kernels

method
1 Break the broccoli into small florets and cook in a pan of lightly salted boiling water for 3 minutes, drain, then plunge into cold water and set aside.

2 Melt the butter in a pan over medium heat, add the onion, rice, and chicken, and cook for 5 minutes, stirring frequently.

3 Remove the pan from the heat and stir in the flour. Return to the heat and cook for 2 minutes, stirring constantly. Stir in the milk and then the stock. Bring to a boil, stirring constantly, then reduce the heat and let simmer for 10 minutes.

4 Drain the broccoli and add to the pan with the corn, salt, and pepper. Let simmer for 5 minutes, or until the rice is tender, then serve.

chicken & tarragon soup

ingredients
SERVES 4

4 tbsp unsalted butter
1 large onion, chopped
10$\frac{1}{2}$ oz/300 g cooked skinless
    chicken, shredded finely
2$\frac{1}{2}$ cups chicken stock
salt and pepper
1 tbsp chopped fresh tarragon
$\frac{2}{3}$ cup heavy cream
fresh tarragon leaves,
    to garnish
deep-fried croutons, to serve

method

1 Melt the butter in a large pan and fry the onion for 3 minutes.

2 Add the chicken to the pan with half of the chicken stock. Bring to a boil, then reduce the heat and let simmer for 20 minutes. Let cool, then process until smooth in a blender or food processor.

3 Add the remainder of the stock and season with salt and pepper.

4 Add the chopped tarragon, then transfer the soup to individual serving bowls and stir in the cream.

5 Garnish the soup with fresh tarragon and serve with deep-fried croutons.

spicy beef & noodle soup

ingredients

SERVES 4

4 cups beef stock

$2/3$ cup vegetable or peanut oil

3 oz/85 g rice vermicelli
     noodles

2 shallots, sliced thinly

2 garlic cloves, crushed

1-inch/2.5-cm piece fresh
     ginger, sliced thinly

8 oz/225 g beef tenderloin, cut
     into thin strips

2 tbsp Thai green curry paste

2 tbsp Thai soy sauce

1 tbsp fish sauce

chopped fresh cilantro,
     to garnish

method

1 Pour the stock into a large pan and bring to a boil. Meanwhile, heat the oil in a wok or large skillet. Add a third of the noodles and cook for 10–20 seconds, until they have puffed up. Lift out with tongs, drain on paper towels, and set aside. Discard all but 2 tablespoons of the oil.

2 Add the shallots, garlic, and ginger to the wok or skillet and stir-fry for 1 minute. Add the beef and curry paste and stir-fry for an additional 3–4 minutes, until tender.

3 Add the beef mixture, the uncooked noodles, soy sauce, and fish sauce to the pan of stock and let simmer for 2–3 minutes, until the noodles have swelled. Serve hot, garnished with the chopped cilantro and the reserved crispy noodles.

fishermen's soup

ingredients
SERVES 6

2 lb/900 g fillets of mixed
    whitefish and shellfish,
    such as cod, flounder,
    halibut, monkfish, sea
    bass, whiting, and peeled
    shrimp
2/3 cup olive oil
2 large onions, sliced
2 celery stalks, sliced thinly
2 garlic cloves, chopped
2/3 cup white wine
4 canned tomatoes, chopped
pared rind of 1 orange
1 tsp chopped fresh thyme
2 tbsp chopped fresh parsley
2 bay leaves
salt and pepper
lemon wedges, to serve
croutons, to garnish

method

1 Cut the fish into large chunks, discarding any skin. Heat the oil in a large saucepan, add the onion, celery, and garlic, and fry for 5 minutes, until softened.

2 Add the fish and shrimp to the saucepan, then add the wine, tomatoes, pared orange rind, thyme, parsley, bay leaves, salt and pepper, and enough cold water to cover. Bring to a boil, then simmer, uncovered, for 15 minutes.

3 Serve the soup hot, with lemon wedges, and garnished with croutons.

shrimp laksa

ingredients

SERVES 4

14 oz/400 g canned coconut
milk

1¼ cups vegetable stock

1¾ oz/50 g vermicelli rice
noodles

1 red bell pepper, seeded and
cut into strips

8 oz/225 g canned bamboo
shoots, drained and rinsed

2-inch/5-cm piece fresh
ginger, sliced thinly

3 scallions, chopped

1 tbsp Thai red curry paste

2 tbsp fish sauce

1 tsp jaggery or light brown
sugar

6 sprigs fresh Thai basil

12 cooked shrimp, in their
shells

method

1 Pour the coconut milk and stock into a pan and bring slowly to a boil. Add the remaining ingredients, except the shrimp, and let simmer gently for 4–5 minutes, until the noodles are cooked.

2 Add the shrimp and let simmer for an additional 1–2 minutes, until heated through. Ladle the soup into small, warmed bowls, dividing the shrimp equally among them, and serve.

corn & crab soup

ingredients

SERVES 4

2 tbsp vegetable or peanut oil

4 garlic cloves, chopped finely

5 shallots, chopped finely

2 lemongrass stalks, chopped
   finely

1-inch/2.5-cm piece fresh
   ginger, chopped finely

4 cups chicken stock

14 oz/400 g canned coconut
   milk

scant 1½ cups frozen corn
   kernels

12 oz/350 g canned crabmeat,
   drained and shredded

2 tbsp fish sauce

juice of 1 lime

1 tsp jaggery or light brown
   sugar

bunch of fresh cilantro,
   chopped, to garnish

method

1 Heat the oil in a large skillet and sauté the garlic, shallots, lemongrass, and ginger over low heat, stirring occasionally, for 2–3 minutes, until softened. Add the stock and coconut milk and bring to a boil. Add the corn, reduce the heat, and let simmer gently for 3–4 minutes.

2 Add the crabmeat, fish sauce, lime juice, and sugar, and let simmer gently for 1 minute. Ladle into warmed bowls, garnish with the chopped cilantro, and serve immediately.

quick clam chowder

ingredients

SERVES 4

2 tsp corn oil

4 oz/115 g rindless lean
    bacon, diced

2 tbsp butter

1 onion, chopped

2 celery stalks, chopped

2 potatoes, chopped

salt and pepper

2 leeks, sliced

14 oz/400 g canned chopped
    tomatoes

3 tbsp chopped fresh parsley

5 cups fish stock

1 lb 4 oz/550 g canned clams,
    drained and rinsed

method

1 Heat the oil in a heavy-bottom pan. Add the bacon and cook over medium heat, stirring, for 5 minutes, or until the fat runs and it begins to crisp. Remove from the pan, drain on paper towels, and reserve.

2 Add the butter to the pan and stir to melt. Add the onion, celery, and potatoes with a pinch of salt. Cover and cook over low heat, stirring occasionally, for 10 minutes, or until soft.

3 Stir in the leeks, the tomatoes and their juices, and 2 tablespoons of the parsley. Pour in the stock, bring to a boil, reduce the heat, and simmer for 10–15 minutes, or until the vegetables are tender. Season to taste with salt and pepper and stir in the clams. Heat the soup through gently for 2–3 minutes, then ladle into warmed bowls, garnish with the remaining parsley and reserved bacon, and serve.

green bean salad with feta cheese

ingredients

SERVES 4

12 oz/350 g green beans

1 red onion, chopped

3–4 tbsp chopped fresh
    cilantro

2 radishes, thinly sliced

2³/₄ oz/75 g feta cheese
    drained weight, crumbled

1 tsp chopped fresh oregano,
    plus extra leaves to garnish
    (optional), or ¹/₂ tsp dried

pepper

2 tbsp red wine or fruit vinegar

¹/₃ cup extra virgin olive oil

3 ripe tomatoes, cut into
    wedges

slices of crusty bread, to serve

method

1 Bring about 2 inches/5 cm of water to a boil in the bottom of a steamer. Add the beans to the top part of the steamer, cover, and steam for 5 minutes, or until just tender.

2 Place the beans in a large bowl and add the onion, cilantro, radishes, and feta cheese.

3 Sprinkle the oregano over the salad, then season to taste with pepper. Mix the vinegar and oil together in a small bowl and pour over the salad. Toss gently to mix well.

4 Transfer to a serving platter, surround with the tomato wedges, and serve immediately with slices of crusty bread.

charbroiled bell pepper salad

ingredients
SERVES 8

3 red bell peppers

3 yellow bell peppers

5 tbsp Spanish extra virgin
   olive oil

2 tbsp dry sherry vinegar or
   lemon juice

2 garlic cloves, crushed

pinch of sugar

salt and pepper

1 tbsp capers

8 small black Spanish olives

2 tbsp chopped fresh
   marjoram, plus extra sprigs
   to garnish

method

1 Preheat the broiler. Place the bell peppers on a wire rack or broiler pan and cook under the hot broiler for 10 minutes, until their skins have blackened and blistered, turning them frequently.

2 Remove the bell peppers from the heat, put them in a bowl, and immediately cover tightly with a clean, damp dish towel. Alternatively, you can put the bell peppers in a plastic bag. Let the peppers stand for about 15 minutes, until they are cool enough to handle.

3 Holding one bell pepper at a time over a clean bowl, use a sharp knife to make a small hole in the base and gently squeeze out the juices and reserve them. Still holding the bell pepper over the bowl, carefully peel off the blackened skin with your fingers or a knife and discard it. Cut the bell peppers in half and remove the stem, core, and seeds, then cut each bell pepper into neat thin strips. Arrange the bell pepper strips attractively on a serving dish.

4 To the reserved pepper juices add the olive oil, sherry vinegar, garlic, sugar, and salt and pepper to taste. Whisk together until combined. Drizzle the dressing evenly over the salad.

5 Sprinkle the capers, olives, and chopped marjoram over the salad, garnish with marjoram sprigs, and serve at room temperature.

avocado salad with lime dressing

ingredients

SERVES 4

2¼ oz/60 g mixed red and
    green lettuce leaves
2¼ oz/60 g wild arugula
4 scallions, finely diced
5 tomatoes, sliced
¼ cup walnuts, toasted and
    chopped
2 avocados
1 tbsp lemon juice

lime dressing

1 tbsp lime juice
1 tsp French mustard
1 tbsp sour cream
1 tbsp chopped fresh parsley
    or cilantro
3 tbsp extra virgin olive oil
pinch of sugar
salt and pepper

method

1 Wash and drain the lettuce and arugula, if necessary. Shred all the leaves and arrange in the bottom of a large salad bowl. Add the scallions, tomatoes, and walnuts.

2 Peel, pit, and thinly slice or dice the avocados. Brush with the lemon juice to prevent discoloration, then transfer to the salad bowl. Gently mix together.

3 To make the dressing, put all the dressing ingredients in a screw-top jar and shake well. Drizzle over the salad and serve immediately.

orange & fennel salad

ingredients

SERVES 4

4 large, juicy oranges

1 large fennel bulb, sliced very
    thinly

1 mild white onion, sliced
    finely

2 tbsp extra virgin olive oil

12 plump black olives, pitted
    and sliced thinly

1 fresh red chile, seeded and
    sliced very thinly (optional)

finely chopped fresh parsley

French bread, to serve

method

1 Finely grate the rind from the oranges into a bowl and aside. Using a small serrated knife, remove all the white pith from the oranges, working over a bowl to catch the juices. Cut the oranges horizontally into thin slices.

2 Toss the orange slices with the fennel and onion slices. Whisk the oil into the reserved orange juice, then spoon over the oranges. Sprinkle the olive slices over the top, add the chile, if using, then sprinkle with the orange rind and parsley. Serve with slices of French bread.

greek salad

ingredients
SERVES 4

4 tomatoes, cut into wedges

1 onion, sliced

1/2 cucumber, sliced

1 1/2 cups kalamata olives,
    pitted

8 oz/225 g feta cheese, cubed

2 tbsp fresh cilantro leaves

fresh flat-leaf parsley sprigs,
    to garnish

pita bread, to serve

dressing

5 tbsp extra virgin olive oil

2 tbsp white wine vinegar

1 tbsp lemon juice

1/2 tsp sugar

1 tbsp chopped fresh cilantro

salt and pepper

method

1 To make the dressing, put all the ingredients for the dressing into a large bowl and mix well together.

2 Add the tomatoes, onion, cucumber, olives, cheese, and cilantro. Toss all the ingredients together, then divide among individual serving bowls. Garnish with parsley sprigs and serve with pita bread.

herby potato salad

ingredients

SERVES 4

1 lb 2 oz/500 g new potatoes

salt and pepper

16 vine-ripened cherry
   tomatoes, halved

generous ¹/₂ cup black
   olives, pitted and coarsely
   chopped

4 scallions, finely sliced

2 tbsp chopped fresh mint

2 tbsp chopped fresh parsley

2 tbsp chopped fresh cilantro

juice of 1 lemon

3 tbsp extra virgin olive oil

method

1 Cook the potatoes in a pan of lightly salted boiling water for 15 minutes, or until tender. Drain, then let cool slightly before peeling off the skins. Cut into halves or quarters, depending on the size of the potato. Combine with the tomatoes, olives, scallions, and herbs in a salad bowl.

2 Mix the lemon juice and oil together in a small bowl or pitcher and pour over the potato salad. Season to taste with salt and pepper before serving.

pasta salad with charbroiled bell peppers

ingredients

SERVES 4

1 red bell pepper

1 orange bell pepper

10 oz/280 g dried conchiglie

5 tbsp extra virgin olive oil

2 tbsp lemon juice

2 tbsp pesto

1 garlic clove, crushed

3 tbsp shredded fresh basil
   leaves

salt and pepper

method

1 Put the whole bell peppers on a baking sheet and place under a preheated broiler, turning frequently, for 15 minutes, until charred all over. Remove with tongs and place in a bowl. Cover with plastic wrap and set aside.

2 Meanwhile, bring a large pan of lightly salted water to a boil. Add the pasta, bring back to a boil, and cook for 8–10 minutes, until tender but still firm to the bite.

3 Combine the olive oil, lemon juice, pesto, and garlic in a bowl, whisking well to mix. Drain the pasta, add it to the pesto mixture while still hot, and toss well. Set aside.

4 When the bell peppers are cool enough to handle, peel off the skins, then cut open and remove the seeds. Chop the flesh coarsely and add to the pasta with the basil. Season to taste with salt and pepper and toss well. Serve at room temperature.

three-color salad

ingredients
SERVES 4
10 oz/280 g buffalo
    mozzarella, drained and
    sliced thinly
8 plum tomatoes, sliced
salt and pepper
20 fresh basil leaves
1/2 cup extra virgin olive oil

method
1 Arrange the cheese and tomato slices on 4 individual serving plates and season to taste with salt. Set aside in a cool place for 30 minutes.

2 Sprinkle the basil leaves over the salad and drizzle with the olive oil. Season with pepper and serve immediately.

sweet potato & mozzarella salad

ingredients

SERVES 4

2 sweet potatoes, peeled and
    cut into chunks
2 tbsp olive oil
pepper
2 garlic cloves, crushed
1 large eggplant, sliced
2 red bell peppers, seeded
    and sliced
7 oz/200 g mixed salad greens
2 x 5 1/2 oz/150 g mozzarella
    cheeses, drained and
    sliced
whole wheat bread, to serve

dressing

1 tbsp balsamic vinegar
1 garlic clove, crushed
3 tbsp olive oil
1 small shallot, finely chopped
2 tbsp chopped mixed fresh
    herbs, such as tarragon,
    chervil, and basil
pepper

method

1 Preheat the oven to 375°F/190°C. Put the sweet potato chunks into a roasting pan with the oil, pepper to taste, and garlic and toss to combine. Roast in the preheated oven for 30 minutes, or until soft and slightly charred.

2 Meanwhile, preheat the broiler to high. Arrange the eggplant and bell pepper slices on the broiler pan and cook under the preheated broiler, turning occasionally, for 10 minutes, or until softened and slightly charred.

3 To make the dressing, whisk the vinegar, garlic, and oil together in a small bowl and stir in the shallot and herbs. Season to taste with pepper.

4 To serve, divide the salad greens among 4 serving plates and arrange the sweet potato, eggplant, bell peppers, and mozzarella on top. Drizzle with the dressing and serve with whole wheat bread.

pasta salad with nuts & gorgonzola

ingredients
SERVES 4

8 oz/225 g dried farfalle

2 tbsp walnut oil

4 tbsp safflower oil

2 tbsp balsamic vinegar

salt and pepper

10 oz/280 g mixed salad
greens

8 oz/225 g Gorgonzola cheese,
diced

1/2 cup walnuts, halved and
toasted

method

1 Bring a large, heavy-bottom pan of lightly salted water to a boil. Add the pasta, return to a boil, and cook for 8–10 minutes, or until tender but still firm to the bite. Drain and refresh in a bowl of cold water. Drain again.

2 Mix the walnut oil, safflower oil, and vinegar together in a measuring cup, whisking well, and season to taste with salt and pepper.

3 Arrange the salad greens in a large serving bowl. Top with the pasta, Gorgonzola cheese, and walnuts. Pour the dressing over the salad, toss lightly, and serve.

warm red lentil salad with goat cheese

ingredients
SERVES 4

2 tbsp olive oil
2 tsp cumin seeds
2 garlic cloves, crushed
2 tsp grated fresh ginger
1½ cups red lentils
3 cups vegetable stock
2 tbsp chopped fresh mint
2 tbsp chopped fresh cilantro
2 red onions, thinly sliced
4½ cups baby spinach leaves
1 tsp hazelnut oil
5½ oz/150 g soft goat cheese
4 tbsp strained plain yogurt
pepper
1 lemon, cut into quarters,
    to garnish
toasted rye bread, to serve

method

1 Heat half the olive oil in a large pan over medium heat, add the cumin seeds, garlic, and ginger, and cook for 2 minutes, stirring constantly.

2 Stir in the lentils, then add the stock, a ladleful at a time, until it is all absorbed, stirring constantly—this will take about 20 minutes. Remove from the heat and stir in the herbs.

3 Meanwhile, heat the remaining olive oil in a skillet over medium heat, add the onions, and cook, stirring frequently, for 10 minutes, or until softened and lightly browned.

4 Toss the spinach in the hazelnut oil in a bowl, then divide among 4 serving plates.

5 Mash the goat cheese with the yogurt in a small bowl and season to taste with pepper.

6 Divide the lentils among the serving plates and top with the onions and goat cheese mixture. Garnish with lemon quarters and serve with toasted rye bread.

cajun chicken salad

ingredients
SERVES 4

4 skinless, boneless chicken
   breasts, about 5 oz/140 g
   each
4 tsp Cajun seasoning
2 tsp corn oil (optional)
1 ripe mango, peeled, pitted,
   and cut into thick slices
7 oz/200 g mixed salad greens
1 red onion, thinly sliced and
   cut in half
6 oz/175 g cooked beet, diced
3 oz/85 g radishes, sliced
scant 1/2 cup walnut halves
4 tbsp walnut oil
1–2 tsp Dijon mustard
1 tbsp lemon juice
salt and pepper
2 tbsp sesame seeds

method

1 Make 3 diagonal slashes across each chicken breast. Put the chicken into a shallow dish and sprinkle all over with the Cajun seasoning. Cover and let chill for at least 30 minutes.

2 When ready to cook, brush a grill pan with the corn oil, if using. Heat over high heat until very hot and a few drops of water sprinkled into the pan sizzle immediately. Add the chicken and cook for 7–8 minutes on each side, or until thoroughly cooked. If still slightly pink in the center, cook a little longer. Remove the chicken and set aside.

3 Add the mango slices to the pan and cook for 2 minutes on each side. Remove from the pan and set aside.

4 Meanwhile, arrange the salad greens in a salad bowl, reserving a few for a garnish, and sprinkle over the onion, beet, radishes, and walnut halves.

5 Put the walnut oil, mustard, lemon juice, salt, and pepper in a screw-top jar and shake until well blended. Pour over the salad and sprinkle with the sesame seeds.

6 Arrange the mango and the salad on a serving plate, top with the chicken breast, and garnish with a few of the salad greens.

spicy chicken salad

ingredients

SERVES 4

2 skinless, boneless chicken
    breast portions, about
    4^1/$_2$ oz/125 g each
2 tbsp butter
1 fresh red chile, seeded and
    chopped
1 tbsp honey
^{1}/$_2$ tsp ground cumin
2 tbsp chopped fresh cilantro
3^1/$_2$ cups diced potatoes
1^3/$_4$ oz/50 g green beans,
    halved
1 red bell pepper, seeded and
    cut into thin strips
2 tomatoes, seeded and diced

dressing
2 tbsp olive oil
pinch of chili powder
1 tbsp garlic wine vinegar
pinch of superfine sugar
1 tbsp chopped fresh cilantro

method

1 Cut the chicken into thin strips. Melt the butter in a heavy pan and add the chicken strips, fresh red chile, honey, and cumin. Cook for 10 minutes, turning until cooked through. Transfer the mixture to a bowl and let cool, then stir in the chopped cilantro.

2 Meanwhile, cook the diced potatoes in a pan of boiling water for 10 minutes, until they are tender. Drain and let cool.

3 Blanch the green beans in a pan of boiling water for 3 minutes. Drain well and let cool. Combine the green beans and potatoes in a mixing bowl. Add the bell pepper strips and tomatoes to the potato mixture. Stir in the chicken mixture.

4 In a small bowl, whisk the dressing ingredients together and pour the dressing over the salad, tossing well. Transfer the spicy chicken salad to a serving bowl or large platter and serve immediately.

indonesian chicken salad

ingredients

SERVES 4

2 lb 12 oz/1.25 kg waxy
 potatoes, cut into small
 dice

10 1/2 oz/300 g fresh
 pineapple, peeled and
 diced

2 carrots, grated

1 3/4 cups bean sprouts

1 bunch of scallions, sliced

1 large zucchini, cut into thin
 sticks

3 celery stalks, cut into thin
 sticks

1 cup unsalted peanuts

2 cooked skinless, boneless
 chicken breasts, about
 4 1/2 oz/125 g each, sliced

dressing

6 tbsp crunchy peanut butter

6 tbsp olive oil

2 tbsp light soy sauce

1 fresh red chile, seeded and
 chopped

2 tsp sesame oil

4 tsp lime juice

method

1 Cook the diced potatoes in the pan for about 10 minutes, or until tender. Drain them thoroughly in a colander and let cool until required. Transfer the cooled potatoes to a salad bowl.

2 Add the diced pineapple, grated carrots, bean sprouts, scallions, zucchini and celery sticks, peanuts, and sliced chicken to the bowl of potatoes. Toss thoroughly to mix all the salad ingredients together.

3 To make the dressing, put the peanut butter in a small mixing bowl and gradually whisk in the olive oil and light soy sauce with a fork or a balloon whisk. Stir in the chopped red chile, sesame oil, and lime juice. Mix well until combined.

4 Pour the spicy dressing over the salad and toss lightly to coat all of the ingredients. Serve the potato and chicken salad immediately.

broiled beef salad

ingredients

SERVES 4

1³/₄ oz/50 g dried oyster
    mushrooms

1 lb 5 oz/600 g rump steak

1 red bell pepper, seeded and
    thinly sliced

scant ¹/₃ cup roasted cashew
    nuts

red and green lettuce leaves

fresh mint leaves, to garnish

dressing

2 tbsp sesame oil

2 tbsp Thai fish sauce

2 tbsp sweet sherry

2 tbsp oyster sauce

1 tbsp lime juice

1 fresh red chile, seeded and
    finely chopped

method

1 Put the mushrooms in a heatproof bowl, cover with boiling water, and let stand for 20 minutes. Drain, then cut into slices.

2 Preheat the broiler to medium or heat a ridged grill pan. To make the dressing, place all the ingredients in a bowl and whisk to combine.

3 Cook the steak under the preheated broiler or in the hot grill pan, turning once, for 5 minutes, or until browned on both sides but still rare in the center. Cook the steak longer if desired.

4 Slice the steak into thin strips and place in a bowl with the mushrooms, bell pepper, and nuts. Add the dressing and toss together.

5 Arrange the lettuce on a large serving platter and place the beef mixture on top. Garnish with mint leaves. Serve at room temperature.

peppered beef salad

ingredients

SERVES 4

4 beef tenderloin steaks,
about 4 oz/115 g each

2 tbsp black peppercorns,
crushed

1 tsp Chinese five spice
powder

3/4 cup bean sprouts

1-inch/2.5-cm piece ginger,
chopped finely

4 shallots, sliced finely

1 red bell pepper, seeded and
sliced thinly

3 tbsp Thai soy sauce

2 fresh red chiles, seeded and
sliced

1/2 lemongrass stalk, chopped
finely

3 tbsp vegetable or peanut oil

1 tbsp sesame oil

method

1 Wash the steaks and pat dry on paper towels. Mix the peppercorns with the five spice and press onto all sides of the steaks. Cook on a grill pan or under a broiler for 2–3 minutes each side, or until cooked to your liking.

2 Meanwhile mix together the bean sprouts, half the ginger, the shallots, and bell pepper and divide among 4 plates.

3 For the dressing, mix together the remaining ginger, soy sauce, chiles, lemongrass, and oils.

4 Slice the beef and arrange on top of the vegetables. Drizzle with the dressing and serve immediately.

mixed antipasto meat platter

ingredients
SERVES 4

1 cantaloupe melon

2 oz/55 g Italian salami, sliced thinly

8 slices prosciutto

8 slices bresaola

8 slices mortadella

4 plum tomatoes, sliced thinly

4 fresh figs, halved

2/3 cup black olives, pitted and sliced

2 tbsp shredded fresh basil leaves

4 tbsp extra virgin olive oil, plus extra for serving

pepper

method

1 Cut the melon in half, scoop out and discard the seeds, then cut the flesh into 8 wedges. Arrange the wedges on one half of a large serving platter.

2 Arrange the salami, prosciutto, bresaola, and mortadella in loose folds on the other half of the platter. Arrange the tomato slices and fig halves along the center of the platter.

3 Sprinkle over the olives and basil and drizzle with the olive oil. Season to taste with pepper, then serve with extra olive oil.

parma ham & figs

ingredients
SERVES 4

6 oz/175 g Parma ham, thinly
    sliced

pepper

4 fresh figs

1 lime

2 fresh basil sprigs

method

1 Using a sharp knife, trim the visible fat from the slices of Parma ham and discard. Arrange the Parma ham on 4 large serving plates, loosely folding it so that it falls into decorative shapes. Season to taste with pepper.

2 Using a sharp knife, cut each fig lengthwise into 4 wedges. Arrange a fig on each serving plate. Cut the lime into 6 wedges, place a wedge on each plate, and reserve the remainder. Remove the leaves from the basil sprigs and divide among the plates. Cover with plastic wrap and let chill in the refrigerator until ready to serve.

3 Just before serving, remove the plates from the refrigerator and squeeze the juice from the remaining lime wedges over the ham.

salad niçoise

ingredients
SERVES 4

2 tuna steaks, about
  $^3/_4$ inch/2 cm thick

olive oil

salt and pepper

9 oz/250 g green beans,
  trimmed

2 hearts of lettuce, leaves
  separated

3 large hard-cooked eggs,
  cut into quarters

2 juicy vine-ripened tomatoes,
  cut into wedges

1$^3/_4$ oz/50 g anchovy fillets in
  oil, drained

2 oz/55 g Niçoise olives

torn fresh basil leaves,
  to garnish

garlic vinaigrette

$^1/_2$ cup olive or other vegetable
  oil

3 tbsp white wine vinegar or
  lemon juice

1 tsp Dijon mustard

$^1/_2$ tsp superfine sugar

salt and pepper

method

1 To make the garlic vinaigrette, put all the ingredients in a screw-top jar, secure the lid, and shake well until an emulsion forms. Taste and adjust the seasoning if necessary.

2 Heat a ridged cast-iron grill pan over high heat until you can feel the heat rising from the surface. Brush the tuna steaks with oil, then place, oiled-side down, on the hot pan and cook for 2 minutes.

3 Lightly brush the top side of the tuna steaks with a little more oil. Use a pair of tongs to turn the tuna steaks over, then season to taste. Continue cooking for an additional 2 minutes for rare or up to 4 minutes for well-done. Let cool.

4 Meanwhile, bring a pan of salted water to a boil. Add the beans to the pan and return to a boil, then boil for 3 minutes, or until tender-crisp. Drain the beans and immediately transfer them to a large bowl. Pour over the garlic vinaigrette and stir together, then let the beans cool in the dressing.

5 To serve, line a platter with lettuce leaves. Lift the beans out of the bowl, leaving the excess dressing behind, and pile them in the center of the platter. Break the tuna into large flakes and arrange it over the beans.

6 Put the hard-cooked eggs and tomatoes around the side and arrange the anchovy fillets, olives, and basil on the salad. Drizzle over the remaining dressing and serve.

tuna & tomato salad with ginger dressing

ingredients
SERVES 4

1/2 cup shredded Chinese
    cabbage
3 tbsp rice wine or dry sherry
2 tbsp Thai fish sauce
1 tbsp finely shredded fresh
    ginger
1 garlic clove, finely chopped
1/2 small fresh red Thai chile,
    finely chopped
2 tsp brown sugar
2 tbsp lime juice
14 oz/400 g fresh tuna steak
corn oil, for brushing
41/2 oz/125 g cherry tomatoes
fresh mint leaves and mint
    sprigs, coarsely chopped,
    to garnish

method

1 Place a small pile of shredded cabbage on a large serving plate. For the dressing, place the rice wine, fish sauce, ginger, garlic, chile, sugar, and 1 tablespoon of the lime juice in a screw-top jar and shake well to combine.

2 Using a sharp knife, cut the tuna into strips of an even thickness. Sprinkle with the remaining lime juice.

3 Brush a wide skillet or ridged grill pan with oil and heat until very hot. Arrange the tuna strips in the skillet and cook until just firm and light golden, turning them over once. Remove the tuna strips from the skillet and reserve.

4 Add the tomatoes to the skillet and cook over high heat until lightly browned. Spoon the tuna and tomatoes over the cabbage, then spoon over the dressing. Garnish with fresh mint and serve warm.

salmon & avocado salad

ingredients

SERVES 4

1 lb/450 g new potatoes

4 salmon steaks, about
    4 oz/115 g each

1 avocado

juice of 1/2 lemon

2 oz/55 g baby spinach leaves

41/2 oz/125 g mixed small
    salad greens, including
    watercress

4 tomatoes, cut into quarters

scant 1/2 cup chopped walnuts

dressing

3 tbsp unsweetened clear
    apple juice

1 tsp balsamic vinegar

pepper

method

1 Cut the new potatoes into bite-size pieces, put into a pan, and cover with cold water. Bring to a boil, then reduce the heat, cover, and let simmer for 10–15 minutes, or until just tender. Drain and keep warm.

2 Meanwhile, preheat the broiler to medium. Cook the salmon steaks under the preheated broiler for 10–15 minutes, depending on the thickness of the steaks, turning halfway through cooking. Remove from the broiler and keep warm.

3 While the potatoes and salmon are cooking, cut the avocado in half, remove and discard the pit, and peel the flesh. Cut the avocado flesh into slices and coat in the lemon juice to prevent discoloration.

4 Toss the spinach leaves and mixed salad greens together in a large serving bowl until combined. Arrange the greens and the tomato quarters on individual serving plates.

5 Remove and discard the skin and any bones from the salmon. Flake the salmon and divide among the plates along with the potatoes. Sprinkle the walnuts over the salads.

6 To make the dressing, mix the apple juice and vinegar together in a small bowl or pitcher and season well with pepper. Drizzle over the salads and serve at once.

mackerel & potato salad

ingredients

SERVES 4

4^1/$_2$ oz/125 g new potatoes, scrubbed and diced

8 oz/225 g mackerel fillets, skinned

5 cups water

1 bay leaf

1 slice of lemon

1 apple, cored and diced

1 shallot, thinly sliced

3 tbsp white wine vinegar

1 tsp sunflower-seed oil

1^1/$_2$ tsp superfine sugar

^{1}/$_4$ tsp Dijon mustard

salt and pepper

to serve

2 tbsp lowfat plain yogurt

^{1}/$_4$ cucumber, thinly sliced

1 bunch of watercress

1 tbsp snipped fresh chives

method

1 Steam the potatoes over a pan of simmering water for 10 minutes, or until tender.

2 Meanwhile, using a sharp knife, remove the skin from the mackerel fillets and discard. Cut the fish into bite-size pieces. Bring the water to a boil in a large, shallow pan, then reduce the heat so that it is just simmering and add the fish pieces, bay leaf, and lemon. Poach for 3 minutes, or until the flesh of the fish is opaque. Remove with a slotted spoon and transfer to a serving dish.

3 Drain the potatoes and transfer to a large bowl. Add the apple and shallot and mix well, then spoon the mixture over the fish.

4 Mix the vinegar, oil, sugar, and mustard together in a pitcher, season to taste with salt and pepper, and whisk thoroughly. Pour the dressing over the potato mixture. Cover and let chill in the refrigerator for up to 6 hours.

5 To serve, spread the yogurt over the salad, then arrange the cucumber decoratively on top. Add sprigs of watercress and sprinkle with the chives.

shrimp & papaya salad

ingredients
SERVES 4

1 papaya, peeled
12 oz/350 g large cooked
    peeled shrimp
assorted baby salad greens

dressing

4 scallions, chopped finely
2 fresh red chiles, seeded and
    chopped finely
1 tsp fish sauce
1 tbsp vegetable or peanut oil
juice of 1 lime
1 tsp jaggery or light brown
    sugar

method

1 Scoop the seeds out of the papaya and slice thinly. Stir gently together with the shrimp.

2 Mix the scallions, chiles, fish sauce, oil, lime juice, and sugar together.

3 Arrange the salad greens in a bowl and top with the papaya and shrimp. Pour over the dressing and serve immediately.

shrimp cocktail

ingredients

SERVES 4

$1/2$ iceberg lettuce, finely
   shredded

$2/3$ cup mayonnaise

2 tbsp light cream

2 tbsp ketchup

few drops of Tabasco sauce,
   or to taste

juice of $1/2$ lemon, or to taste

salt and pepper

6 oz/175 g cooked peeled
   shrimp

paprika, for sprinkling

4 cooked shrimp, in their
   shells, and 4 lemon slices,
   to garnish

thin buttered brown bread
   slices (optional), to serve

method

1 Divide the lettuce among 4 small serving dishes (traditionally, stemmed glass ones, but any small dishes will be fine).

2 For the dressing, mix together the mayonnaise, cream, and ketchup in a bowl. Add the Tabasco sauce and lemon juice and season well with salt and pepper.

3 Divide the peeled shrimp equally among the dishes and pour over the dressing. Cover and let chill in the refrigerator for 30 minutes.

4 Sprinkle over a little paprika and garnish each dish with a shrimp and a lemon slice. Serve with slices of brown bread and butter.

sautéed garlic mushrooms

ingredients

SERVES 6

1 lb/450 g white mushrooms

5 tbsp Spanish olive oil

2 garlic cloves, finely chopped

squeeze of lemon juice

salt and pepper

4 tbsp chopped fresh flat-leaf
   parsley

crusty bread, to serve

method

1 Wipe or brush clean the mushrooms, then trim off the stalks close to the caps. Cut any large mushrooms in half or into quarters. Heat the olive oil in a large, heavy-bottom skillet, add the garlic, and cook for 30 seconds–1 minute, or until lightly browned. Add the mushrooms and sauté over high heat, stirring most of the time, until the mushrooms have absorbed all the oil in the skillet.

2 Reduce the heat to low. When the juices have come out of the mushrooms, increase the heat again and sauté for 4–5 minutes, stirring most of the time, until the juices have almost evaporated. Add a squeeze of lemon juice and season to taste with salt and pepper. Stir in the parsley and cook for an additional minute.

3 Transfer the sautéed mushrooms to a warmed serving dish and serve piping hot or warm. Accompany with chunks or slices of crusty bread for mopping up the garlic cooking juices.

zucchini fritters with yogurt dip

ingredients
SERVES 4

2–3 zucchini, about
14 oz/400 g
1 garlic clove, crushed
3 scallions, finely sliced
4$\frac{1}{2}$ oz/125 g feta cheese,
crumbled
2 tbsp finely chopped fresh
parsley
2 tbsp finely chopped fresh
mint
1 tbsp finely chopped fresh dill
$\frac{1}{2}$ tsp freshly grated nutmeg
2 tbsp all-purpose flour
pepper
2 eggs
2 tbsp olive oil
1 lemon, cut into quarters,
to garnish

yogurt dip
scant 1$\frac{1}{4}$ cups strained plain
yogurt
$\frac{1}{4}$ cucumber, diced
1 tbsp finely chopped fresh dill
pepper

method

1 Grate the zucchini straight onto a clean dish towel and cover with another. Pat well and let stand for 10 minutes until the zucchini are dry.

2 Meanwhile, to make the dip, mix the yogurt, cucumber, dill, and pepper to taste in a serving bowl. Cover and let chill.

3 Tip the zucchini into a large bowl. Stir in the garlic, scallions, cheese, herbs, nutmeg, flour, and pepper to taste. Beat the eggs in a separate bowl and stir into the zucchini batter—the batter will be quite lumpy and uneven but this is fine.

4 Heat the oil in a large skillet over medium heat. Drop 4 tablespoonfuls of the batter into the skillet, with space in between, and cook for 2–3 minutes on each side. Remove, drain on paper towels, and keep warm. Cook the second batch of fritters in the same way. (There should be 8 fritters in total.)

5 Serve the fritters hot with the dip, garnished with lemon quarters.

sweet potato, mint & feta rösti

ingredients

SERVES 4

1 lb 5 oz/600 g sweet
   potatoes, peeled and
   grated
1 egg, lightly beaten
$1/3$ cup all-purpose flour
5 tbsp butter, melted
$3^1/2$ oz/100 g feta cheese,
   crumbled
3 tbsp chopped fresh mint
salt and pepper
1 tbsp vegetable oil
4 tbsp sour cream
2 tbsp chopped fresh parsley,
   to garnish

method

1 Preheat the oven to 325°F/160°C. Cover a baking sheet with parchment paper. Mix the grated sweet potato with the egg, flour, melted butter, feta, and mint until well combined. Season to taste with salt and pepper.

2 Heat the oil in a large nonstick skillet over medium heat. Spoon large tablespoons of the mixture into patties, flattening slightly, and cook on both sides in batches until golden.

3 Slide the rösti onto the prepared baking sheet and bake for 15 minutes, or until crisp. Place 2 rösti on each plate, top with a tablespoon of sour cream, and garnish with a little chopped parsley. Serve immediately.

vegetable rösti

ingredients

SERVES 4

1 carrot, grated

1 zucchini, grated

1 sweet potato, grated

8 scallions, finely chopped or
     shredded

pepper

1 egg white, beaten

2 tsp extra virgin olive oil

8 lean Canadian bacon slices,
     to serve (optional)

method

1 Mix all the vegetables together and season with pepper to taste, then stir in the egg white. Using clean hands, form into 8 small patties. Press them firmly together.

2 Heat the oil in a nonstick skillet and cook the patties over gentle heat for 5–6 minutes, or until golden. Turn over halfway through the cooking time and press down with the back of a spatula. Do this in 2 batches to prevent the skillet from being overcrowded.

3 Meanwhile, preheat the broiler and line the broiler pan with foil. Place the bacon under the broiler and cook for 5–8 minutes, until crisp, or cook to personal preference. Turn the slices over halfway through the cooking time.

4 As soon as the patties and bacon are cooked, serve immediately.

falafel with tahini sauce

ingredients

SERVES 4

1 lb/450 g canned cannellini
    beans, drained
12 oz/350 g canned
    chickpeas, drained
1 onion, finely chopped
2 garlic cloves, chopped
1 small fresh red chile, seeded
    and chopped
1 tsp baking powder
1 oz/25 g fresh parsley,
    chopped, plus extra sprigs
    to garnish
pinch of cayenne pepper
2 tbsp water
salt and pepper
vegetable oil, for deep-frying
pita bread, thick plain yogurt,
    or tzatziki and lemon
    wedges, to serve

tahini sauce

scant 1 cup tahini
1 garlic clove, chopped
1–2 tbsp water
2–3 tsp lemon juice, to taste

method

1 To make the tahini sauce, put the tahini and garlic in a bowl. Gradually stir in the water until a fairly smooth consistency is reached, then stir in lemon juice to taste. Add more water or lemon juice, if necessary. Cover with plastic wrap and let chill in the refrigerator until required.

2 To make the falafel, rinse and drain the beans and chickpeas. Put them in a food processor with the onion, garlic, chile, baking powder, chopped parsley, and cayenne pepper. Process to a coarse paste, then add the water and season with plenty of salt and pepper. Process again briefly.

3 Heat about 2¹/₂ inches/6 cm of oil in a deep-fat fryer, large, heavy-bottom pan, or wok over high heat. Deep-fry rounded tablespoonfuls of the mixture in batches for 2–2¹/₂ minutes, until golden and crispy on the outside. Remove with a slotted spoon and drain well on paper towels. Serve hot or cold, garnished with parsley sprigs and accompanied by the tahini sauce, pita bread, yogurt, or tzatziki, and lemon wedges.

crispy spring rolls

ingredients

SERVES 4

2 tbsp vegetable or peanut oil

6 scallions, cut into
2-inch/5-cm lengths

1 fresh green chile, seeded
and chopped

1 carrot, cut into thin sticks

1 zucchini, cut into thin sticks

1/2 red bell pepper, seeded
and thinly sliced

3/4 cup bean sprouts

4 oz/115 g canned bamboo
shoots, drained and rinsed

3 tbsp Thai soy sauce

1–2 tbsp chili sauce

8 egg roll skins

vegetable or peanut oil, for
deep-frying

method

1 Heat the oil in a wok and stir-fry the scallions and chile for 30 seconds. Add the carrot, zucchini, and red bell pepper and stir-fry for an additional minute. Remove the wok from the heat and stir in the bean sprouts, bamboo shoots, soy sauce, and chili sauce. Taste and add more soy sauce or chili sauce if necessary.

2 Place an egg roll skin on a counter and spoon some of the vegetable mixture diagonally across the center. Roll one corner over the filling and flip the sides of the skin over the top to enclose the filling. Continue to roll up to make an enclosed package. Repeat with the remaining skins and filling to make 8 egg rolls.

3 Heat the oil for deep-frying in a wok or large skillet. Deep-fry the egg rolls, 3–4 at a time, until crisp and golden brown. Remove with a slotted spoon, drain on paper towels while you cook the remainder, then serve immediately.

thai tofu cakes with chile dip

ingredients
SERVES 8

$10^1/2$ oz/300 g firm tofu,
   drained weight, coarsely
   grated
1 lemongrass stalk, outer layer
   discarded, finely chopped
2 garlic cloves, chopped
1-inch/2.5-cm piece fresh
   ginger, grated
2 kaffir lime leaves, finely
   chopped (optional)
2 shallots, finely chopped
2 fresh red chiles, seeded and
   finely chopped
4 tbsp chopped fresh cilantro
scant $3/4$ cup all-purpose flour,
   plus extra for flouring
$1/2$ tsp salt
corn oil, for cooking

chile dip
3 tbsp white distilled vinegar
   or rice wine vinegar
2 scallions, finely sliced
1 tbsp superfine sugar
2 fresh chiles, finely chopped
2 tbsp chopped fresh cilantro
pinch of salt

method

1 To make the chili dip, mix all the ingredients together in a small serving bowl and set aside.

2 Mix the tofu with the lemongrass, garlic, ginger, lime leaves, if using, shallots, chiles, and cilantro in a mixing bowl. Stir in the flour and salt to make a coarse, sticky paste. Cover and let chill in the refrigerator for 1 hour to let the mixture firm up slightly.

3 Form the mixture into large walnut-size balls and, using floured hands, flatten into circles until you have 8 cakes. Heat enough oil to cover the bottom of a large, heavy-bottom skillet over medium heat. Cook the cakes in 2 batches, turning halfway through, for 4–6 minutes, or until golden brown. Drain on paper towels and serve warm with the chili dip.

chile bean cakes with avocado salsa

ingredients
SERVES 4

scant 1/2 cup pine nuts

15 oz/425 g canned mixed
  beans, drained and rinsed

1/2 red onion, finely chopped

1 tbsp tomato paste

1/2 fresh red chile, seeded and
  finely chopped

1 cup fresh brown bread
  crumbs

1 egg, beaten

1 tbsp finely chopped fresh
  cilantro

2 tbsp corn oil

1 lime, cut into quarters,
  to garnish

4 toasted whole wheat bread
  rolls, to serve (optional)

salsa

1 avocado, pitted, peeled, and
  chopped

3 1/2 oz/100 g tomatoes,
  seeded and chopped

2 garlic cloves, crushed

2 tbsp finely chopped fresh
  cilantro

1 tbsp olive oil

pepper

juice of 1/2 lime

method

1 Heat a nonstick skillet over medium heat, add the pine nuts, and cook, turning, until just browned. Tip into a bowl and set aside.

2 Put the beans into a large bowl and coarsely mash. Add the onion, tomato paste, chile, pine nuts, and half the bread crumbs and mix well. Add half the egg and the cilantro and mash together, adding a little more egg, if needed, to bind the mixture.

3 Form the mixture into 4 flat cakes. Coat with the remaining bread crumbs, cover, and let chill in the refrigerator for 30 minutes.

4 To make the salsa, mix all the ingredients together in a serving bowl, cover, and let chill in the refrigerator until required.

5 Heat the oil in a skillet over medium heat, add the bean cakes, and cook for 4–5 minutes on each side, or until crisp and heated through. Remove from the skillet and drain on paper towels.

6 Serve each bean cake in a toasted whole wheat roll, if desired, with the salsa, garnished with a lime quarter.

deviled eggs

ingredients

SERVES 8

8 large eggs

2 whole pimientos from a jar
    or can

8 green olives

5 tbsp mayonnaise

8 drops Tabasco sauce

large pinch cayenne pepper

salt and pepper

paprika, for dusting

sprigs of fresh dill, to garnish

method

1 To cook the eggs, put them in a pan, cover with cold water, and slowly bring to a boil. Immediately reduce the heat to very low, cover, and let simmer gently for 10 minutes. As soon as the eggs are cooked, drain and put under cold running water to prevent a black ring from forming around the yolk. Gently tap the eggs to crack the shells and let stand until cold. When cold, remove the shells.

2 Using a stainless steel knife, halve the eggs lengthwise, then carefully remove the yolks. Put the yolks in a nylon strainer, set over a bowl, and rub through, then mash them with a wooden spoon or fork. If necessary, rinse the egg whites under cold water and dry very carefully.

3 Drain the pimientos on paper towels, then chop them finely, reserving 16 strips. Finely chop the olives, reserving 16 larger pieces to garnish. Add the chopped pimientos and chopped olives to the mashed egg yolks. Add the mayonnaise, mix well together, then add the Tabasco sauce, cayenne pepper, and salt and pepper to taste.

4 Use a teaspoon to spoon the prepared filling into each egg half. Arrange the eggs on a serving plate. Add a small strip of the reserved pimientos and a piece of olive to the top of each stuffed egg. Dust with a little paprika and garnish with dill sprigs.

lime-drizzled shrimp

ingredients
SERVES 6

4 limes

12 raw jumbo shrimp, in their
    shells

3 tbsp Spanish olive oil

2 garlic cloves, finely chopped

splash of fino sherry

salt and pepper

4 tbsp chopped fresh flat-leaf
    parsley

method

1 Grate the rind and squeeze the juice from 2 of the limes. Cut the remaining 2 limes into wedges and set aside for later.

2 To prepare the shrimp, remove the head and legs, leaving the shells and tails intact. Using a sharp knife, make a shallow slit along the underside of each shrimp, then pull out the dark vein and discard. Rinse the shrimp under cold water and dry well on paper towels.

3 Heat the olive oil in a large, heavy-bottom skillet, then add the garlic and cook for 30 seconds. Add the shrimp and cook for 5 minutes, stirring from time to time, or until they turn pink and start to curl. Mix in the lime rind, juice, and a splash of sherry to moisten, then stir well together.

4 Transfer the cooked shrimp to a serving dish, season to taste with salt and pepper, and sprinkle with the parsley. Serve piping hot, accompanied by the reserved lime wedges for squeezing over the shrimp.

calamares

ingredients
SERVES 6

1 lb/450 g prepared squid

all-purpose flour, for coating

sunflower-seed oil, for deep-
 frying

salt

lemon wedges, to garnish

garlic mayonnaise, to serve

method

1 Slice the squid into 1/2-inch/1-cm rings and halve the tentacles if large. Rinse under cold running water and dry well with paper towels. Dust the squid rings with flour so that they are lightly coated.

2 Heat the oil in a deep-fat fryer, large, heavy-bottom pan, or wok to 350–375°F/180–190°C, or until a cube of bread browns in 30 seconds. Deep-fry the squid rings in small batches for 2–3 minutes, or until golden brown and crisp all over, turning several times (if you deep-fry too many squid rings at one time, the oil temperature will drop and they will be soggy). Do not overcook or the squid will become tough and rubbery rather than moist and tender.

3 Remove with a slotted spoon and drain well on paper towels. Keep warm in a low oven while you deep-fry the remaining squid rings.

4 Sprinkle the fried squid rings with salt and serve piping hot, garnished with lemon wedges for squeezing over. Accompany with a bowl of garlic mayonnaise for dipping.

guacamole

ingredients

SERVES 4

2 large, ripe avocados

juice of 1 lime, or to taste

2 tsp olive oil

1/2 onion, finely chopped

1 fresh green chile, such as
  poblano, seeded and finely
  chopped

1 garlic clove, crushed

1/4 tsp ground cumin

1 tbsp chopped fresh cilantro,
  plus extra to garnish
  (optional)

salt and pepper

method

1 Cut the avocados in half lengthwise and twist the 2 halves in opposite directions to separate. Stab the pit with the point of a sharp knife and lift out.

2 Peel, then coarsely chop the avocado halves and place in a nonmetallic bowl. Squeeze over the lime juice and add the oil.

3 Mash the avocados with a fork until the desired consistency—either chunky or smooth. Blend in the onion, chile, garlic, cumin, and chopped cilantro, then season to taste with salt and pepper.

4 Transfer to a serving dish and serve immediately, to avoid discoloration, sprinkled with extra chopped cilantro, if liked.

eggplant dip

ingredients

SERVES 6–8

5 tbsp olive oil

1 large eggplant, about
    14 oz/400 g, sliced

2 scallions, chopped finely

1 large garlic clove, crushed

2 tbsp finely chopped fresh
    parsley

salt and pepper

smoked sweet Spanish
    paprika, to garnish

French bread, to serve

method

1 Heat 4 tablespoons of the oil in a large skillet over medium–high heat. Add the eggplant slices and cook on both sides until soft and starting to brown. Remove from the skillet and set aside to cool. The slices will release the oil again as they cool.

2 Heat another tablespoon of oil in the skillet. Add the scallions and garlic and cook for 3 minutes, until the scallions become soft. Remove from the heat and set aside with the eggplant slices to cool.

3 Transfer the cooled scallions, garlic, and eggplant to a food processor and process just until a coarse paste forms. Transfer to a serving bowl and stir in the parsley. Taste and adjust the seasoning, if necessary. Serve at once, or cover and let chill until 15 minutes before required. Sprinkle with paprika and serve with slices of French bread.

tapenade

ingredients

SERVES 6

9 oz/250 g black olives, such
    as Nyons or Niçoise, pitted
3 anchovy fillets in oil, drained
1 large garlic clove, halved,
    with the green center
    removed, if necessary
2 tbsp pine nuts
1/2 tbsp capers in brine, rinsed
1/2 cup extra virgin olive oil
freshly squeezed lemon or
    orange juice, to taste
pepper

garlic croûtes

12 slices French bread, about
    1/4 inch/5 mm thick
extra virgin olive oil
2 garlic cloves, peeled and
    halved

method

1 Put the olives, anchovy fillets, garlic, pine nuts, and capers in a food processor or blender and process until well blended. With the motor still running, pour the olive oil through the feed tube and continue blending until a loose paste forms.

2 Add the lemon juice and pepper to taste. It shouldn't need any salt because of the saltiness of the anchovies. Cover and chill until required.

3 To make the garlic croûtes, preheat the broiler to high. Place the bread slices on the broiler rack and toast 1 side for 1–2 minutes, or until golden brown. Flip the bread slices over, lightly brush the untoasted side with olive oil, then toast for 1–2 minutes.

4 Rub 1 side of each bread slice with the garlic cloves while it is still hot, then set aside and let cool completely. Store in an airtight container for up to 2 days.

5 Serve the tapenade with the garlic croûtes.

moorish fava bean dip

ingredients

SERVES 6

1 lb 2 oz/500 g shelled fresh
    or frozen fava beans
5 tbsp olive oil
1 garlic clove, finely chopped
1 onion, finely chopped
1 tsp ground cumin
1 tbsp lemon juice
3/4 cup water
1 tbsp chopped fresh mint
salt and pepper
paprika, to garnish
raw vegetables, crusty bread,
    or breadsticks, to serve

method

1 If using fresh fava beans, bring a large pan of lightly salted water to a boil. Add the beans, then reduce the heat and simmer, covered, for 7 minutes. Drain well, then refresh under cold running water and drain again. Remove and discard the outer skins. If using frozen beans, let thaw completely, then remove and discard the outer skins.

2 Heat 1 tablespoon of the olive oil in a skillet. Add the garlic, onion, and cumin and cook over low heat, stirring occasionally, until the onion is softened and translucent. Add the fava beans and cook, stirring frequently, for 5 minutes.

3 Remove the skillet from the heat and transfer the mixture to a food processor or blender. Add the lemon juice, the remaining olive oil, water, and mint and process to a paste. Season to taste with salt and pepper.

4 Scrape the paste back into the skillet and heat gently until warm. Transfer to individual serving bowls and dust lightly with paprika. Serve with dippers of your choice.

chicken

Chicken is a great choice for family meals because it is astonishingly versatile and it goes well with such a wide variety of other ingredients—it tastes as good in a creamy sauce as it does in a spicy curry. In addition, it can be cooked in lots of different ways—for example, broiled, roasted, pan-fried, or poached—and is as appetizing in risotto as it is on kebab skewers. It's always a popular option and is ideal for adding variety to the family menu.

For health reasons, it is important that chicken is cooked all the way through. Timings vary depending on the cooking method and cut of chicken, but an approximate guide is given in each recipe. To test whether chicken is fully cooked, pierce the thickest part with the point of a sharp knife or skewer— the chicken is ready if the juices run clear, but will need additional cooking if there is any trace of pink. It is not a good idea to attempt to speed up the cooking process by increasing the heat because this is likely to cause the meat to dry out in a thoroughly unappetizing way.

Chicken does cook much more quickly if a boneless cut is diced, sliced, or cut into strips, making it ideal for stir-fries and pasta sauces. Flattening a whole breast portion by covering it with plastic wrap and beating it to an even thickness with a rolling pin or meat mallet also enables it to

be cooked more speedily. If a recipe suggests marinating chicken before cooking, it is worth doing this even if time is short because chicken readily absorbs the flavors of spices, herbs, and sauces and this will also help to keep the chicken moist.

chicken with basil & pine nut pesto

ingredients

SERVES 4

2 tbsp vegetable oil

4 boneless, skinless chicken breasts

12 oz/350 g dried farfalle

salt and pepper

sprig of fresh basil, to garnish

pesto

2 cups shredded fresh basil

1/2 cup extra virgin olive oil

3 tbsp pine nuts

3 garlic cloves, crushed

1/2 cup freshly grated Parmesan

2 tbsp freshly grated pecorino

method

1 To make the pesto, put the basil, olive oil, pine nuts, garlic, and a generous pinch of salt in a food processor or blender. Process the ingredients until smooth. Scrape the mixture into a bowl and stir in the cheeses.

2 Heat the vegetable oil in a skillet over medium heat. Fry the chicken breasts, turning once, for 8–10 minutes, until the juices are no longer pink. Cut into small cubes.

3 Cook the pasta in plenty of boiling salted water until al dente. Drain and transfer to a warm serving dish. Add the chicken and pesto, then season with pepper. Toss well to mix.

4 Garnish with a sprig of basil and serve warm.

farfalle with chicken, broccoli & roasted red bell peppers

ingredients

SERVES 4

4 tbsp olive oil

5 tbsp butter

3 garlic cloves, chopped very finely

1 lb/450 g boneless, skinless chicken breasts, diced

1/4 tsp dried chile flakes

salt and pepper

1 lb/450 g small broccoli florets

10¼ oz/300 g dried farfalle or fusilli

6 oz/175 g bottled roasted red bell peppers, drained and diced

1 cup chicken stock

freshly grated Parmesan, to serve (optional)

method

1 Bring a large pan of salted water to a boil. Meanwhile, heat the olive oil, butter, and garlic in a large skillet over medium–low heat. Cook the garlic until just beginning to color.

2 Add the diced chicken, raise the heat to medium, and stir-fry for 4–5 minutes, until the chicken is no longer pink. Add the chile flakes and season with salt and pepper. Remove from the heat.

3 Plunge the broccoli into the boiling water and cook for 2 minutes, until tender-crisp. Remove with a slotted spoon and set aside. Bring the water back to a boil. Add the pasta and cook until al dente. Drain and add to the chicken mixture in the pan. Add the broccoli and roasted peppers. Pour in the stock. Simmer briskly over medium–high heat, stirring frequently, until most of the liquid has been absorbed.

4 Sprinkle with the Parmesan, if using, and serve.

fettuccine with chicken & onion cream sauce

ingredients

SERVES 4

1 tbsp olive oil

2 tbsp butter

1 garlic clove, chopped very
finely

4 boneless, skinless chicken
breasts

salt and pepper

1 onion, chopped finely

1 chicken bouillon cube,
crumbled

$1/2$ cup water

$1^1/4$ cups heavy cream

$3/4$ cup milk

6 scallions, green part
included, sliced diagonally

scant $1/3$ cup freshly grated
Parmesan

1 lb/450 g dried fettuccine

chopped fresh flat-leaf parsley,
to garnish

method

1 Heat the oil and butter with the garlic in a large skillet over medium–low heat. Cook the garlic until just beginning to color. Add the chicken breasts and raise the heat to medium. Cook for 4–5 minutes on each side, or until the juices are no longer pink. Season with salt and pepper. Remove from the heat. Lift out the chicken breasts, leaving the oil in the skillet. Slice the breasts diagonally into thin strips and set aside.

2 Reheat the oil in the skillet. Add the onion and gently cook for 5 minutes, or until softened. Add the crumbled bouillon cube and the water. Bring to a boil, then let simmer over medium–low heat for 10 minutes. Stir in the cream, milk, scallions, and Parmesan. Let simmer until heated through and slightly thickened.

3 Cook the fettucine in boiling salted water until al dente. Drain and transfer to a warm serving dish. Layer the chicken slices over the pasta. Pour on the sauce, then garnish with parsley and serve.

spaghetti with parsley chicken

ingredients

SERVES 4

1 tbsp olive oil

thinly pared zest of 1 lemon, cut into julienne strips

1 tsp finely chopped fresh ginger

1 tsp sugar

salt

1 cup chicken stock

9 oz/250 g dried spaghetti

4 tbsp butter

8 oz/225 g skinless, boneless chicken breasts, diced

1 red onion, finely chopped

leaves from 2 bunches of flat-leaf parsley

method

1 Heat the olive oil in a heavy-bottom pan. Add the lemon zest and cook over low heat, stirring frequently, for 5 minutes. Stir in the ginger and sugar, season with salt, and cook, stirring constantly, for an additional 2 minutes. Pour in the chicken stock, bring to a boil, then cook for 5 minutes, or until the liquid has reduced by half.

2 Meanwhile, bring a large, heavy-bottom pan of lightly salted water to a boil. Add the pasta, return to a boil, and cook for 8–10 minutes, or until tender but still firm to the bite.

3 Meanwhile, melt half the butter in a skillet. Add the chicken and onion and cook, stirring frequently, for 5 minutes, or until the chicken is light brown all over. Stir in the lemon and ginger mixture and cook for 1 minute. Stir in the parsley leaves and cook, stirring constantly, for an additional 3 minutes.

4 Drain the pasta and transfer to a warmed serving dish, then add the remaining butter and toss well. Add the chicken sauce, toss again, and serve.

pasta with chicken & feta

ingredients

SERVES 4

2 tbsp olive oil

1 lb/450 g skinless, boneless
    chicken breasts, cut into
    thin strips

6 scallions, chopped

8 oz/225 g feta cheese, diced

4 tbsp chopped fresh chives

salt and pepper

1 lb/450 g dried garganelli

tomato focaccia, to serve

method

1 Heat the olive oil in a heavy-bottom skillet. Add the chicken and cook over medium heat, stirring frequently, for 5–8 minutes, or until golden all over and cooked through. Add the scallions and cook for 2 minutes. Stir the feta cheese into the skillet with half the chives and season with salt and pepper.

2 Meanwhile, bring a large, heavy-bottom pan of lightly salted water to a boil. Add the pasta, return to a boil, and cook for 8–10 minutes, or until tender but still firm to the bite. Drain well, then transfer to a warmed serving dish.

3 Spoon the chicken mixture onto the pasta, toss lightly, and serve immediately, garnished with the remaining chives and accompanied by tomato focaccia.

fruity chicken fusilli

ingredients

SERVES 4

1 lb/450 g skinless, boneless
   chicken, diced

1 tsp ground turmeric

1/4 tsp ground cinnamon

1/4 tsp ground cumin

1/4 tsp ground cardamom

pinch of cayenne pepper

2 tbsp peanut oil

1 onion, finely chopped

2 garlic cloves, finely chopped

1 1/2 cups chicken stock

salt

2 tbsp raisins

1 ripe mango, peeled, pitted,
   and diced

10 oz/280 g dried fusilli

2 tbsp chopped fresh cilantro,
   to garnish

method

1 Place the chicken in a shallow dish. Sprinkle with the turmeric, cinnamon, cumin, cardamom, and cayenne and toss well to coat. Cover with plastic wrap and let stand in the refrigerator for 30 minutes.

2 Heat the peanut oil in a heavy-bottom skillet. Add the onion and garlic and cook over low heat, stirring occasionally, for 5 minutes, or until softened. Add the spiced chicken and cook, stirring frequently, for 5 minutes, or until golden brown all over. Pour in the chicken stock and season with salt. Bring to a boil, add the raisins and mango, partially cover, and let simmer for 25 minutes.

3 Meanwhile, bring a large, heavy-bottom pan of lightly salted water to a boil. Add the pasta, return to a boil, and cook for 8–10 minutes, or until tender but still firm to the bite. Drain and transfer to a warmed serving dish. Add the chicken mixture, toss lightly, and serve, garnished with the cilantro.

sweet-&-sour chicken

ingredients

SERVES 4–6

1 lb/450 g chicken, cubed

5 tbsp vegetable or peanut oil

1/2 tsp minced garlic

1/2 tsp finely chopped fresh
   ginger

1 green bell pepper, coarsely
   chopped

1 onion, coarsely chopped

1 carrot, finely sliced

1 tsp sesame oil

1 tbsp finely chopped scallions

marinade

2 tsp light soy sauce

1 tsp Shaoxing rice wine

pinch of white pepper

1/2 tsp salt

dash of sesame oil

sauce

8 tbsp rice vinegar

4 tbsp sugar

2 tsp light soy sauce

6 tbsp ketchup

method

1 Place all the marinade ingredients in a bowl and marinate the chicken pieces for at least 20 minutes.

2 To prepare the sauce, heat the vinegar in a pan and add the sugar, light soy sauce, and ketchup. Stir to dissolve the sugar, then set aside.

3 In a preheated wok or deep pan, heat 3 tablespoons of the oil and stir-fry the chicken until it starts to turn golden brown. Remove and set aside.

4 In the clean wok or deep pan, heat the remaining oil and cook the garlic and ginger until fragrant. Add the vegetables and cook for 2 minutes. Add the chicken and cook for 1 minute. Finally add the sauce and sesame oil, then stir in the scallions and serve.

chicken with cashews

ingredients

SERVES 4–6

1 lb/450 g boneless chicken
    meat, cut into bite-size
    pieces
3 dried Chinese mushrooms,
    soaked in warm water for
    20 minutes
2 tbsp vegetable or peanut oil
4 slices of fresh ginger
1 tsp finely chopped garlic
1 red bell pepper, cut into
    1-inch/2.5-cm squares
1 tbsp light soy sauce
generous 1/2 cup cashews,
    roasted

m a r i n a d e
2 tbsp light soy sauce
1 tsp Shaoxing rice wine
pinch of sugar
1/2 tsp salt

method

1 Marinate the chicken in the light soy sauce, Shaoxing, sugar, and salt for at least 20 minutes.

2 Squeeze any excess water from the mushrooms and finely slice, discarding any tough stems. Reserve the soaking water.

3 In a preheated wok or deep pan, heat 1 tablespoon of the oil. Add the ginger and stir-fry until fragrant. Stir in the chicken and cook for 2 minutes, or until it begins to turn brown. Before the chicken is cooked through, remove and set aside.

4 In the clean wok or deep pan, heat the remaining oil and stir-fry the garlic until fragrant. Add the mushrooms and red bell pepper and stir-fry for 1 minute. Add about 2 tablespoons of the mushroom soaking water and cook for about 2 minutes, or until the water has evaporated. Return the chicken to the wok, then add the light soy sauce and the cashews and stir-fry for 2 minutes, or until the chicken is cooked through.

chicken fried rice

ingredients

SERVES 4

1/2 tbsp sesame oil

6 shallots, peeled and cut into
    fourths

1 lb/450g cooked, cubed
    chicken meat

3 tbsp soy sauce

2 carrots, diced

1 stalk celery, diced

1 red bell pepper, diced

1 1/2 cups fresh peas

3 1/2 oz/100 g canned corn

2 cups cooked long-grain rice

2 large eggs, scrambled

method

1 Heat the oil in a large skillet over medium heat. Add the shallots and fry until softened, then add the chicken and 2 tablespoons of the soy sauce and stir-fry for 5–6 minutes.

2 Stir in the carrots, celery, red bell pepper, peas, and corn and stir-fry for an additional 5 minutes. Add the rice and stir thoroughly.

3 Finally, stir in the scrambled eggs and the remaining tablespoon of soy sauce. Serve immediately.

chicken chow mein

ingredients

SERVES 4

9 oz/250 g dried medium egg noodles

2 tbsp sunflower-seed oil

10 oz/280 g cooked chicken breasts, shredded

1 garlic clove, finely chopped

1 red bell pepper, seeded and thinly sliced

3½ oz/100 g shiitake mushrooms, sliced

6 scallions, sliced

¾ cup bean sprouts

3 tbsp soy sauce

1 tbsp sesame oil

method

1 Place the egg noodles in a large bowl or dish and break them up slightly. Pour enough boiling water over the noodles to cover and let stand while preparing the other ingredients.

2 Preheat a wok over medium heat. Add the oil and swirl it around to coat the sides of the wok. When the oil is hot, add the shredded chicken, garlic, bell pepper, mushrooms, scallions, and bean sprouts to the wok and stir-fry for about 5 minutes.

3 Drain the noodles then add them to the wok, toss well, and stir-fry for an additional 5 minutes. Drizzle over the soy sauce and sesame oil and toss until thoroughly combined.

4 Transfer to warmed serving bowls and serve immediately.

yaki soba

ingredients

SERVES 2

14 oz/400 g ramen noodles

1 onion, finely sliced

1^1/$_3$ cups bean sprouts

1 red bell pepper, seeded and
   finely shredded

1 boneless, skin-on cooked
   chicken breast, about
   5^1/$_2$ oz/150 g, sliced

12 cooked peeled shrimp

1 tbsp oil

2 tbsp shoyu (Japanese soy
   sauce)

^{1}/$_2$ tbsp mirin

1 tsp sesame oil

1 tsp roasted sesame seeds

2 scallions, finely sliced

method

1 Cook the noodles according to the package instructions, drain well, and tip into a bowl.

2 Mix the onion, bean sprouts, red bell pepper, chicken, and shrimp together in a separate bowl. Stir through the noodles.

3 Preheat a wok over high heat. Add the oil and heat until very hot. Add the noodle mixture and stir-fry for 4 minutes, or until golden, then add the shoyu, mirin, and sesame oil and toss together.

4 Divide the mixture between 2 plates, sprinkle with the sesame seeds and scallions, and serve immediately.

gong bau chicken

ingredients

SERVES 4

2 boneless chicken breasts,
    with or without skin, cut
    into 1/2-inch/1-cm cubes
1 tbsp vegetable or peanut oil
10 dried red chiles or more,
    to taste, snipped into 2 or
    3 pieces
1 tsp Sichuan peppers
3 garlic cloves, finely sliced
1-inch/2.5-cm piece of fresh
    ginger, finely sliced
1 tbsp coarsely chopped
    scallion, white part only
generous 1/2 cup peanuts,
    roasted

marinade

2 tsp light soy sauce
1 tsp Shaoxing rice wine
1/2 tsp sugar

sauce

1 tsp light soy sauce
1 tsp dark soy sauce
1 tsp black Chinese rice
    vinegar
a few drops of sesame oil
2 tbsp chicken stock
1 tsp sugar

method

1 Combine all the ingredients for the marinade in a bowl and marinate the chicken, covered, for at least 20 minutes. Mix together all the ingredients for the sauce and set aside.

2 In a preheated wok or deep pan, heat the oil and stir-fry the chiles and peppers until crisp and fragrant. Toss in the chicken pieces. When they begin to turn white, add the garlic, ginger, and scallion. Stir-fry for about 5 minutes, or until the chicken is cooked.

3 Pour in the sauce, and when everything is well mixed, stir in the peanuts. Serve immediately.

shredded chicken & mixed mushrooms

ingredients

SERVES 4

2 tbsp vegetable or peanut oil

2 skinless, boneless chicken breasts

1 red onion, sliced

2 garlic cloves, chopped finely

1-inch/2.5-cm piece fresh ginger, grated

4 oz/115 g baby white mushrooms

4 oz/115 g shiitake mushrooms, halved

4 oz/115 g cremini mushrooms, sliced

2–3 tbsp Thai green curry paste

2 tbsp Thai soy sauce

4 tbsp chopped fresh parsley

boiled noodles or rice, to serve

method

1 Heat the oil in a wok and cook the chicken on all sides until lightly browned and cooked through. Remove with a slotted spoon, shred into even-size pieces, and set aside.

2 Pour off any excess oil, then stir-fry the onion, garlic, and ginger for 1–2 minutes, or until softened. Add all the mushrooms and stir-fry for 2–3 minutes, until they start to brown.

3 Add the curry paste, soy sauce, and shredded chicken to the wok and stir-fry for 1–2 minutes. Stir in the parsley and serve immediately with boiled noodles or rice.

five-spice chicken with vegetables

ingredients

SERVES 4

2 tbsp sesame oil

1 garlic clove, chopped

3 scallions, trimmed and
    sliced

1 tbsp cornstarch

2 tbsp rice wine

4 skinless chicken breasts,
    cut into strips

1 tbsp Chinese five-spice
    powder

1 tbsp grated fresh ginger

$^1/_2$ cup chicken stock

3$^1/_2$ oz/100 g baby corn, sliced

3 cups bean sprouts

finely chopped scallions,
    to garnish (optional)

freshly cooked jasmine rice,
    to serve

method

1 Heat the oil in a preheated wok or large skillet. Add the garlic and scallions and stir-fry over medium–high heat for 1 minute.

2 In a bowl, mix together the cornstarch and rice wine, then add the mixture to the pan. Stir-fry for 1 minute, then add the chicken, five-spice powder, ginger, and chicken stock and cook for another 4 minutes. Add the baby corn and cook for 2 minutes, then add the bean sprouts and cook for another minute.

3 Remove from the heat, garnish with chopped scallions, if using, and serve with freshly cooked jasmine rice.

chicken & ginger stir-fry

ingredients

SERVES 4

3 tbsp vegetable oil

1 lb 9 oz/700 g lean skinless,
    boneless chicken breasts,
    cut into 2-inch/5-cm strips

3 garlic cloves, crushed

1 tsp pomegranate seeds,
    crushed

1½-inch/4-cm piece fresh
    ginger, cut into strips

½ tsp ground turmeric

1 tsp garam masala

2 fresh green chiles, sliced

½ tsp salt

4 tbsp lemon juice

grated rind of 1 lemon

6 tbsp chopped fresh cilantro,
    plus extra to garnish

½ cup chicken stock

naan bread, to serve

method

1 Heat the oil in a preheated wok or large skillet. Add the chicken and stir-fry until golden brown all over. Remove from the wok and set aside.

2 Add the garlic, pomegranate seeds, and ginger to the wok and stir-fry in the oil for 1 minute, taking care not to let the garlic burn.

3 Stir in the turmeric, garam masala, and chiles and fry for 30 seconds.

4 Return the chicken to the wok and add the salt, lemon juice, lemon rind, cilantro, and stock. Stir the chicken well to make sure it is coated in the sauce.

5 Bring the mixture to a boil, then reduce the heat and let simmer for 10–15 minutes, or until the chicken is thoroughly cooked. Garnish with chopped cilantro and serve with warm naan bread.

chicken with bok choy

ingredients

SERVES 4

6 oz/175 g broccoli

1 tbsp peanut oil

1-inch/2.5-cm piece fresh
    ginger, finely grated

1 fresh red Thai chile, seeded
    and chopped

2 garlic cloves, crushed

1 red onion, cut into wedges

1 lb/450 g skinless, boneless
    chicken breast, cut into
    thin strips

6 oz/175 g bok choy,
    shredded

4 oz/115 g baby corn, halved

1 tbsp light soy sauce

1 tbsp Thai fish sauce

1 tbsp chopped fresh cilantro

1 tbsp toasted sesame seeds

method

1 Break the broccoli into small florets and cook in a pan of lightly salted boiling water for 3 minutes. Drain and set aside.

2 Heat a wok over high heat until almost smoking, add the oil, and then add the ginger, chile, and garlic. Stir-fry for 1 minute. Add the onion and chicken and stir-fry for an additional 3–4 minutes, or until the chicken is sealed on all sides.

3 Add the remaining vegetables to the wok, including the broccoli, and stir-fry for 3–4 minutes, or until tender.

4 Add the soy and Thai fish sauces to the wok and stir-fry for an additional 1–2 minutes, then serve immediately, sprinkled with the cilantro and sesame seeds.

chicken with yellow curry sauce

ingredients

SERVES 4

spice paste

6 tbsp Thai yellow curry paste

2/3 cup plain yogurt

1 3/4 cups water

handful of fresh cilantro, chopped, plus extra to garnish

handful of fresh Thai basil leaves, shredded, plus extra to garnish

stir-fry

2 tbsp vegetable or peanut oil

2 onions, cut into thin wedges

2 garlic cloves, chopped finely

2 skinless, boneless chicken breasts, cut into strips

6 oz/175 g baby corn, halved lengthwise

method

1 To make the spice paste, stir-fry the yellow curry paste in a wok for 2–3 minutes, then stir in the yogurt, water, and herbs. Bring to a boil, then let simmer for 2–3 minutes.

2 Meanwhile, heat the oil in a wok and stir-fry the onions and garlic for 2–3 minutes. Add the chicken and baby corn and stir-fry for 3–4 minutes, until the meat and baby corn are tender.

3 Stir in the spice paste and bring to a boil. Let simmer for 2–3 minutes, until heated through. Serve immediately, garnished with the extra herbs.

ginger chicken with noodles

ingredients

SERVES 4

2 tbsp vegetable or peanut oil

1 onion, sliced

2 garlic cloves, chopped finely

2-inch/5-cm piece fresh
   ginger, sliced thinly

2 carrots, sliced thinly

4 skinless, boneless chicken
   breasts, cut into cubes

1$1/4$ cups chicken stock

4 tbsp Thai soy sauce

8 oz/225 g canned bamboo
   shoots, drained and rinsed

2$3/4$ oz/75 g flat rice noodles

4 scallions, chopped, and
   4 tbsp chopped fresh
   cilantro, to garnish

method

1 Heat the oil in a wok and stir-fry the onion, garlic, ginger, and carrots for 1–2 minutes, until softened. Add the chicken and stir-fry for 3–4 minutes, until the chicken is cooked through and lightly browned.

2 Add the stock, soy sauce, and bamboo shoots to the wok and gradually bring to a boil. Let simmer for 2–3 minutes. Meanwhile, soak the noodles in boiling water for 6–8 minutes. Drain well. Garnish with the scallions and cilantro and serve immediately with the chicken stir-fry.

sweet-&-sour noodles with chicken

ingredients

SERVES 4

9 oz/250 g dried medium egg
    noodles

2 tbsp peanut or corn oil

1 onion, thinly sliced

4 boneless chicken thighs,
    skinned and cut into thin
    strips

1 carrot, peeled and cut into
    thin half-moon slices

1 red bell pepper, cored,
    seeded, and finely
    chopped

3½ oz/100 g canned bamboo
    shoots (drained weight)

scant ½ cup cashews

sweet-&-sour sauce

½ cup water

1½ tsp arrowroot

4 tbsp rice vinegar

3 tbsp brown sugar

2 tsp dark soy sauce

2 tsp tomato paste

2 large garlic cloves, very
    finely chopped

½-inch/1-cm piece fresh
    ginger, peeled and very
    finely chopped

pinch of salt

method

1 Cook the noodles in a large pan of boiling water for 3 minutes, or according to the package instructions, until soft. Drain, rinse, and drain again, then set aside.

2 Meanwhile, to make the sauce, stir half of the water into the arrowroot and set aside. Stir the remaining sauce ingredients and the remaining water together in a small pan and bring to a boil. Stir in the arrowroot mixture and continue boiling until the sauce becomes clear, glossy, and thick. Remove from the heat and set aside.

3 Heat a wok or large skillet over high heat. Add the oil and heat it until it shimmers. Add the onion and stir-fry for 1 minute. Stir in the chicken, carrot, and bell pepper and continue stir-frying for about 3 minutes, or until the chicken is cooked through.

4 Add the bamboo shoots and cashews and stir them around to brown the nuts lightly. Stir the sauce into the wok and heat until it starts to bubble. Add the noodles and use 2 forks to mix them with the chicken and vegetables. Serve immediately.

rice noodles with chicken, shrimp & tofu

ingredients

SERVES 4

8 oz/225 g rice noodles

3¼ oz/90 g peanuts, roughly
   chopped, plus extra,
   to garnish

2 tbsp lime juice

1 tbsp superfine sugar

6 tbsp Thai fish sauce

1 tsp hot chili sauce, to taste

9 oz/250 g firm tofu (drained
   weight), cubed

vegetable oil, for deep-frying

3 tbsp peanut oil

1 garlic clove, crushed

1 onion, finely sliced

1 red bell pepper, seeded and
   thinly sliced

9 oz/250 g skinless, boneless
   chicken breast, cut into
   thin strips

3 oz/85 g bean sprouts

4½ oz/125 g snow peas

6 oz/175 g cooked peeled
   shrimp, cut in half
   lengthwise

3 eggs, beaten

lemon wedges, 4 finely
   chopped scallions, and
   1 tbsp chopped fresh basil,
   to garnish

method

1 Soak the noodles in a bowl of warm water for about 20 minutes, or until soft. Drain thoroughly in a colander and set aside. Mix the peanuts, lime juice, sugar, fish sauce, and hot chili sauce together in a small bowl and set aside.

2 Rinse the tofu in cold water, place between layers of paper towels, and pat dry. Heat the oil for deep-frying in a large skillet or wok. Deep-fry the tofu over medium heat for 2 minutes, until light brown and crisp. Remove from the heat, lift the tofu out with a slotted spoon, and let drain thoroughly on paper towels.

3 Heat another large skillet or preheated wok and add the peanut oil, garlic, onion, red bell pepper, and chicken strips. Cook for 2–3 minutes. Stir in the bean sprouts and snow peas and cook for 1 minute, then add the shrimp, noodles, eggs, and tofu and stir-fry for 4–5 minutes. Finally, add the peanut and lime juice mixture and cook for 3–4 minutes. Transfer to warmed dishes, garnish with the lemon, scallions, peanuts, and basil, and serve.

balti chicken

ingredients

SERVES 6

3 tbsp ghee or vegetable oil

2 large onions, sliced

3 tomatoes, sliced

1/2 tsp kalonji seeds

4 black peppercorns

2 cardamom pods

1 cinnamon stick

1 tsp chili powder

1 tsp garam masala

1 tsp garlic paste

1 tsp ginger paste

salt

1 lb 9 oz/700 g skinless,
   boneless chicken breasts
   or thighs, diced

2 tbsp plain yogurt

2 tbsp chopped fresh cilantro,
   plus extra to garnish

2 fresh green chiles, seeded
   and finely chopped

2 tbsp lime juice

naan bread, to serve

method

1 Heat the ghee in a large, heavy-bottom skillet. Add the onions and cook over low heat, stirring occasionally, for 10 minutes, or until golden. Add the sliced tomatoes, kalonji seeds, peppercorns, cardamoms, cinnamon stick, chili powder, garam masala, garlic paste, and ginger paste and season with salt. Cook, stirring constantly, for 5 minutes.

2 Add the chicken and cook, stirring constantly, for 5 minutes, or until well coated in the spice paste. Stir in the yogurt. Cover and let simmer, stirring occasionally, for 10 minutes.

3 Stir in the chopped cilantro, chiles, and lime juice. Transfer to a warmed serving dish, sprinkle with more chopped cilantro, and serve immediately with naan bread.

chicken pasanda

ingredients

SERVES 4

4 cardamom pods
6 black peppercorns
$^{1}/_{2}$ cinnamon stick
$^{1}/_{2}$ tsp cumin seeds
2 tsp garam masala
1 tsp chili powder
1 tsp grated fresh ginger
1 garlic clove, very finely
    chopped
4 tbsp thick plain yogurt
pinch of salt
1 lb 8 oz/675 g skinless,
    boneless chicken, diced
5 tbsp peanut oil
2 onions, finely chopped
3 fresh green chiles, seeded
    and chopped
2 tbsp chopped fresh cilantro
$^{1}/_{2}$ cup light cream
fresh cilantro sprigs,
    to garnish

method

1 Place the cardamom pods in a nonmetallic dish with the peppercorns, cinnamon, cumin, garam masala, chili powder, ginger, garlic, yogurt, and salt. Add the chicken pieces and stir well to coat. Cover and let marinate in the refrigerator for 2–3 hours.

2 Heat the oil in a preheated wok. Add the onions and cook over low heat, stirring occasionally, for 5 minutes, or until softened, then add the chicken pieces and marinade and cook over medium heat, stirring, for 15 minutes, or until the chicken is cooked through.

3 Stir in the fresh chiles and cilantro and pour in the cream. Heat through gently, but do not let boil. Garnish with fresh cilantro and serve immediately.

thai red chicken curry

ingredients

SERVES 4

6 garlic cloves, chopped

2 fresh red chiles, chopped

2 tbsp chopped fresh
    lemongrass

1 tsp finely grated lime rind

1 tbsp chopped fresh kaffir
    lime leaves

1 tbsp Thai red curry paste

1 tbsp coriander seeds,
    toasted and crushed

1 tbsp chili oil

4 skinless, boneless chicken
    breasts, sliced

1¼ cups coconut milk

1¼ cups chicken stock

1 tbsp soy sauce

⅓ cup shelled unsalted
    peanuts, toasted and
    ground

3 scallions, diagonally sliced

1 red bell pepper, seeded and
    sliced

3 Thai eggplants, sliced

2 tbsp chopped fresh Thai
    basil or fresh cilantro

fresh cilantro, to garnish

freshly cooked jasmine rice,
    to serve

method

1 Place the garlic, chiles, lemongrass, lime rind, lime leaves, curry paste, and coriander seeds in a food processor and process until the mixture is smooth.

2 Heat the oil in a preheated wok or large skillet over high heat. Add the chicken and the garlic mixture and stir-fry for 5 minutes. Add the coconut milk, stock, and soy sauce and bring to a boil. Reduce the heat and cook, stirring, for an additional 3 minutes. Stir in the ground peanuts and let simmer for 20 minutes.

3 Add the scallions, bell pepper, and eggplants and let simmer, stirring occasionally, for an additional 10 minutes. Remove from the heat, stir in the basil, and garnish with cilantro. Serve immediately with freshly cooked jasmine rice.

red hot chili chicken

ingredients

SERVES 4

1 tbsp curry paste

2 fresh green chiles, chopped

5 dried red chiles

2 tbsp tomato paste

2 garlic cloves, chopped

1 tsp chili powder

pinch of sugar

pinch of salt

2 tbsp peanut or corn oil

$1/2$ tsp cumin seeds

1 onion, chopped

2 curry leaves

1 tsp ground cumin

1 tsp ground coriander

$1/2$ tsp ground turmeric

14 oz/400 g canned chopped
    tomatoes

$2/3$ cup chicken stock

4 skinless, boneless chicken
    breasts

1 tsp garam masala

freshly cooked rice and plain
    yogurt garnished with
    mint sprigs and diced
    cucumber, to serve

method

1 To make the chili paste, place the curry paste, fresh and dried chiles, tomato paste, garlic, chili powder, and sugar in a blender or food processor with the salt. Process to a smooth paste.

2 Heat the oil in a large, heavy-bottom pan. Add the cumin seeds and cook over medium heat, stirring constantly, for 2 minutes, or until they begin to pop and release their aroma. Add the onion and curry leaves and cook, stirring, for 5 minutes.

3 Add the chili paste, cook for 2 minutes, then stir in the ground cumin, coriander, and turmeric and cook for an additional 2 minutes.

4 Add the tomatoes and their juices and the stock. Bring to a boil, then reduce the heat and simmer for 5 minutes. Add the chicken and garam masala, cover, and simmer gently for 20 minutes, or until the chicken is cooked through and tender. Serve immediately with freshly cooked rice and yogurt.

creamy chicken curry with lemon rice

ingredients

SERVES 4

2 tbsp vegetable oil

4 skinless, boneless chicken breasts, 1 lb 12 oz/800 g in total, cut into 1-inch/ 2.5-cm pieces

1½ tsp cumin seeds

1 large onion, grated

2 fresh green chiles, finely chopped

2 large garlic cloves, grated

1 tbsp grated fresh ginger

1 tsp ground turmeric

1 tsp ground coriander

1 tsp garam masala

1¼ cups coconut milk

9 oz/250 g canned chopped tomatoes

2 tsp lemon juice

salt

2 tbsp chopped fresh cilantro, to garnish

lemon rice

scant 1¾ cups basmati rice, rinsed

5 cups water

juice and grated rind of 1 lemon

3 cloves

method

1 Heat the oil in a large, heavy-bottom pan over medium heat. Add the chicken and cook for 5–8 minutes, turning frequently, until lightly browned and cooked through. Remove from the pan and set aside. Add the cumin seeds and cook until they start to darken and sizzle. Stir in the onion, partially cover, and cook over medium–low heat, stirring frequently, for 10 minutes, or until softened and golden. Add the chiles, garlic, ginger, turmeric, ground coriander, and garam masala and cook for 1 minute.

2 Return the chicken to the pan and stir in the coconut milk and tomatoes. Partially cover and cook over medium heat for 15 minutes, until the sauce has reduced and thickened. Stir in the lemon juice and season with salt.

3 Meanwhile, cook the rice. Put the rice into a pan and cover with the water. Add the lemon juice and cloves. Bring to a boil, then reduce the heat, cover, and let simmer over very low heat for 15 minutes, or until the rice is tender and all the water has been absorbed. Remove the pan from the heat and stir in the lemon rind. Let the rice stand, covered, for 5 minutes.

4 Serve the curry with the lemon rice, sprinkled with fresh cilantro.

chicken & peanut curry

ingredients

SERVES 4

1 tbsp vegetable or peanut oil

2 red onions, sliced

2 tbsp Penang curry paste

1³/4 cups coconut milk

²/3 cup chicken stock

4 kaffir lime leaves, torn
coarsely

1 lemongrass stalk, chopped
finely

6 skinless, boneless chicken
thighs, chopped

1 tbsp fish sauce

2 tbsp Thai soy sauce

1 tsp jaggery or light brown
sugar

¹/2 cup unsalted peanuts,
roasted and chopped,
plus extra to garnish

6 oz/175 g fresh pineapple,
chopped coarsely

6-inch/15-cm piece
cucumber, peeled, seeded,
and sliced thickly, plus
extra to garnish

method

1 Heat the oil in a wok and stir-fry the onions for 1 minute. Add the curry paste and stir-fry for 1–2 minutes.

2 Pour in the coconut milk and stock. Add the lime leaves and lemongrass and let simmer for 1 minute. Add the chicken and gradually bring to a boil. Let simmer for 8–10 minutes, until the chicken is tender.

3 Stir in the fish sauce, soy sauce, and sugar, and let simmer for 1–2 minutes. Stir in the peanuts, pineapple, and cucumber and cook for 30 seconds. Serve immediately, sprinkled with the extra nuts and cucumber.

green chicken curry

ingredients

SERVES 4

1 tbsp vegetable or peanut oil

1 onion, sliced

1 garlic clove, chopped finely

2–3 tbsp Thai green curry
   paste

1³/₄ cups coconut milk

²/₃ cup chicken stock

4 kaffir lime leaves

4 skinless, boneless chicken
   breasts, cut into cubes

1 tbsp fish sauce

2 tbsp Thai soy sauce

grated rind and juice of
   ¹/₂ lime

1 tsp jaggery or light brown
   sugar

4 tbsp chopped fresh cilantro,
   to garnish

freshly cooked rice, to serve

method

1 Heat the oil in a wok or large skillet and stir-fry the onion and garlic for 1–2 minutes, until starting to soften. Add the curry paste and stir-fry for 1–2 minutes.

2 Add the coconut milk, stock, and lime leaves, bring to a boil, and add the chicken. Reduce the heat and let simmer gently for 15–20 minutes, until the chicken is tender.

3 Add the fish sauce, soy sauce, lime rind and juice, and sugar. Cook for 2–3 minutes, until the sugar has dissolved. Garnish with chopped cilantro and serve immediately, with rice.

spiced cilantro chicken

ingredients

SERVES 4

4 skinless, boneless chicken
    breasts
2 garlic cloves
1 fresh green chile, seeded
3/4-inch/2-cm piece fresh
    ginger
4 tbsp chopped cilantro
finely grated rind of 1 lime
3 tbsp lime juice
2 tbsp light soy sauce
1 tbsp superfine sugar
3/4 cup coconut milk

to garnish
finely chopped cilantro
cucumber slices
radish slices
1/2 fresh red chile, seeded and
    sliced into rings
freshly cooked rice, to serve

method

1 Using a sharp knife, cut 3 deep slashes into the skinned side of each chicken breast. Place the breasts in a single layer in a nonmetallic dish.

2 Place the garlic, chile, ginger, cilantro, lime rind and juice, soy sauce, sugar, and coconut milk in a food processor and process to a smooth paste.

3 Spread the paste over both sides of the chicken breasts, coating them evenly. Cover with plastic wrap and let marinate in the refrigerator for 1 hour.

4 Preheat the broiler to medium. Lift the chicken from the marinade, then drain off the excess and place on a broiler pan. Cook under the hot broiler for 12–15 minutes, or until thoroughly and evenly cooked.

5 Meanwhile, place the remaining marinade in a pan and bring to a boil. Reduce the heat and simmer for several minutes. Transfer the chicken breasts to serving plates and pour over the cooked marinade. Garnish with chopped cilantro, cucumber slices, radish slices, and chile rings and serve with rice.

lime chicken with mint

ingredients

SERVES 6

3 tbsp finely chopped fresh
   mint
4 tbsp honey
4 tbsp lime juice
salt and pepper
12 boneless chicken thighs
mixed salad, to serve

s a u c e
2/3 cup lowfat thick plain
   yogurt
1 tbsp finely chopped fresh
   mint
2 tsp finely grated lime rind

method

1 Mix the mint, honey, and lime juice in a large bowl and season with salt and pepper. Use toothpicks to keep the chicken thighs in neat shapes and add the chicken to the marinade, turning to coat evenly.

2 Cover with plastic wrap and let the chicken marinate in the refrigerator for at least 30 minutes. Remove the chicken from the marinade and drain. Set aside the marinade.

3 Preheat the broiler to medium. Place the chicken on a broiler rack and cook under the hot broiler for 15–18 minutes, or until the chicken is tender and the juices run clear when the tip of a knife is inserted into the thickest part of the meat, turning the chicken frequently and basting with the marinade.

4 Meanwhile, combine all the sauce ingredients in a bowl. Remove the toothpicks and serve with a mixed salad and the sauce, for dipping.

grilled chicken with lemon

ingredients

SERVES 4

4 chicken parts

grated rind and juice of
2 lemons

4 tbsp olive oil

2 garlic cloves, crushed

2 sprigs fresh thyme, plus
extra to garnish

salt and pepper

method

1 Prick the skin of the chicken parts all over with a fork. Put the chicken parts in a dish, add the lemon juice, oil, garlic, thyme, salt, and pepper, and mix well. Cover and let marinate in the refrigerator for at least 2 hours.

2 To cook the chicken, preheat the barbecue or broiler. Put the chicken on the barbecue grill or in a broiler pan and baste with the marinade. Cook for 30–40 minutes, basting and turning occasionally, until the chicken is tender. (To test if the chicken is cooked, pierce the thickest part of the meat with a skewer. If the juices run clear, it is ready.) Serve hot, garnished with thyme sprigs and the grated lemon rind.

sticky lime chicken

ingredients

SERVES 4

4 part-boned, skinless chicken
   breasts, about 5 oz/140 g
   each
grated rind and juice of 1 lime
1 tbsp honey
1 tbsp olive oil
1 garlic clove, chopped
   (optional)
1 tbsp chopped fresh thyme
pepper
boiled new potatoes and
   lightly cooked seasonal
   vegetables, to serve

method

1 Preheat the oven to 375°F/190°C. Arrange the chicken breasts in a shallow roasting pan.

2 Put the lime rind and juice, honey, oil, garlic, if using, and thyme in a small bowl and combine thoroughly. Spoon the mixture evenly over the chicken breasts and season with pepper.

3 Roast the chicken in the preheated oven, basting every 10 minutes, for 35–40 minutes, or until the chicken is tender and the juices run clear when a skewer is inserted into the thickest part of the meat. If the juices still run pink, return the chicken to the oven and cook for an additional 5 minutes, then test again. As the chicken cooks, the liquid in the pan thickens to give a tasty, sticky coating.

4 Serve with boiled new potatoes and lightly cooked seasonal vegetables.

chicken pinwheels with bleu cheese & herbs

ingredients

SERVES 4

2 tbsp pine nuts, lightly
    toasted
2 tbsp chopped fresh parsley
2 tbsp chopped fresh thyme
1 garlic clove, chopped
1 tbsp grated lemon rind
salt and pepper
4 large, skinless chicken
    breasts
9 oz/250 g bleu cheese, such
    as Stilton, crumbled
twists of lemon and sprigs of
    fresh thyme, to garnish
fresh green and red salad
    leaves, to serve

method

1 Put the pine nuts into a food processor with the parsley, thyme, garlic, and lemon rind. Season with salt and pepper.

2 Pound the chicken breasts lightly to flatten them. Spread them on one side with the pine nut mixture, then top with the cheese. Roll them up from one short end to the other, so that the filling is enclosed. Wrap the rolls individually in aluminum foil and seal well. Transfer to a steamer, or a metal colander placed over a pan of boiling water, cover tightly, and steam for 10–12 minutes, or until cooked through.

3 Arrange the salad leaves on a large serving platter. Remove the chicken from the heat, discard the foil, and cut the chicken rolls into slices. Arrange the slices over the salad leaves, garnish with twists of lemon and sprigs of thyme, and serve.

chicken rolls with cheese & pine nuts

ingredients

SERVES 6

3 slices white bread, crusts removed

6 skinless, boneless chicken breasts, about 6 oz/175 g each

2 shallots, finely chopped

2 garlic cloves, finely chopped

2 tbsp finely chopped fresh flat-leaf parsley

2 tbsp freshly grated Parmesan cheese

1/3 cup pine nuts

pinch of ground mace

salt and pepper

tarragon-flavored oil or olive oil, for brushing

a few sprigs of fresh flat-leaf parsley, to garnish

method

1 Tear the bread into pieces, place in a bowl, and add cold water to cover. Set aside to soak for 10 minutes.

2 Meanwhile, place the chicken breasts between 2 sheets of plastic wrap and pound gently with a meat mallet or the side of a rolling pin to flatten.

3 Drain the bread and squeeze out the excess liquid. Mix together the bread, shallots, garlic, parsley, Parmesan, pine nuts, and mace in a bowl. Season with salt and pepper.

4 Preheat the broiler to medium. Spread the filling evenly over the chicken breasts and roll up. Secure each roll with a wooden toothpick. Brush with the oil, then place the chicken on a broiler rack and cook under the hot broiler, turning frequently and brushing with more oil as necessary, for 25–30 minutes, or until cooked through and tender. Serve immediately, garnished with parsley.

chicken kiev

ingredients

SERVES 4

4 tbsp butter, softened

1 garlic clove, finely chopped

1 tbsp finely chopped fresh
   parsley

1 tbsp finely chopped fresh
   oregano

salt and pepper

4 skinless, boneless chicken
   breasts

1 1/2 cups fresh white or whole
   wheat bread crumbs

3 tbsp freshly grated
   Parmesan cheese

1 egg, beaten

vegetable oil, for deep-frying

slices of lemon and flat-leaf
   parsley sprigs, to garnish

freshly cooked new potatoes
   and selection of cooked
   vegetables, to serve

method

1 Place the butter and garlic in a bowl and mix together well. Stir in the chopped herbs and season well with salt and pepper. Pound the chicken breasts to flatten them to an even thickness, then place a tablespoon of herb butter in the center of each one. Fold in the sides to enclose the butter, then secure with wooden toothpicks.

2 Combine the bread crumbs and grated Parmesan on a plate. Dip the chicken parcels into the beaten egg, then coat in the bread crumb mixture. Transfer to a plate, cover, and let chill for 30 minutes. Remove from the refrigerator and coat in the egg and then the breadcrumb mixture for a second time.

3 Pour the oil into a deep-fryer to a depth that will cover the chicken parcels. Heat until it reaches 350–375°F/180–190°C, or until a cube of bread browns in 30 seconds. Transfer the chicken to the hot oil and deep-fry for 5 minutes, or until cooked through. Lift out the chicken and drain on paper towels.

4 Divide the chicken among 4 serving plates, garnish with lemon slices and parsley sprigs, and serve with new potatoes and a selection of vegetables.

roasted chicken with sun-blush tomato pesto

ingredients

SERVES 4

4 skinless, boneless chicken breasts, about 1 lb 12 oz/ 800 g in total
1 tbsp olive oil
salt and pepper
2 tbsp pine nuts, lightly toasted, to garnish

sun-blush tomato pesto

$4^{1}/_{2}$ oz/125 g sun-blush tomatoes in oil (drained weight), chopped
2 garlic cloves, crushed
4 tbsp pine nuts, lightly toasted
$^{2}/_{3}$ cup extra virgin olive oil

method

1 Preheat the oven to 400°F/200°C. To make the sun-blush tomato pesto, put the tomatoes, garlic, pine nuts, and oil into a food processor and process to a coarse paste.

2 Arrange the chicken in a large, ovenproof dish or roasting pan. Brush each breast with the oil, then place a tablespoon of red pesto over each breast. Using the back of a spoon, spread the pesto so that it covers the top of each breast. (Store the remaining pesto in an airtight container in the refrigerator for up to 1 week.)

3 Roast the chicken in the preheated oven for 30 minutes, or until tender and the juices run clear when a skewer is inserted into the thickest part of the meat.

4 Serve sprinkled with toasted pine nuts.

pesto & ricotta chicken with tomato vinaigrette

ingredients

SERVES 4

1 tbsp pesto sauce
1/2 cup ricotta cheese
4 x 6 oz/175 g boneless
    chicken breasts
1 tbsp olive oil
ground black pepper
salad greens, to garnish

tomato vinaigrette
scant 1/2 cup olive oil
1 bunch fresh chives
1 lb 2 oz/500 g tomatoes,
    peeled, seeded, and
    chopped
juice and finely grated rind
    of 1 lime
salt and pepper

method

1 Mix together the pesto and ricotta in a small bowl until well combined. Using a sharp knife, cut a deep slit in the side of each chicken breast to make a pocket. Spoon the ricotta mixture into the pockets and re-shape the chicken breasts to enclose it. Place the chicken on a plate, cover, and let chill for 30 minutes.

2 To make the vinaigrette, pour the olive oil into a blender or food processor, add the chives, and process until smooth. Scrape the mixture into a bowl and stir in the tomatoes, lime juice, and rind. Season to taste with salt and pepper.

3 Brush the chicken with the olive oil and season with pepper. Grill on a fairly hot barbecue for about 8 minutes on each side, or until cooked through and tender. Transfer to serving plates, spoon over the vinaigrette, and serve immediately, garnished with salad greens.

chicken with saffron mash

ingredients

SERVES 4

1 lb 4 oz/550 g mealy
  potatoes, cut into chunks
1 garlic clove, peeled
1 tsp saffron threads, crushed
5 cups chicken or vegetable
  stock
4 skinless, boneless chicken
  breasts, trimmed of all
  visible fat
2 tbsp olive oil
1 tbsp lemon juice
1 tbsp chopped fresh thyme
1 tbsp chopped fresh cilantro
1 tbsp coriander seeds,
  crushed
$1/3$ cup hot milk
salt and pepper
fresh thyme sprigs, to garnish

method

1 Put the potatoes, garlic, and saffron in a large, heavy-bottom pan, add the stock, and bring to a boil. Cover and let simmer for 20 minutes, or until tender.

2 Meanwhile, brush the chicken breasts all over with half the olive oil and all of the lemon juice. Sprinkle with the fresh thyme, cilantro, and the crushed coriander seeds. Heat a grill pan, add the chicken, and cook over medium–high heat for 5 minutes on each side, or until the juices run clear when the meat is pierced with the tip of a sharp knife. Alternatively, cook the chicken breasts under a preheated medium–hot broiler for 5 minutes on each side, or until cooked through.

3 Drain the potatoes and return the contents of the strainer to the pan. Add the remaining olive oil and the milk, season with salt and pepper, and mash until smooth. Divide the saffron mash among 4 large, warmed serving plates, top with a piece of chicken, and garnish with a few sprigs of fresh thyme. Serve.

tarragon chicken

ingredients

SERVES 4

4 skinless, boneless chicken
    breasts, about 6 oz/175 g
    each
salt and pepper
1/2 cup dry white wine
1–11/4 cups chicken stock
1 garlic clove, finely chopped
1 tbsp dried tarragon
3/4 cup heavy cream
1 tbsp chopped fresh tarragon
fresh tarragon sprigs,
    to garnish

method

1 Season the chicken with salt and pepper and place in a single layer in a large, heavy-bottom skillet. Pour in the wine and just enough chicken stock to cover and add the garlic and dried tarragon. Bring to a boil, reduce the heat, and cook gently for 10 minutes, or until the chicken is tender and cooked through.

2 Remove the chicken with a slotted spoon or tongs, cover, and keep warm. Strain the poaching liquid into a clean skillet and skim off any fat from the surface. Bring to a boil and cook for 12–15 minutes, or until reduced by about two-thirds.

3 Stir in the cream, return to a boil, and cook until reduced by about half. Stir in the fresh tarragon. Slice the chicken breasts and arrange on warmed plates. Spoon over the sauce, garnish with tarragon sprigs, and serve immediately.

chicken with goat cheese & basil

ingredients

SERVES 4

4 skinned chicken breast
   fillets
3^1/$_2$ oz/100 g soft goat cheese
small bunch fresh basil
salt and pepper
2 tbsp olive oil

method

1 Using a sharp knife, slit along one long edge of each chicken breast, then carefully open out each breast to make a small pocket. Divide the cheese equally among the pockets and tuck 3 or 4 basil leaves in each. Close the openings and season the breasts with salt and pepper.

2 Heat the oil in a skillet, add the chicken breasts, and fry gently for 15–20 minutes, turning several times, until golden and tender.

3 Serve warm, garnished with a sprig of basil.

chicken with walnut sauce

ingredients

SERVES 4

4–8 skinned chicken pieces

1/2 lemon, cut into wedges

3 tbsp olive oil

2/3 cup dry white wine

1 1/4 cups chicken stock

1 bay leaf

salt and pepper

3/4 cup walnut pieces

2 garlic cloves

2/3 cup strained plain yogurt

chopped fresh flat-leaf parsley,
    to garnish

rice and pita bread, to serve

method

1 Rub the chicken pieces with the lemon. Heat the oil in a large skillet, add the chicken pieces, and fry quickly until lightly browned on all sides.

2 Pour the wine into the skillet and bring to a boil. Add the stock, bay leaf, and salt and pepper to taste and simmer for about 20 minutes, turning several times, until the chicken is tender.

3 Meanwhile, put the walnuts and garlic in a food processor and blend to form a fairly smooth paste.

4 When the chicken is cooked, transfer to a warmed serving dish and keep warm. Stir the walnut mixture and yogurt into the pan juices and heat gently for about 5 minutes, until the sauce is quite thick. (Do not boil or the sauce will curdle.) Season with salt and pepper.

5 Pour the walnut sauce over the chicken pieces and serve hot with rice and pita bread. Garnish with chopped fresh parsley.

paprika chicken on a bed of onions & ham

ingredients

SERVES 4

4 chicken breast fillets, skin on

$2/3$ cup freshly squeezed lemon juice

$1–1^1/2$ tsp mild or hot Spanish paprika, to taste

salt and pepper

about 2 tbsp olive oil

$2^1/2$ oz/70 g serrano ham or prosciutto, diced

4 large onions, sliced thinly

$1/2$ cup dry white wine

$1/2$ cup chicken stock

fresh thyme or chopped fresh parsley, to garnish

method

1 To marinate the chicken, put the breasts in a nonmetallic bowl. Pour over the lemon juice and let marinate in the fridge overnight.

2 Remove the chicken breasts from the marinade and pat dry. Rub the skins with the paprika and salt and pepper to taste. Heat 2 tablespoons of the oil in a large, lidded, heavy-bottom skillet over medium–high heat. Add the chicken breasts, skin-side down, and cook for 5 minutes, or until the skins are crisp and golden. Remove from the skillet.

3 Stir the ham into the skillet, cover, and cook for about 2 minutes, until it renders any fat. Add the onions and cook for 5 minutes, stirring occasionally and adding extra oil if necessary, until the onions are softened, but not browned.

4 Add the wine and stock and bring to a boil, stirring. Return the chicken to the skillet and season to taste. Reduce the heat, cover, and let simmer for 20 minutes, or until the chicken is cooked through and the juices run clear.

5 Transfer the chicken to a plate and keep warm in a preheated oven. Bring the sauce to a boil and let bubble until the juices reduce. Taste and adjust the seasoning. Divide the onion mixture among 4 warmed plates and arrange a chicken breast on top of each. Garnish with the herbs and serve.

chicken with garlic

ingredients

SERVES 4–6

4 tbsp all-purpose flour

Spanish paprika, either hot or
    smoked sweet, to taste

salt and pepper

1 large chicken, about
    3 lb 14 oz/1.75 kg, cut into
    8 pieces, rinsed, and
    patted dry

4–6 tbsp olive oil

24 large garlic cloves, peeled
    and halved

scant 2 cups chicken stock

4 tbsp dry white wine, such as
    white Rioja

2 sprigs fresh parsley,
    1 bay leaf, and 1 sprig
    fresh thyme, tied together

fresh parsley and thyme
    leaves, to garnish

method

1 Sift the flour onto a large plate and season with paprika and salt and pepper to taste. Dredge the chicken pieces with the flour on both sides, shaking off the excess.

2 Heat 4 tablespoons of the oil in a large, deep skillet or flameproof casserole over medium heat. Add the garlic pieces and cook, stirring frequently, for about 2 minutes to flavor the oil. Remove with a slotted spoon and set aside to drain on paper towels.

3 Add as many chicken pieces, skin-side down, as will fit in a single layer. (Work in batches, if necessary, to avoid overcrowding the skillet, adding a little extra oil if necessary.) Cook for 5 minutes, until the skin is golden brown. Turn over and cook for 5 minutes longer.

4 Pour off any excess oil. Return the garlic and chicken pieces to the skillet and add the chicken stock, wine, and herbs. Bring to a boil, then reduce the heat, cover, and let simmer for 20–25 minutes, until the chicken is cooked through and tender and the garlic very soft.

5 Transfer the chicken pieces to a serving platter and keep warm. Bring the cooking liquid to a boil, with the garlic and herbs, and boil until reduced to about 1$1/2$ cups. Remove and discard the herbs. Taste and adjust the seasoning, if necessary. Spoon the sauce and the garlic cloves over the chicken pieces. Garnish with the parsley and thyme, and serve.

lemongrass chicken skewers

ingredients

SERVES 4

2 long or 4 short lemongrass
  stems

2 large skinless, boneless
  chicken breasts, about
  14 oz/400 g in total

1 small egg white

1 carrot, finely grated

1 small fresh red chile, seeded
  and chopped

2 tbsp snipped fresh garlic
  chives

2 tbsp chopped cilantro

salt and pepper

1 tbsp corn oil

cilantro sprigs and lime slices,
  to garnish

mixed salad leaves, to serve

method

1 If the lemongrass stems are long, cut them in half across the center to make 4 short lengths. Cut each stem in half lengthwise, so that you have 8 sticks.

2 Coarsely chop the chicken and place in a food processor with the egg white. Process to a smooth paste, then add the carrot, chile, chives, cilantro, and salt and pepper to taste. Process for a few seconds to mix well. Transfer the mixture to a large bowl. Cover and chill in the refrigerator for 15 minutes.

3 Preheat the broiler to medium. Divide the mixture into 8 equal-size portions and use your hands to shape the mixture around the lemongrass "skewers."

4 Brush the skewers with oil and cook under the hot broiler for 4–6 minutes, turning them occasionally, until golden brown and thoroughly cooked. Alternatively, grill over medium–hot coals.

5 Transfer to serving plates. Garnish with cilantro sprigs and lime slices and serve hot with salad greens.

chicken kebabs with yogurt sauce

ingredients

SERVES 4

1¼ cups strained plain yogurt

2 garlic cloves, crushed

juice of ½ lemon juice

1 tbsp chopped fresh herbs,
    such as oregano, dill,
    tarragon, or parsley

salt and pepper

4 large skinned, boned
    chicken breasts

corn oil, for oiling

8 firm stems of fresh rosemary
    (optional)

lemon wedges, to garnish

shredded romaine lettuce,
    to serve

method

1 To make the sauce, put the yogurt, garlic, lemon juice, oregano, and salt and pepper to taste in a large bowl and mix together well.

2 Cut the chicken breasts into chunks measuring about 1½ inches/4 cm square. Add to the yogurt mixture and toss together well until the chicken pieces are coated. Cover and let marinate in the refrigerator for about 1 hour. If you are using wooden skewers, soak them in cold water for 30 minutes before use.

3 Preheat the broiler. Thread the pieces of chicken onto 8 flat, greased, metal kebab skewers, wooden skewers, or rosemary stems and place on a greased broiler pan.

4 Cook the kebabs under the broiler for about 15 minutes, turning and basting with the remaining marinade occasionally, until lightly browned and tender.

5 Pour the remaining marinade into a saucepan and heat gently but do not boil. Serve the kebabs on a bed of shredded lettuce and garnish with lemon wedges. Accompany with the yogurt sauce.

chicken satay

ingredients

SERVES 4

2 tbsp vegetable or peanut oil

1 tbsp sesame oil

juice of 1/2 lime

2 skinless, boneless chicken
  breasts, cut into small
  cubes

d i p

2 tbsp vegetable or peanut oil

1 small onion, chopped finely

1 small fresh green chile,
  seeded and chopped

1 garlic clove, chopped finely

1/2 cup crunchy peanut butter

6–8 tbsp water

juice of 1/2 lime

method

1 Combine both the oils and the lime juice in a nonmetallic dish. Add the chicken cubes, cover with plastic wrap, and let chill for 1 hour. Soak 8–12 wooden skewers in cold water for 30 minutes before use, to prevent burning.

2 To make the dip, heat the oil in a skillet and sauté the onion, chile, and garlic over low heat, stirring occasionally, for about 5 minutes, until just softened. Add the peanut butter, water, and lime juice and let simmer gently, stirring constantly, until the peanut butter has softened enough to make a dip—you may need to add extra water to make a thinner consistency.

3 Meanwhile, drain the chicken cubes and thread them onto the wooden skewers. Put under a hot broiler or on a barbecue, turning frequently, for about 10 minutes, until cooked and browned. Serve hot with the warm dip.

gingered chicken kebabs

ingredients

SERVES 4

3 skinless, boneless chicken
  breasts, cut into small
  cubes
juice of 1 lime
1-inch/2.5-cm piece ginger,
  peeled and chopped
1 fresh red chile, seeded and
  sliced
2 tbsp vegetable or peanut oil
1 onion, sliced
2 garlic cloves, chopped
1 eggplant, cut into chunks
2 zucchini, cut into thick slices
1 red bell pepper, seeded and
  cut into squares
2 tbsp Thai red curry paste
2 tbsp Thai soy sauce
1 tsp jaggery or light brown
  sugar
boiled rice, with chopped
  cilantro, to serve

method

1 Put the chicken cubes in a shallow dish. Mix the lime, ginger, and chile together and pour over the chicken pieces. Stir gently to coat. Cover and let chill in the refrigerator for at least 3 hours to marinate.

2 Soak 8–12 wooden skewers in cold water for 30 minutes before use, to prevent burning.

3 Thread the chicken pieces onto the soaked wooden skewers and cook under a hot broiler for 3–4 minutes, turning frequently, until they are cooked through.

4 Meanwhile, heat the oil in a wok or large skillet and sauté the onion and garlic for 1–2 minutes, until softened, but not browned. Add the eggplant, zucchini, and bell pepper and cook for 3–4 minutes, until cooked but still firm. Add the curry paste, soy sauce, and sugar, and cook for 1 minute.

5 Serve hot with boiled rice, stirred through with chopped cilantro.

moroccan chicken

ingredients

SERVES 4

4 skinless, boneless chicken
    breasts, about 5 oz/140 g
    each
salt and pepper
toasted flat breads, to serve

m a r i n a d e
3 tbsp olive oil
4 tbsp lemon juice
2 tbsp chopped fresh parsley
2 tbsp chopped fresh cilantro
1 garlic clove, finely chopped
1 tsp ground coriander
1/2 tsp ground cumin
1 tsp sweet paprika
pinch of chili powder

s a l a d
4 carrots
1/2 small head white cabbage
1 cup bean sprouts
1/2 cup alfalfa sprouts
1/3 cup golden raisins
1/3 cup raisins
1 tbsp lemon juice

method

1 Mix together the oil, lemon juice, parsley, fresh cilantro, garlic, ground coriander, cumin, paprika, and chili powder in a large, shallow, nonmetallic dish.

2 Using a sharp knife, score the chicken breasts 3–4 times. Add the chicken to the dish, turning to coat. Cover with plastic wrap and let marinate in a cool place, turning occasionally, for 2–3 hours.

3 Drain the chicken, reserving the marinade. Broil, brushing occasionally with the reserved marinade, for 20–30 minutes, or until tender and cooked through. Season with salt and pepper.

4 Meanwhile, to make the salad, trim and peel the carrots, then grate them into a large salad bowl. Trim the white cabbage, then shred it finely. Transfer it to a large colander and rinse under cold running water. Drain well, then add it to the carrots. Put the bean sprouts and alfalfa sprouts into the colander and rinse well, then drain and add to the salad. Rinse and drain the golden raisins and raisins and add them to the bowl. Pour in the lemon juice and toss the salad.

5 Serve the Moroccan chicken with the salad and toasted flat breads.

chicken fajitas

ingredients

SERVES 4

3 tbsp olive oil, plus extra for drizzling

3 tbsp maple syrup or honey

1 tbsp red wine vinegar

2 garlic cloves, crushed

2 tsp dried oregano

1–2 tsp dried red pepper flakes

salt and pepper

4 skinless, boneless chicken breasts

2 red bell peppers, seeded and cut into 1-inch/2.5-cm strips

8 flour tortillas, warmed

guacamole and salsa, to serve

method

1 Place the oil, maple syrup, vinegar, garlic, oregano, pepper flakes, and salt and pepper to taste in a large, shallow plate or bowl and mix together.

2 Slice the chicken across the grain into slices 1 inch/2.5 cm thick. Toss in the marinade until well coated. Cover and let chill in the refrigerator for 2–3 hours, turning occasionally.

3 Heat a grill pan until hot. Lift the chicken slices from the marinade with a slotted spoon, lay on the grill pan, and cook over medium–high heat for 3–4 minutes on each side, or until cooked through. Remove the chicken to a warmed serving plate and keep warm.

4 Add the bell peppers, skin-side down, to the grill pan, and cook for 2 minutes on each side. Transfer to the serving plate.

5 Divide the chicken and bell peppers among the tortillas, top with guacamole and salsa, and roll up. Serve immediately.

chicken tacos from puebla

ingredients

SERVES 4

8 soft corn tortillas

2 tsp vegetable oil

8–12 oz/225–350 g leftover cooked chicken, diced or shredded

salt and pepper

8 oz/225 g canned refried beans, warmed with 2 tbsp water to thin

1/4 tsp ground cumin

1/4 tsp dried oregano

1 avocado, pitted, peeled, sliced, and tossed with lime juice

salsa of your choice

1 canned chipotle chile in adobo marinade, chopped, or bottled chipotle salsa

3/4 cup sour cream

1/2 onion, chopped

handful of lettuce leaves

5 radishes, diced

method

1 Heat the tortillas through, in an unoiled nonstick skillet, in a stack, alternating the tortillas from the top to the bottom so that they warm evenly. Wrap in foil or a clean dish towel to keep them warm.

2 Heat the oil in a skillet. Add the chicken and heat through. Season with salt and pepper.

3 Combine the warmed refried beans with the cumin and oregano.

4 Spread one tortilla with the refried beans, then top with a spoonful of the chicken, a slice or two of avocado, a little salsa, chipotle to taste, a spoonful of sour cream, and a sprinkling of onion, lettuce, and radishes. Season with salt and pepper, then roll up as tightly as you can. Repeat with the remaining tortillas and serve immediately.

bacon-wrapped chicken burgers

ingredients

SERVES 4

1 lb/450 g fresh ground
   chicken
1 onion, grated
2 garlic cloves, crushed
1/2 cup pine nuts, toasted
2 oz/55 g Gruyère cheese,
   grated
2 tbsp fresh snipped chives
salt and pepper
2 tbsp whole wheat flour
8 lean bacon slices
1–2 tbsp corn oil
crusty rolls, chopped lettuce,
   and red onion rings,
   to serve
mayonnaise and snipped
   chives, to garnish

method

1 Place the ground chicken, onion, garlic, pine nuts, cheese, chives, and salt and pepper in a food processor. Using the pulse button, blend the mixture together using short, sharp bursts. Scrape out onto a board and shape into 4 even-size burgers. Coat in the flour, then cover and let chill for 1 hour.

2 Wrap each burger with 2 bacon slices, securing in place with a wooden toothpick.

3 Heat a heavy-bottom skillet and add the oil. When hot, add the burgers and cook over medium heat for 5–6 minutes on each side, or until thoroughly cooked through.

4 Serve the burgers immediately in crusty rolls on a bed of lettuce and red onion rings and topped with mayonnaise and chives.

chicken tagine

ingredients

SERVES 4

1 tbsp olive oil

1 onion, cut into small wedges

2–4 garlic cloves, sliced

1 lb/450 g skinless, boneless
   chicken breast, diced

1 tsp ground cumin

2 cinnamon sticks, lightly
   bruised

1 tbsp all-purpose whole
   wheat flour

8 oz/225 g eggplant, diced

1 red bell pepper, seeded and
   chopped

3 oz/85 g white mushrooms,
   sliced

1 tbsp tomato paste

2$^1/_2$ cups chicken stock

10 oz/280 g canned
   chickpeas, drained and
   rinsed

$^1/_3$ cup plumped dried
   apricots, chopped

salt and pepper

1 tbsp chopped fresh cilantro

method

1 Heat the oil in a large pan over medium heat, add the onion and garlic, and cook for 3 minutes, stirring frequently. Add the chicken and cook, stirring constantly, for an additional 5 minutes, or until sealed on all sides. Add the cumin and cinnamon sticks to the pan halfway through sealing the chicken.

2 Sprinkle in the flour and cook, stirring constantly, for 2 minutes. Add the eggplant, red bell pepper, and mushrooms and cook for an additional 2 minutes, stirring constantly.

3 Blend the tomato paste with the stock, stir into the pan, and bring to a boil. Reduce the heat and add the chickpeas and apricots. Cover and let simmer for 15–20 minutes, or until the chicken is tender.

4 Season with salt and pepper and serve immediately, sprinkled with cilantro.

chicken risotto with saffron

ingredients

SERVES 4

generous $1/2$ cup butter

2 lb/900 g skinless, boneless
    chicken breasts, thinly
    sliced

1 large onion, chopped

$2^1/2$ cups Arborio rice

$2/3$ cup white wine

1 tsp crumbled saffron threads

generous $5^1/2$ cups simmering
    chicken stock

salt and pepper

$1/2$ cup freshly grated
    Parmesan cheese

method

1 Heat 4 tbsp of the butter in a deep pan, add the chicken and onion, and cook, stirring frequently, for 8 minutes, or until golden brown. Add the rice and mix to coat in the butter. Cook, stirring constantly for 2–3 minutes, or until the grains are translucent. Add the wine and cook, stirring constantly, for 1 minute, until reduced.

2 Mix the saffron with 4 tablespoons of the hot stock. Add the liquid to the rice and cook, stirring constantly, until it is absorbed. Gradually add the remaining hot stock, a ladleful at a time. Stir constantly and add more liquid as the rice absorbs each addition. Cook for 20 minutes, or until all the liquid is absorbed and the rice is creamy. Season with salt and pepper.

3 Remove the risotto from the heat and add the remaining butter. Mix well, then stir in the Parmesan until it melts. Spoon the risotto onto warmed plates and serve immediately.

chicken, mushroom & cashew risotto

ingredients

SERVES 4

4 tbsp butter

1 onion, chopped

9 oz/250 g skinless, boneless
chicken breasts, diced

1³/₄ cups Arborio rice

1 tsp ground turmeric

²/₃ cup white wine

generous 5¹/₂ cups simmering
chicken stock

2³/₄ oz/75 g cremini
mushrooms, sliced

scant ¹/₃ cup cashews, halved

salt and pepper

wild arugula, fresh Parmesan
cheese shavings, and fresh
basil leaves, to garnish

method

1 Melt the butter in a large pan over medium heat. Add the onion and cook, stirring occasionally, for 5 minutes, or until softened. Add the chicken and cook, stirring frequently, for an additional 5 minutes. Reduce the heat, add the rice, and mix to coat in butter. Cook, stirring constantly, for 2–3 minutes, or until the grains are translucent. Stir in the turmeric, then add the wine. Cook, stirring constantly, for 1 minute until reduced.

2 Gradually add the hot stock, a ladleful at a time. Stir constantly and add more liquid as the rice absorbs each addition. Increase the heat to medium so that the liquid bubbles. Cook for 20 minutes, or until all the liquid is absorbed and the rice is creamy. About 3 minutes before the end of the cooking time, stir in the mushrooms and cashews. Season with salt and pepper.

3 Arrange the arugula leaves on 4 individual serving plates. Remove the risotto from the heat and spoon it over the arugula. Sprinkle over the Parmesan shavings and basil leaves and serve.

chicken & duck paella with orange

ingredients

SERVES 4–6

1/2 tsp saffron threads

2 tbsp hot water

6 oz/175 g skinless, boneless
   chicken breast

4 large skinless, boneless
   duck breasts

salt and pepper

2 tbsp olive oil

1 large onion, chopped

2 garlic cloves, crushed

1 tsp paprika

8 oz/225 g tomato wedges

1 orange bell pepper, broiled,
   peeled, seeded, and
   chopped

6 oz/175 g canned red kidney
   beans (drained weight)

generous 1 1/2 cups paella rice

1 tbsp chopped fresh flat-leaf
   parsley, plus extra sprigs to
   garnish

1 tbsp freshly grated orange
   rind

2 tbsp orange juice

generous 1/3 cup white wine

5 cups simmering chicken
   stock

orange wedges, to garnish

method

1 Put the saffron threads and water in a small bowl and let infuse for a few minutes.

2 Cut the chicken and duck into bite-size chunks and season. Heat the oil in a paella pan and cook the chicken and duck over medium–high heat, stirring, until golden all over. Transfer to a bowl and set aside.

3 Add the onion and cook over medium heat, stirring, until softened. Add the garlic, paprika, and saffron and its soaking liquid and cook, stirring constantly, for 1 minute. Add the tomato wedges, orange bell pepper, and beans and cook, stirring, for an additional 2 minutes.

4 Add the rice and parsley and cook, stirring, for 1 minute. Add the orange rind and juice, the wine, and most of the hot stock. Bring to a boil, then let simmer, uncovered, for 10 minutes. Do not stir during cooking, but shake the pan once or twice, and when adding ingredients. Return the chicken and duck to the pan and season. Cook for 10–15 minutes, or until the rice grains are plump and cooked, adding a little more stock if necessary.

5 When all the liquid has been absorbed and you detect a faint toasty aroma coming from the rice, remove from the heat. Cover with foil and let stand for 5 minutes. Garnish with parsley sprigs and orange wedges to serve.

jambalaya

ingredients

SERVES 4

14 oz/400 g skinless, boneless chicken breast, diced

1 red onion, diced

1 garlic clove, crushed

2¹/₂ cups chicken stock

14 oz/400 g canned chopped tomatoes in tomato juice

generous 1¹/₂ cups brown rice

1–2 tsp hot chili powder

¹/₂ tsp paprika

1 tsp dried oregano

1 red bell pepper, seeded and diced

1 yellow bell pepper, seeded and diced

¹/₂ cup frozen corn kernels

¹/₂ cup frozen peas

3 tbsp chopped fresh parsley

pepper

crisp salad greens, to serve (optional)

method

1 Put the chicken, onion, garlic, stock, tomatoes, and rice into a large, heavy-bottom pan. Add the chili powder, paprika, and oregano and stir well. Bring to a boil, then reduce the heat, cover, and let simmer for 25 minutes.

2 Add the red and yellow bell peppers, corn, and peas to the rice mixture and return to a boil. Reduce the heat, cover, and let simmer for an additional 10 minutes, or until the rice is just tender (brown rice retains a 'nutty' texture when cooked) and most of the stock has been absorbed but is not completely dry.

3 Stir in 2 tablespoons of the parsley and season with pepper. Transfer the jambalaya to a warmed serving dish, garnish with the remaining parsley, and serve with crisp salad greens, if using.

egg-fried rice with chicken

ingredients

SERVES 4

generous 1 cup jasmine rice

3 skinless, boneless chicken
  breasts, cut into cubes

2 cups canned coconut milk

2–3 cilantro roots, chopped

thinly pared zest of 1 lemon

1 fresh green chile, seeded
  and chopped

3 fresh Thai basil leaves

1 tbsp fish sauce

1 tbsp oil

3 eggs, beaten

fresh chives and sprigs fresh
  cilantro, to garnish

method

1 Cook the rice in boiling water for 12–15 minutes, drain well, then let cool and chill overnight.

2 Put the chicken into a pan and cover with the coconut milk. Add the cilantro roots, lemon zest, and chile, and bring to a boil. Let simmer for 8–10 minutes, until the chicken is tender. Remove from the heat. Stir in the basil and fish sauce.

3 Meanwhile, heat the oil in a wok and stir-fry the rice for 2–3 minutes. Pour in the eggs and stir until they have cooked and mixed with the rice. Line 4 small ovenproof bowls or ramekins with plastic wrap and pack with the rice. Turn out carefully onto serving plates and remove the plastic wrap. Garnish with long chives and sprigs of cilantro. Serve with the chicken.

chicken with vegetables & cilantro rice

ingredients

SERVES 4

2 tbsp vegetable or peanut oil

1 red onion, chopped

2 garlic cloves, chopped

1-inch/2.5-cm piece ginger, peeled and chopped

2 skinless, boneless chicken breasts, cut into strips

4 oz/115 g white mushrooms

14 oz/400 g canned coconut milk

2 oz/50 g snow peas, trimmed and halved lengthwise

2 tbsp soy sauce

1 tbsp fish sauce

rice

1 tbsp vegetable or peanut oil

1 red onion, sliced

3 cups rice, cooked and cooled

8 oz/250 g bok choy, torn into large pieces

handful of fresh cilantro, chopped

2 tbsp Thai soy sauce

method

1 Heat the oil in a wok or large skillet and sauté the onion, garlic, and ginger together for 1–2 minutes.

2 Add the chicken and mushrooms and cook over high heat until browned. Add the coconut milk, snow peas, and sauces, and bring to a boil. Let simmer gently for 4–5 minutes, until tender.

3 Heat the oil for the rice in a separate wok or large skillet and cook the onion until softened, but not browned. Add the cooked rice, bok choy, and fresh cilantro, and heat gently until the leaves have wilted and the rice is hot. Sprinkle over the soy sauce and serve immediately with the chicken.

meat

Meat is the mainstay of many family menus but it is incredibly easy to get stuck in a rut of chops, steak, sausages, and ground meat because these are all straightforward to prepare and cook quickly. Of course there's nothing wrong with that, but you may be surprised to find out how with a little know-how, and a handful of additional ingredients, you can transform these simple cuts and meat products into truly special meals in minutes.

All these recipes have been inspired by everyday dishes from across the world. Even in countries where it was once traditional to lavish hours on preparing the day's main meal, twenty-first century cooks have busy lives and so have developed straightforward, speedy dishes that still retain all the character of their local cuisine. So it's really easy to extend your repertoire and surprise your family with Italian pasta, Thai stir-fry, Greek kebabs, or Spanish sausage casserole, for example.

There's a wealth of recipes for beef, lamb, and pork, as well as delicious dishes based on bacon and sausages. You're sure to find an easy-to-cook dish that suits your taste and budget and there are also intriguing international versions of familiar favorites. As many of them include pasta, noodles, rice, or potatoes and vegetables, they constitute a complete main course and you won't have to spend time and energy preparing

accompaniments. Lots of others require nothing more complicated than a simple salad and some fresh bread to turn them into a veritable feast.

spaghetti with meatballs

ingredients

SERVES 6

1 potato, diced

14 oz/400 g ground steak

1 onion, finely chopped

1 egg

4 tbsp chopped fresh flat-leaf
    parsley

all-purpose flour, for dusting

5 tbsp virgin olive oil

1³/4 cups strained tomatoes

2 tbsp tomato paste

14 oz/400 g dried spaghetti

salt and pepper

6 fresh basil leaves, shredded

freshly grated Parmesan
    cheese, to garnish

method

1 Place the potato in a small pan, add cold water to cover and a pinch of salt, and bring to a boil. Cook for 10–15 minutes, until tender, then drain. Either mash thoroughly with a potato masher or fork or pass through a potato ricer.

2 Combine the potato, steak, onion, egg, and parsley in a bowl and season to taste with salt and pepper. Spread out the flour on a plate. With dampened hands, shape the meat mixture into walnut-size balls and roll in the flour. Shake off any excess.

3 Heat the oil in a heavy-bottom skillet, add the meatballs, and cook over medium heat, stirring and turning frequently, for 8–10 minutes, until golden all over.

4 Add the strained tomatoes and tomato paste and cook for an additional 10 minutes, until the sauce is reduced and thickened.

5 Meanwhile, bring a large pan of lightly salted water to a boil. Add the pasta, bring back to a boil, and cook for 8–10 minutes, until tender but still firm to the bite.

6 Drain well and add to the meatball sauce, tossing well to coat. Transfer to a warmed serving dish, garnish with the basil leaves and Parmesan, and serve immediately.

tagliatelle with a rich meat sauce

ingredients

SERVES 4

4 tbsp olive oil, plus extra for
    serving
3 oz/85 g pancetta or rindless
    lean bacon, diced
1 onion, chopped
1 garlic clove, chopped finely
1 carrot, chopped
1 celery stalk, chopped
8 oz/225 g ground steak
4 oz/115 g chicken livers,
    chopped
2 tbsp strained tomatoes
$1/2$ cup dry white wine
1 cup beef stock or water
1 tbsp chopped fresh oregano
1 bay leaf
salt and pepper
1 lb/450 g dried tagliatelle
freshly grated Parmesan
    cheese, to serve

method

1 Heat the olive oil in a large, heavy-bottom pan. Add the pancetta or bacon and cook over medium heat, stirring occasionally, for 3–5 minutes, until it is just turning brown. Add the onion, garlic, carrot, and celery and cook, stirring occasionally, for an additional 5 minutes.

2 Add the steak and cook over high heat, breaking up the meat with a wooden spoon, for 5 minutes, until browned. Stir in the chicken livers and cook, stirring occasionally, for an additional 2–3 minutes. Add the strained tomatoes, wine, stock, oregano, and bay leaf, and season to taste with salt and pepper. Bring to a boil, reduce the heat, cover, and simmer for 30–35 minutes.

3 When the sauce is almost cooked, bring a large pan of lightly salted water to a boil. Add the pasta, bring back to a boil, and cook for 8–10 minutes, until tender but still firm to the bite. Drain, transfer to a warmed serving dish, drizzle with a little olive oil, and toss well.

4 Remove and discard the bay leaf from the sauce, then pour it over the pasta, toss again, and serve immediately with grated Parmesan.

grilled steak with tomatoes & garlic

ingredients

SERVES 4

3 tbsp olive oil, plus extra for
   brushing

1 lb 9 oz/700 g tomatoes,
   peeled and chopped

1 red bell pepper, seeded and
   chopped

1 onion, chopped

2 garlic cloves, chopped finely

1 tbsp chopped fresh flat-leaf
   parsley

1 tsp dried oregano

1 tsp sugar

salt and pepper

4 x 6-oz/175-g entrecôte or
   rump steaks

method

1 Place the oil, tomatoes, red bell pepper, onion, garlic, parsley, oregano, and sugar in a heavy-bottom pan and season to taste with salt and pepper. Bring to a boil, reduce the heat, and let simmer for 15 minutes.

2 Meanwhile, trim any fat around the outsides of the steaks. Season each generously with pepper (but no salt) and brush with olive oil. Cook in a preheated ridged grill pan according to taste: 2–3 minutes each side for rare; 3–4 minutes each side for medium; 4–5 minutes on each side for well done.

3 Transfer the steaks to warmed individual plates and spoon the sauce over them. Serve immediately.

beef chop suey

ingredients

SERVES 4

1 lb/450 g ribeye or sirloin
    steak, finely sliced

1 head of broccoli, cut into
    small florets

2 tbsp vegetable or peanut oil

1 onion, finely sliced

2 celery stalks, finely sliced
    diagonally

2 cups snow peas, sliced in
    half lengthwise

1/2 cup fresh or canned
    bamboo shoots, rinsed and
    julienned (if using fresh
    shoots, boil in water first for
    30 minutes)

8 water chestnuts, finely sliced

4 cups finely sliced
    mushrooms

1 tbsp oyster sauce

1 tsp salt

marinade

1 tbsp Shaoxing rice wine

pinch of white pepper

pinch of salt

1 tbsp light soy sauce

1/2 tsp sesame oil

method

1 Combine all the marinade ingredients in a bowl and marinate the beef for at least 20 minutes. Blanch the broccoli florets in a large pan of boiling water for 30 seconds. Drain and set aside.

2 In a preheated wok or deep pan, heat 1 tablespoon of the oil and stir-fry the beef until the color has changed. Remove and set aside.

3 In the clean wok or deep pan, heat the remaining oil and stir-fry the onion for 1 minute. Add the celery and broccoli and cook for 2 minutes. Add the snow peas, bamboo shoots, chestnuts, and mushrooms and cook for 1 minute. Add the beef, then season with the oyster sauce and salt and serve immediately.

hot sesame beef

ingredients

SERVES 4

1 lb 2 oz/500 g beef
   tenderloin, cut into thin
   strips
1¹/₂ tbsp sesame seeds
¹/₂ cup beef stock
2 tbsp soy sauce
2 tbsp grated fresh ginger
2 garlic cloves, chopped finely
1 tsp cornstarch
¹/₂ tsp chile flakes
3 tbsp sesame oil
1 large head of broccoli, cut
   into florets
1 orange bell pepper, sliced
   thinly
1 red chile, seeded and sliced
   finely
1 tbsp chili oil (optional)

method

1 Mix the beef strips with 1 tablespoon of the sesame seeds in a small bowl. In a separate bowl, whisk together the beef stock, soy sauce, ginger, garlic, cornstarch, and chile flakes.

2 Heat 1 tablespoon of the sesame oil in a large skillet or wok. Stir-fry the beef strips for 2–3 minutes. Remove and set aside.

3 Discard any oil left in the pan, then wipe with paper towels to remove any stray sesame seeds. Heat the remaining oil, add the broccoli, orange bell pepper, chile, and chili oil, if using, and stir-fry for 2–3 minutes. Stir in the beef stock mixture, cover, and let simmer for 2 minutes.

4 Return the beef to the skillet and let simmer until the juices thicken, stirring occasionally. Cook for another 1–2 minutes.

5 Sprinkle with the remaining sesame seeds. Serve garnished with chopped cilantro.

rice sticks with beef in black bean sauce

ingredients

SERVES 4

8 oz/225 g rump steak, finely
   sliced
8 oz/225 g rice sticks
2–3 tbsp vegetable or peanut
   oil
1 small onion, finely sliced
1 green bell pepper, finely
   sliced
1 red bell pepper, finely sliced
2 tbsp black bean sauce
2–3 tbsp light soy sauce

marinade
1 tbsp dark soy sauce
1 tsp Shaoxing rice wine
1/2 tsp sugar
1/2 tsp white pepper

method

1 Combine all the marinade ingredients in a bowl, add the beef, and let marinate for at least 20 minutes.

2 Cook the rice sticks according to the directions on the package. When cooked, drain and set aside.

3 In a preheated wok or deep pan, heat the oil and stir-fry the beef for 1 minute, or until the meat has changed color. Drain the meat and set aside.

4 Pour off any excess oil from the wok and stir-fry the onion and bell peppers for 1 minute. Add the black bean sauce and stir well, then pour in the light soy sauce. Toss the rice sticks in the vegetables and when fully incorporated, add the beef and stir until warmed through. Serve immediately.

beef stir-fry

ingredients

SERVES 4

2 tbsp vegetable or peanut oil

2 medium red onions, sliced
    thinly

2 garlic cloves, chopped

1-inch/2.5-cm piece ginger,
    cut into thin sticks

2 x 4-oz/115-g beef
    tenderloins, sliced thinly

1 green bell pepper, seeded
    and sliced

5$^1/_2$ oz/150 g canned bamboo
    shoots

$^3/_4$ cup bean sprouts

2 tbsp magic paste

1 tbsp Thai red curry paste

handful of fresh cilantro,
    chopped

a few sprigs Thai basil

boiled rice, to serve

method

1 Heat the oil in a wok or large skillet and stir-fry the onions, garlic, and ginger for 1 minute. Add the beef strips and stir-fry over high heat until browned all over. Add the vegetables and the two pastes and cook for 2–3 minutes, until blended and cooked.

2 Stir in the cilantro and basil and serve immediately with rice.

beef with fresh noodles

ingredients

SERVES 4

6 dried black cloud Chinese
   mushrooms
2 tbsp vegetable or peanut oil
2 x 8-oz/225-g sirloin steaks,
   sliced thickly
1 onion, cut into thin wedges
2 garlic cloves, chopped
1 green bell pepper, seeded
   and chopped
3 celery stalks, sliced
2 tbsp Thai green curry paste
1¼ cups beef stock
4 tbsp black bean sauce
8 oz/225 g fresh egg noodles
4 tbsp chopped fresh parsley

method

1 Put the mushrooms in a bowl, cover with boiling water, and set aside to soak for 30 minutes. Drain. Break up any larger pieces.

2 Heat the oil in a wok and stir-fry the steak over high heat until browned. Add the mushrooms, onion, garlic, bell pepper, and celery, and stir-fry for 3–4 minutes. Add the curry paste, beef stock, and black bean sauce and stir-fry for 2–3 minutes.

3 Meanwhile, cook the noodles in boiling water for 3–4 minutes, drain well, and stir into the wok. Sprinkle over the parsley and stir. Serve immediately.

beef chow mein

ingredients

SERVES 4

10 oz/280 g tenderloin steak,
   cut into slivers
8 oz/225 g dried egg noodles
2 tbsp vegetable or peanut oil
1 onion, finely sliced
1 green bell pepper, finely
   sliced
1 cup bean sprouts, trimmed
1 tsp salt
pinch of sugar
2 tsp Shaoxing rice wine
2 tbsp light soy sauce
1 tbsp dark soy sauce
1 tbsp finely shredded scallion

marinade
1 tsp light soy sauce
dash of sesame oil
$^1/_2$ tsp Shaoxing rice wine
pinch of white pepper

method

1 Combine all the marinade ingredients in a bowl and marinate the beef for at least 20 minutes.

2 Cook the noodles according to the directions on the package. When cooked, rinse under cold water and set aside.

3 In a preheated wok, heat the oil and stir-fry the beef for about 1 minute, or until the meat has changed color, then add the onion and cook for 1 minute, followed by the bell pepper and bean sprouts. Evaporate off any water from the vegetables. Add the salt, sugar, Shaoxing, and soy sauces. Stir in the noodles and toss for 1 minute. Finally, stir in the scallion and serve.

beef with onions & broccoli

ingredients

SERVES 4

2 tbsp vegetable or peanut oil

2 tbsp Thai green curry paste

2 x 6-oz/175-g sirloin steaks,
     sliced thinly

2 onions, sliced

6 scallions, chopped

2 shallots, chopped finely

8 oz/225 g broccoli, cut into
     florets

1³/₄ cups coconut milk

3 kaffir lime leaves, chopped
     coarsely

4 tbsp chopped fresh cilantro

a few Thai basil leaves

method

1 Heat the oil in a wok and stir-fry the curry paste for 1–2 minutes. Add the meat, in batches if necessary, and stir-fry until starting to brown.

2 Add the onions, scallions, and shallots, and stir-fry for 2–3 minutes. Add the broccoli and stir-fry for 2–3 minutes.

3 Pour in the coconut milk, add the lime leaves, and bring to a boil. Let simmer gently for 8–10 minutes, until the meat is tender. Stir in the cilantro and basil and serve immediately.

stir-fried beef with bean sprouts

ingredients

SERVES 4

1 bunch of scallions

2 tbsp corn oil

1 garlic clove, crushed

1 tsp finely chopped fresh
   ginger

1 lb 2 oz/500 g lean beef
   tenderloin, cut into thin
   strips

1 large red bell pepper,
   seeded and sliced

1 small fresh red chile, seeded
   and chopped

3 cups fresh bean sprouts

1 small lemongrass stem,
   finely chopped

2 tbsp smooth peanut butter

4 tbsp coconut milk

1 tbsp rice vinegar or white
   wine vinegar

1 tbsp soy sauce

1 tsp brown sugar

9 oz/250 g medium egg
   noodles

salt and pepper

method

1 Thinly slice the scallions, reserving some slices to use as a garnish.

2 Heat the oil in a skillet or preheated wok over high heat. Add the scallions, garlic, and ginger and stir-fry for 2–3 minutes to soften. Add the beef and continue stir-frying for 4–5 minutes, or until evenly browned.

3 Add the bell pepper and stir-fry for an additional 3–4 minutes. Add the chile and bean sprouts and stir-fry for 2 minutes. Mix the lemongrass, peanut butter, coconut milk, rice vinegar, soy sauce, and sugar together in a bowl, then stir into the skillet.

4 Meanwhile, cook the egg noodles in boiling salted water for 4 minutes, or according to the package directions. Drain and stir into the skillet, tossing to mix evenly.

5 Season to taste with salt and pepper. Sprinkle with the reserved scallions and serve hot.

spicy beef with potato

ingredients

SERVES 4

1 lb/450 g beef tenderloin

2 tbsp Thai soy sauce

2 tbsp fish sauce

2 tbsp vegetable or peanut oil

3–4 cilantro roots, chopped

1 tbsp crushed black
    peppercorns

2 garlic cloves, chopped

1 tbsp jaggery or light brown
    sugar

12 oz/350 g potatoes, diced

2/3 cup water

bunch of scallions, chopped

5 cups baby spinach leaves

cooked rice or noodles,
    to serve

method

1 Cut the beef into thick slices and place in a shallow dish. Put the soy sauce, fish sauce, 1 tablespoon of the oil, the cilantro roots, peppercorns, garlic, and sugar in a food processor and process to a thick paste. Scrape the paste into the dish and toss the beef to coat. Cover with plastic wrap and set aside to marinate in the refrigerator for at least 3 hours, preferably overnight.

2 Heat the remaining oil in a wok. Lift the beef out of the marinade, reserving the marinade, and cook for 3–4 minutes on each side, until browned. Add the reserved marinade and the potatoes with the measured water and gradually bring to a boil. Let simmer for 6–8 minutes, or until the potatoes are tender.

3 Add the scallions and spinach. Cook gently until the greens have wilted. Serve immediately with rice or noodles.

mussaman curry

ingredients

SERVES 4

1 tbsp vegetable or peanut oil

1 lb/450 g beef top round,
    cut into cubes

2 tbsp Mussaman curry paste

2 large onions, cut into
    wedges

2 large potatoes, cut into
    chunks

1^3/$_4$ cups coconut milk

^{2}/$_3$ cup water

2 cardamom pods

2 tbsp tamarind paste

2 tsp jaggery or light brown
    sugar

^{2}/$_3$ cup unsalted peanuts,
    toasted or dry-fried

1 fresh red chile, sliced thinly

boiled rice, to serve

method

1 Heat the oil in a wok and cook the meat, in batches, until browned all over. Remove with a slotted spoon and set aside.

2 Add the curry paste to the wok and stir-fry for 1–2 minutes. Add the onions and potatoes and stir–fry for 4–5 minutes, until golden brown. Remove with a slotted spoon and set aside.

3 Pour the coconut milk into the wok with the measured water and bring to a boil. Reduce the heat and let simmer for 8–10 minutes.

4 Return the meat and cooked vegetables to the wok. Add the cardamom, tamarind paste, and sugar, and let simmer for 15–20 minutes, until the meat is tender. Stir in the peanuts and chile and serve with rice.

hot beef & coconut curry

ingredients

SERVES 4

1 3/4 cups coconut milk

2 tbsp Thai red curry paste

2 garlic cloves, crushed

1 lb 2 oz/500 g braising beef

2 fresh kaffir lime leaves,
    shredded

3 tbsp lime juice

2 tbsp Thai fish sauce

1 large fresh red chile, seeded
    and sliced

1/2 tsp ground turmeric

salt and pepper

2 tbsp chopped fresh basil
    leaves

2 tbsp chopped cilantro leaves

shredded coconut, to garnish

freshly cooked rice, to serve

method

1 Place the coconut milk in a large pan and bring to a boil. Reduce the heat and simmer gently for 10 minutes, or until it has thickened. Stir in the curry paste and garlic and simmer for an additional 5 minutes.

2 Cut the beef into 3/4-inch/2-cm chunks. Add to the pan and bring to a boil, stirring constantly. Reduce the heat and add the kaffir lime leaves, lime juice, fish sauce, sliced chile, turmeric, and 1/2 teaspoon of salt.

3 Cover the pan and continue simmering for 20–25 minutes, or until the meat is tender, adding a little water if the sauce looks too dry.

4 Stir in the basil and cilantro and season to taste with salt and pepper. Sprinkle with shredded coconut and serve with freshly cooked rice.

egg-fried rice with seven-spice beef

ingredients

SERVES 4

generous 1 cup long-grain
     white rice
2¹/₂ cups water
12 oz/350 g beef tenderloin
2 tbsp dark soy sauce
2 tbsp ketchup
1 tbsp seven-spice seasoning
2 tbsp peanut oil
1 onion, diced
3 small carrots, diced
1 cup frozen peas
2 eggs, beaten
2 tbsp cold water

method

1 Rinse the rice under cold running water, then drain thoroughly. Place the rice in a pan with the water, bring to a boil, cover, and let simmer for 12 minutes. Turn the cooked rice out onto a cookie sheet and let cool.

2 Using a sharp knife, thinly slice the beef tenderloin and place in a large, shallow dish. Mix the soy sauce, ketchup, and seven-spice seasoning. Spoon over the beef and toss well to coat.

3 Heat the peanut oil in a preheated wok. Add the beef and stir-fry for 3–4 minutes. Add the onion, carrots, and peas and stir-fry for a further 2–3 minutes. Add the cooked rice to the wok and mix together.

4 Beat the eggs with 2 tablespoons of cold water. Drizzle the egg mixture over the rice and stir-fry for 3–4 minutes, or until the rice is heated through and the egg has set. Transfer the rice and beef to a warmed serving bowl and serve immediately.

greek-style beef kebabs

ingredients

SERVES 4

1 small onion, finely chopped
1 tbsp chopped fresh cilantro
large pinch of paprika
$1/4$ tsp ground allspice
$1/4$ tsp ground coriander
$1/4$ tsp brown sugar
1 lb/450 g ground beef
salt and pepper
vegetable oil, for brushing
fresh cilantro leaves,
    to garnish
freshly cooked bulgur wheat
    and mixed salad, to serve

method

1 If you are using wooden skewers, soak them in cold water for 30 minutes before use.

2 Put the onion, fresh cilantro, spices, sugar, and beef into a large bowl and mix until well combined. Season with salt and pepper.

3 On a clean counter, use your hands to shape the mixture into sausages around the skewers. Brush them lightly with vegetable oil.

4 Barbecue the kebabs over hot coals, turning them frequently, for 15–20 minutes, or until cooked through. Arrange the kebabs on a platter of freshly cooked bulgur wheat and garnish with fresh cilantro leaves. Serve with a mixed salad.

beef skewers with orange & garlic

ingredients

SERVES 6–8

3 tbsp white wine

2 tbsp olive oil

3 garlic cloves, finely chopped

juice of 1 orange

1 lb/450 g rump steak, cubed

salt and pepper

1 lb/450 g pearl onions,
      halved

2 orange bell peppers, seeded
      and cut into squares

8 oz/225 g cherry tomatoes,
      halved

method

1 Mix the wine, olive oil, garlic, and orange juice together in a shallow, nonmetallic dish. Add the cubes of steak, season to taste with salt and pepper, and toss to coat. Cover with plastic wrap and let marinate in the refrigerator for 2–8 hours.

2 Preheat the broiler to high. Drain the steak, reserving the marinade. Thread the steak, onions, bell peppers, and tomatoes alternately onto several small skewers.

3 Cook the skewers under the hot broiler, turning and brushing frequently with the marinade, for 10 minutes, or until cooked through. Transfer to warmed serving plates and serve immediately.

red lamb curry

ingredients

SERVES 4

2 tbsp vegetable oil

1 large onion, sliced

2 garlic cloves, crushed

1 lb 2 oz/500 g lean boneless
   leg of lamb, cut into
   1 1/4-inch/3-cm cubes

2 tbsp Thai red curry paste

2/3 cup coconut milk

1 tbsp brown sugar

1 large red bell pepper,
   seeded and thickly sliced

1/2 cup lamb or beef stock

1 tbsp Thai fish sauce

2 tbsp lime juice

generous 1 cup canned water
   chestnuts, drained

2 tbsp chopped cilantro

2 tbsp chopped fresh basil

salt and pepper

fresh basil leaves, to garnish

freshly cooked jasmine rice,
   to serve

method

1 Heat the oil in a large skillet or preheated wok over high heat. Add the onion and garlic and stir-fry for 2–3 minutes to soften. Add the meat and stir-fry the mixture quickly until lightly browned.

2 Stir in the curry paste and cook for a few seconds, then add the coconut milk and sugar and bring to a boil. Reduce the heat and simmer for 15 minutes, stirring occasionally.

3 Stir in the bell pepper, stock, fish sauce, and lime juice, then cover and simmer for an additional 15 minutes, or until the meat is tender.

4 Add the water chestnuts, cilantro, and basil and season to taste with salt and pepper. Transfer to serving plates, then garnish with basil leaves and serve with jasmine rice.

stir-fried lamb with mint

ingredients

SERVES 4

2 tbsp vegetable oil

2 garlic cloves, finely sliced

2 fresh red chiles, seeded and
    cut into thin strips

1 onion, thinly sliced

1$^1/_2$ tbsp Madras curry paste

1 lb 2 oz/500 g lamb
    tenderloin, cut into thin
    strips

8 oz/225 g canned baby corn,
    drained

4 scallions, finely chopped

generous $^1/_3$ cup fresh mint
    leaves, coarsely shredded

1 tbsp Thai fish sauce

freshly cooked rice, to serve

method

1 Heat half the oil in a preheated wok or large skillet. Add the garlic and chiles and cook until softened. Remove and reserve. Add the onion and cook for 5 minutes, or until softened. Remove and reserve.

2 Heat the remaining oil in the wok. Add the curry paste and cook for 1 minute. Add the lamb, in batches if necessary, and cook for 5–8 minutes, or until cooked through and tender.

3 Return the onion to the wok with the baby corn, scallions, mint, and fish sauce. Cook until heated through. Sprinkle over the garlic and chiles and serve with rice.

lamb skewers with lemon

ingredients

SERVES 8

2 garlic cloves, finely chopped

1 Spanish onion, finely
    chopped

2 tsp finely grated lemon rind

2 tbsp lemon juice

1 tsp fresh thyme leaves

1 tsp ground coriander

1 tsp ground cumin

2 tbsp red wine vinegar

$^{1}/_{2}$ cup olive oil

2 lb 4 oz/1 kg lamb
    tenderloin, cut into
    $^{3}/_{4}$-inch/2-cm pieces

orange or lemon slices,
    to garnish

method

1 If you are using wooden skewers, soak them in cold water for 30 minutes before use.

2 Mix the garlic, onion, lemon rind, lemon juice, thyme, coriander, cumin, vinegar, and olive oil together in a large, shallow, nonmetallic dish, whisking well until thoroughly combined.

3 Thread the pieces of lamb onto the skewers and add to the dish, turning well to coat. Cover with plastic wrap and let marinate in the refrigerator for 2–8 hours, turning occasionally.

4 Preheat the broiler to medium. Drain the skewers, reserving the marinade. Cook under the hot broiler, turning frequently and brushing with the marinade, for 10 minutes, or until tender and cooked to your liking. Serve immediately, garnished with orange slices.

marinated lamb & vegetable kebabs

ingredients

SERVES 4

juice of 2 large lemons

1/3 cup olive oil, plus extra for oiling

1 garlic clove, crushed

1 tbsp chopped fresh oregano or mint

salt and pepper

1 lb 9 oz/700 g boned leg of lamb, trimmed and cut into 1 1/2-inch/4-cm cubes

2 green bell peppers

2 zucchini

12 pearl onions, peeled and left whole

8 large bay leaves

freshly cooked rice, to serve

cucumber & yogurt dip

1 small cucumber

1 1/4 cups strained plain yogurt

1 large garlic clove, crushed

1 tbsp chopped fresh mint or dill

salt and pepper

method

1 To make the cucumber and yogurt dip, peel then coarsely grate the cucumber. Put in a strainer and squeeze out as much of the water as possible. Put the cucumber into a bowl. Add the yogurt, garlic, and chopped mint, season with pepper, and mix thoroughly. Let chill in the refrigerator for 2 hours. Sprinkle with salt just before serving.

2 Put the lemon juice, oil, garlic, oregano or mint, and salt and pepper to taste in a bowl and whisk together. Add the lamb to the marinade.

3 Toss the lamb in the marinade, cover, and let chill overnight or for at least 8 hours. Stir occasionally to coat the lamb.

4 When ready to serve, seed the bell peppers and cut into 1 1/4-inch/3-cm cubes. Cut the zucchini into 1-inch/2.5-cm pieces. Thread the lamb, bell peppers, zucchini, onions, and bay leaves onto 8 flat, greased metal kebab skewers, alternating and dividing the ingredients as evenly as possible. Place on a greased broiler pan.

5 Preheat the broiler then put the kebabs under the broiler for 10–15 minutes, turning frequently and basting with any remaining marinade, until cooked. Serve with rice and the cucumber and yogurt dip.

grecian meatballs

ingredients

SERVES 4

1 lb/450 g lean, finely ground
    lamb
1 medium onion
1 garlic clove, crushed
$1/2$ cup fresh white or brown
    bread crumbs
1 tbsp chopped fresh mint
1 tbsp chopped fresh parsley
salt and pepper
1 egg, beaten
olive oil, for brushing
rice or warm pita bread,
    to serve

method

1 Put the ground lamb in a bowl. Grate in the onion, then add the garlic, bread crumbs, mint, and parsley. Season well with salt and pepper. Mix the ingredients well, then add the beaten egg and mix to bind the mixture together.

2 With damp hands, form the mixture into 16 small balls and thread onto 4 flat metal skewers. Lightly oil a broiler pan and brush the meatballs with oil.

3 Preheat the broiler and cook the meatballs under a medium heat for 10 minutes, turning frequently and brushing with more oil if necessary, until browned. Serve the meatballs with rice or tucked into warm pita bread.

moussaka

ingredients

SERVES 4

2 eggplants, thinly sliced

1 lb/450 g fresh lean ground
    beef

2 onions, thinly sliced

1 tsp finely chopped garlic

14 oz/400 g canned tomatoes

2 tbsp chopped fresh parsley

salt and pepper

2 eggs

1¼ cups lowfat plain yogurt

1 tbsp freshly grated
    Parmesan cheese

method

1 Preheat the oven to 350°F/180°C. Dry-fry the eggplant slices, in batches, in a nonstick skillet on both sides until browned. Remove from the skillet.

2 Add the beef to the skillet and cook for 5 minutes, stirring, until browned. Stir in the onions and garlic and cook for 5 minutes, or until browned. Add the tomatoes, parsley, salt and pepper, then bring to a boil and let simmer for 20 minutes, or until the meat is tender.

3 Arrange half the eggplant slices in a layer in an ovenproof dish. Add the meat mixture, then a final layer of the remaining eggplant slices.

4 Beat the eggs in a bowl, then beat in the yogurt and add salt and pepper to taste. Pour the mixture over the eggplants and sprinkle the grated cheese on top.

5 Bake the moussaka in the preheated oven for 45 minutes, or until golden brown. Serve straight from the dish.

lamb with balsamic & rosemary marinade

ingredients

SERVES 4

6 racks of lamb, each with
  3 chops
fresh rosemary sprigs,
  to garnish

marinade

3 tbsp chopped fresh
  rosemary
1 small onion, finely chopped
3 tbsp olive oil
1 tbsp balsamic vinegar
1 tbsp lemon juice
salt and pepper

method

1 Put the lamb in a large, shallow dish and sprinkle with the chopped rosemary and onion. Whisk together the olive oil, balsamic vinegar, and lemon juice and season with salt and pepper.

2 Pour the balsamic mixture over the lamb, turning well to coat. Cover with plastic wrap and set aside in a cool place to marinate for 1–2 hours.

3 Drain the lamb, reserving the marinade. Broil the racks, brushing frequently with the reserved marinade, for 8–10 minutes on each side. Serve garnished with rosemary sprigs.

lamb with zucchini & tomatoes

ingredients

SERVES 4

4–8 lamb chops

salt and pepper

2 tbsp olive oil

1 onion, chopped finely

1 garlic clove, chopped finely

4 tbsp ouzo (optional)

14 oz/400 g canned tomatoes
   in juice

pinch of sugar

9 oz/250 g zucchini, sliced

2 tbsp chopped fresh thyme

method

1 Season the lamb chops with pepper. Heat the oil in a large, flameproof casserole or Dutch oven, add the onion and garlic, and fry for 5 minutes, until softened. Add the lamb chops and fry until browned on both sides.

2 Stir the ouzo into the saucepan, if using, then add the tomatoes with their juice, the sugar, zucchini, thyme, and salt.

3 Bring to a boil and then simmer for 30–45 minutes, stirring occasionally and turning the chops once during cooking, until the lamb and zucchini are tender. If necessary, add a little water during cooking if the sauce becomes too thick.

4 Serve hot.

lamb stew with chickpeas

ingredients

SERVES 4–6

6 tbsp olive oil

8 oz/225 g chorizo sausage, cut into 1/4-inch/5-mm thick slices, casings removed

2 large onions, chopped

6 large garlic cloves, crushed

2 lb/900 g boned leg of lamb, cut into 2-inch/5-cm chunks

scant 1 1/4 cups lamb stock or water

1/2 cup red wine, such as Rioja or Tempranillo

2 tbsp sherry vinegar

1 lb 12 oz/800 g canned chopped tomatoes

salt and pepper

4 sprigs fresh thyme

2 bay leaves

1/2 tsp sweet Spanish paprika

1 lb 12 oz/800 g canned chickpeas, rinsed and drained

sprigs fresh thyme, to garnish

method

1 Preheat the oven to 325°F/160°C. Heat 4 tablespoons of the oil in a large, heavy-bottom flameproof casserole over medium–high heat. Reduce the heat, add the chorizo, and cook for 1 minute. Add the onions to the casserole and cook for 2 minutes, then add the garlic and continue cooking for 3 minutes, or until the onions are softened, but not browned. Remove from the casserole and set aside.

2 Heat the remaining oil in the casserole. Add the lamb chunks in a single layer without overcrowding the casserole, and cook until browned on each side; work in batches, if necessary.

3 Return the onion mixture to the casserole with all the lamb. Stir in the stock, wine, vinegar, tomatoes with their juices, and salt and pepper to taste. Bring to a boil, scraping any glazed bits from the bottom of the casserole. Reduce the heat and stir in the thyme, bay leaves, and paprika.

4 Transfer to the preheated oven, covered, for 40–45 minutes until the lamb is tender. Stir in the chickpeas and return to the oven, uncovered, for 10 minutes, or until they are heated through and the juices are reduced.

5 Taste and adjust the seasoning. Garnish with thyme and serve.

xinjiang rice pot with lamb

ingredients

SERVES 6–8

2 tbsp vegetable or peanut oil

10½ oz/300 g lamb or
    mutton, cut into bite-size
    cubes

2 carrots, coarsely chopped

2 onions, coarsely chopped

1 tsp salt

1 tsp ground ginger

1 tsp Szechuan peppers,
    lightly roasted and lightly
    crushed

generous 2 cups short- or
    medium-grain rice

3¾ cups water

method

1 In a large casserole, heat the oil and stir-fry the meat for 1–2 minutes, or until the pieces are sealed on all sides. Add the carrot and onion and stir-fry until the vegetables are beginning to soften. Add the salt, ginger, and Szechuan peppers and mix well.

2 Finally, add the rice and water and bring to a boil. Cover the pan and cook over low heat for 30 minutes, or until the rice has absorbed all the water. Serve alone or as part of a meal.

xinjiang lamb casserole

ingredients

SERVES 5–6

1–2 tbsp vegetable or peanut
  oil
14 oz/400 g lamb or mutton,
  cut into bite-size cubes
1 onion, coarsely chopped
1 green bell pepper, coarsely
  chopped
1 carrot, coarsely chopped
1 turnip, coarsely chopped
2 tomatoes, coarsely chopped
1-inch/2.5-cm piece fresh
  ginger, finely sliced
1¹/₄ cups water
1 tsp salt

method

1 In a preheated wok or deep pan, heat the oil and stir-fry the lamb for 1–2 minutes, or until the meat is sealed on all sides.

2 Transfer the meat to a large casserole and add all the other ingredients. Bring to a boil, then cover and let simmer over low heat for 35 minutes.

hot pepper lamb in red wine risotto

ingredients

SERVES 4

8 pieces neck of lamb or lamb chops

4 tbsp seasoned all-purpose flour

4 tbsp olive oil

1 green bell pepper, seeded and thinly sliced

1–2 fresh green chiles, seeded and thinly sliced

2 small onions, 1 thinly sliced and 1 finely chopped

2 garlic cloves, thinly sliced

2 tbsp torn fresh basil

1/4 cup red wine

4 tbsp red wine vinegar

8 cherry tomatoes

1/4 cup water

3 tbsp butter

1 1/4 cups Arborio rice

5 cups simmering chicken stock

3/4 cup freshly grated Parmesan or Grana Padano cheese

salt and pepper

method

1 Coat the lamb in the seasoned flour, shaking off any excess. Heat 3 tablespoons of the oil in a large ovenproof casserole over high heat. Add the lamb and cook until browned all over. Remove from the casserole and set aside.

2 Toss the bell pepper, chiles, sliced onion, garlic, and basil in the oil left in the casserole until lightly browned. Add the wine and vinegar, bring to a boil, and cook for 3–4 minutes to reduce the liquid to 2 tablespoons. Add the tomatoes and the water, stir, and bring to a boil. Return the meat, cover, and cook over low heat for 30 minutes, or until the meat is tender, turning occasionally.

3 To make the risotto, melt 2 tablespoons of the butter with the remaining oil in a pan over medium heat. Add the chopped onion and cook, stirring, until soft and starting to turn golden. Reduce the heat, add the rice, and mix to coat in oil and butter. Cook, stirring, for 2–3 minutes, or until translucent. Add the hot stock, a ladleful at a time, stirring constantly, until all the liquid is absorbed and the rice is creamy. Season to taste.

4 Remove the risotto from the heat and stir in the remaining butter and the Parmesan. Serve topped with bell peppers, tomatoes, and lamb.

linguine with lamb & bell pepper sauce

ingredients

SERVES 4

4 tbsp olive oil

10 oz/280 g boneless lamb, cubed

1 garlic clove, finely chopped

1 bay leaf

1 cup dry white wine

salt and pepper

2 large yellow bell peppers, seeded and diced

4 tomatoes, peeled and chopped

9 oz/250 g dried linguine

method

1 Heat half the olive oil in a large, heavy-bottom skillet. Add the lamb and cook over medium heat, stirring frequently, until browned on all sides. Add the garlic and cook for an additional 1 minute. Add the bay leaf, pour in the wine, and season to taste with salt and pepper. Bring to a boil and cook for 5 minutes, or until reduced.

2 Stir in the remaining oil, bell peppers, and tomatoes. Reduce the heat, cover, and let simmer, stirring occasionally, for 45 minutes.

3 Meanwhile, bring a large, heavy-bottom pan of lightly salted water to a boil. Add the pasta, return to a boil, and cook for 8–10 minutes, or until tender but still firm to the bite. Drain and transfer to a warmed serving dish. Remove and discard the bay leaf from the lamb sauce and spoon the sauce onto the pasta. Toss well and serve immediately.

pan-fried pork with mozzarella

ingredients

SERVES 4

1 lb/450 g loin of pork

2–3 garlic cloves, chopped
finely

6 oz/175 g buffalo mozzarella,
drained

salt and pepper

12 slices prosciutto

12 fresh sage leaves

4 tbsp unsalted butter

flat-leaf parsley sprigs and
lemon slices, to garnish

mostarda di Verona, to serve

method

1 Trim any excess fat from the meat, then slice it crosswise into 12 pieces, each about 1 inch/ 2.5 cm thick. Stand each piece on end and beat with the flat end of a meat mallet or the side of a rolling pin until thoroughly flattened. Rub each piece all over with garlic, transfer to a plate, and cover with plastic wrap. Set aside in a cool place for 30 minutes–1 hour.

2 Cut the mozzarella into 12 slices. Season the pork to taste with salt and pepper, then place a slice of cheese on top of each slice of meat. Top with a slice of prosciutto, letting it fall in folds. Place a sage leaf on each portion and secure with a toothpick.

3 Melt the butter in a large, heavy-bottom skillet. Add the pork, in batches if necessary, and cook for 2–3 minutes on each side, until the meat is tender and the cheese has melted. Remove with a slotted spoon and keep warm while you cook the remaining batch.

4 Remove and discard the toothpicks. Transfer the pork to 4 warmed individual plates, garnish with parsley and lemon slices, and serve immediately with mostarda di Verona.

pork with fennel & juniper

ingredients

SERVES 4

1/2 fennel bulb

1 tbsp juniper berries

about 2 tbsp olive oil

finely grated rind and juice of
    1 orange

4 pork chops, about
    5 1/2 oz/150 g each

crisp salad and fresh bread,
    to serve

method

1 Finely chop the fennel bulb, discarding the green parts.

2 Grind the juniper berries in a mortar and pestle. Mix the crushed juniper berries with the fennel flesh, olive oil, and orange rind.

3 Using a sharp knife, score a few cuts all over each pork chop. Place the chops in a roasting pan or ovenproof dish. Spoon the fennel and juniper mixture over the top. Pour over the orange juice, cover, and let marinate in the refrigerator for 2 hours.

4 Preheat the broiler to medium. Cook the pork chops under the preheated broiler for 10–15 minutes, depending on the thickness of the meat, or until the meat is tender and cooked through, turning occasionally.

5 Transfer the chops to serving plates and serve with a crisp, fresh salad and plenty of fresh bread to mop up the cooking juices.

pork tenderloin with fennel

ingredients

SERVES 4

1 lb/450 g pork tenderloin

2–3 tbsp virgin olive oil

2 tbsp sambuca

1 large fennel bulb, sliced,
    fronds reserved

3 oz/85 g Gorgonzola cheese,
    crumbled

2 tbsp light cream

1 tbsp chopped fresh sage

1 tbsp chopped fresh thyme

salt and pepper

method

1 Trim any fat from the pork and cut into 1/4 inch/5 mm thick slices. Place the slices between 2 sheets of plastic wrap and beat with the flat end of a meat mallet or with a rolling pin to flatten slightly.

2 Heat 2 tablespoons of the oil in a heavy-bottom skillet and add the pork, in batches. Cook over medium heat for 2–3 minutes on each side, until tender. Remove from the skillet and keep warm. Cook the remaining batches, adding more oil if necessary.

3 Stir the sambuca into the skillet, increase the heat, and cook, stirring constantly and scraping up the glazed bits from the bottom. Add the fennel and cook, stirring and turning frequently, for 3 minutes. Remove from the skillet and keep warm.

4 Reduce the heat, add the Gorgonzola and cream, and cook, stirring constantly, until smooth. Remove the skillet from the heat, stir in the sage and thyme, and season to taste with salt and pepper.

5 Divide the pork and fennel among 4 warmed individual serving plates and pour over the sauce. Garnish with the reserved fennel fronds and serve immediately.

spaghetti alla carbonara

ingredients

SERVES 4

1 lb/450 g dried spaghetti

1 tbsp olive oil

8 oz/225 g rindless pancetta
    or lean bacon, chopped

4 eggs

5 tbsp light cream

4 tbsp freshly grated
    Parmesan cheese

salt and pepper

method

1 Bring a large, heavy-bottom pan of lightly salted water to a boil. Add the pasta, return to a boil, and cook for 8–10 minutes, or until tender but still firm to the bite.

2 Meanwhile, heat the olive oil in a heavy-bottom skillet. Add the chopped pancetta and cook over medium heat, stirring frequently, for 8–10 minutes.

3 Beat the eggs with the cream in a small bowl and season to taste with salt and pepper. Drain the pasta and return it to the pan. Tip in the contents of the skillet, then add the egg mixture and half the Parmesan cheese. Stir well, then transfer to a warmed serving dish. Serve immediately, sprinkled with the remaining Parmesan cheese.

linguine with bacon & olives

ingredients

SERVES 4

3 tbsp olive oil

2 onions, thinly sliced

2 garlic cloves, finely chopped

6 oz/175 g rindless lean
    bacon, diced

8 oz/225 g mushrooms, sliced

5 canned anchovy fillets,
    drained

6 black olives, pitted and
    halved

salt and pepper

1 lb/450 g dried linguine

1/2 cup freshly grated
    Parmesan cheese

method

1 Heat the olive oil in a large skillet. Add the onions, garlic, and bacon, and cook over low heat, stirring occasionally, until the onions are softened. Stir in the mushrooms, anchovies, and olives, then season to taste with salt, if necessary, and pepper. Simmer for 5 minutes.

2 Meanwhile, bring a large, heavy-bottom pan of lightly salted water to a boil. Add the pasta, return to a boil, and cook for 8–10 minutes, or until tender but still firm to the bite.

3 Drain the pasta and transfer to a warmed serving dish. Spoon the sauce on top, toss lightly, and sprinkle with the Parmesan cheese. Serve immediately.

pepperoni pasta

ingredients

SERVES 4

3 tbsp olive oil

1 onion, chopped

1 red bell pepper, seeded and
diced

1 orange bell pepper, seeded
and diced

1 lb 12 oz/800 g canned
chopped tomatoes

1 tbsp sun-dried tomato paste

1 tsp paprika

8 oz/225 g pepperoni, sliced

2 tbsp chopped fresh flat-leaf
parsley, plus extra
to garnish

salt and pepper

1 lb/450 g dried garganelli

mixed salad greens, to serve

method

1 Heat 2 tablespoons of the olive oil in a large, heavy-bottom skillet. Add the onion and cook over low heat, stirring occasionally, for 5 minutes, or until softened. Add the red and orange bell peppers, tomatoes and their can juices, sun-dried tomato paste, and paprika to the pan and bring to a boil.

2 Add the pepperoni and parsley and season to taste with salt and pepper. Stir well and bring to a boil, then reduce the heat and simmer for 10–15 minutes.

3 Meanwhile, bring a large, heavy-bottom pan of lightly salted water to a boil. Add the pasta, return to a boil, and cook for 8–10 minutes, or until tender but still firm to the bite. Drain well and transfer to a warmed serving dish. Add the remaining olive oil and toss. Add the sauce and toss again. Sprinkle with parsley and serve immediately with mixed salad greens.

chile pork with tagliatelle

ingredients

SERVES 4

1 lb/450 g dried tagliatelle

3 tbsp peanut oil

12 oz/350 g pork tenderloin,
   cut into thin strips

1 garlic clove, finely chopped

1 bunch of scallions, sliced

1-inch/2.5-cm piece fresh
   ginger, grated

2 fresh Thai chiles, seeded
   and finely chopped

1 red bell pepper, seeded
   and cut into thin sticks

1 yellow bell pepper, seeded
   and cut into thin sticks

3 zucchini, cut into thin sticks

2 tbsp finely chopped peanuts

1 tsp ground cinnamon

1 tbsp oyster sauce

2 tbsp coconut cream

salt and pepper

2 tbsp chopped fresh cilantro,
   to garnish

method

1 Bring a large, heavy-bottom pan of lightly salted water to a boil. Add the pasta, return to a boil, and cook for 8–10 minutes, or until tender but still firm to the bite.

2 Meanwhile, heat the peanut oil in a preheated wok or large, heavy-bottom skillet. Add the pork and stir-fry for 5 minutes. Add the garlic, scallions, ginger, and Thai chiles, and stir-fry for 2 minutes.

3 Add the red and yellow bell peppers and the zucchini and stir-fry for 1 minute. Add the peanuts, cinnamon, oyster sauce, and coconut cream, and stir-fry for an additional 1 minute. Season to taste with salt and pepper. Drain the pasta and transfer to a serving dish. Top with the chile pork, sprinkle with the chopped cilantro, and serve.

macaroni with sausage, pepperoncini & olives

ingredients

SERVES 4

1 tbsp olive oil

1 large onion, chopped finely

2 garlic cloves, chopped

1 lb/450 g pork sausage, peeled and chopped coarsely

3 canned pepperoncini, or other hot red peppers, drained and sliced

14 oz/400 g canned chopped tomatoes

2 tsp dried oregano

1/2 cup chicken stock or red wine

salt and pepper

1 lb/450 g dried macaroni

12–15 black olives, pitted and quartered

1/3 cup freshly grated cheese, such as cheddar or Gruyère

method

1 Heat the oil in a large skillet over medium heat. Add the onion and fry for 5 minutes, until softened. Add the garlic and fry for a few seconds, until just beginning to color. Add the sausage and fry until evenly browned.

2 Stir in the pepperoncini, tomatoes, oregano, and stock. Season with salt and pepper. Bring to a boil, then simmer over medium heat for 10 minutes, stirring occasionally.

3 Cook the macaroni in plenty of boiling salted water until al dente. Drain and transfer to a warmed serving dish.

4 Add the olives and half the cheese to the sauce, then stir until the cheese has melted. Pour the sauce over the pasta. Toss well to mix. Sprinkle with the remaining cheese and serve immediately.

rigatoni with ham, tomato & chile sauce

ingredients

SERVES 4

1 tbsp olive oil

2 tbsp butter

1 onion, chopped finely

5$^{1}/_{2}$ oz/150 g ham, diced

2 garlic cloves, chopped very
finely

1 fresh red chile, seeded and
chopped finely

1 lb 12 oz/800 g canned
chopped tomatoes

salt and pepper

1 lb/450 g rigatoni or penne

2 tbsp chopped fresh flat-leaf
parsley

6 tbsp freshly grated
Parmesan

method

1 Put the olive oil and 1 tablespoon of the butter in a large saucepan over a medium–low heat. Add the onion and fry for 10 minutes, until softened and golden. Add the ham and fry for 5 minutes, until lightly browned. Stir in the garlic, chile, and tomatoes. Season with a little salt and pepper. Bring to a boil, then simmer over medium–low heat for 30–40 minutes, until thickened.

2 Cook the pasta in plenty of boiling salted water until al dente. Drain and transfer to a warmed serving dish.

3 Pour the sauce over the pasta. Add the parsley, Parmesan, and the remaining butter. Toss well to mix. Serve immediately.

pork lo mein

ingredients

SERVES 4–6

6 oz/175 g boneless lean pork, shredded

8 oz/225 g egg noodles

1¹/₂ tbsp vegetable or peanut oil

2 tsp finely chopped garlic

1 tsp finely chopped fresh ginger

1 carrot, julienned

4 cups finely sliced mushrooms

1 green bell pepper, seeded and thinly sliced

1 tsp salt

¹/₂ cup hot chicken stock

1¹/₃ cups bean sprouts

2 tbsp finely chopped scallions

marinade

1 tsp light soy sauce

dash of sesame oil

pinch of white pepper

method

1 Combine all the marinade ingredients in a bowl, add the pork, and let marinate for at least 20 minutes.

2 Cook the noodles according to the package instructions. When cooked, drain and set aside.

3 In a preheated wok or deep pan, heat 1 teaspoon of the oil and stir-fry the pork until it has changed color. Remove and set aside.

4 In the clean wok or pan, heat the remaining oil and stir-fry the garlic and ginger until fragrant. Add the carrot and cook for 1 minute, then add the mushrooms and cook for an additional 1 minute. Toss in the bell pepper and cook for 1 minute more. Add the pork, salt, and stock and heat through. Finally, toss in the noodles, followed by the bean sprouts, and stir well. Sprinkle with the scallions and serve.

red curry pork with bell peppers

ingredients

SERVES 4

2 tbsp vegetable or peanut oil

1 onion, coarsely chopped

2 garlic cloves, chopped

1 lb/450 g pork tenderloin,
    sliced thickly

1 red bell pepper, seeded and
    cut into squares

6 oz/175 g mushrooms,
    quartered

2 tbsp Thai red curry paste

2½ cups coconut cream

1 tsp pork or vegetable
    bouillon powder

2 tbsp Thai soy sauce

4 tomatoes, peeled, seeded,
    and chopped

handful of fresh cilantro,
    chopped

boiled noodles or rice, to serve

method

1 Heat the oil in a wok or large skillet and sauté the onion and garlic for 1–2 minutes, until they are softened, but not browned.

2 Add the pork slices and stir-fry for 2–3 minutes, until browned all over. Add the bell pepper, mushrooms, and curry paste.

3 Add the coconut cream to the wok with the bouillon powder and soy sauce. Bring to a boil and let simmer for 4–5 minutes, until the liquid has reduced and thickened.

4 Add the tomatoes and cilantro and cook for 1–2 minutes, before serving with noodles or rice.

pad thai

ingredients

SERVES 4

8 oz/225 g thick rice stick
noodles

2 tbsp vegetable or peanut oil

2 garlic cloves, chopped

2 fresh red chiles, seeded and
chopped

6 oz/175 g pork tenderloin,
sliced thinly

4 oz/115 g raw peeled shrimp,
chopped

8 fresh Chinese chives,
snipped

2 tbsp fish sauce

juice of 1 lime

2 tsp jaggery or light brown
sugar

2 eggs, beaten

3/4 cup bean sprouts

4 tbsp chopped fresh cilantro

3/4 cup unsalted peanuts,
chopped, plus extra
to serve

crispy fried onions, to serve

method

1 Soak the noodles in warm water for 10 minutes, drain well, and set aside.

2 Heat the oil in a wok and stir-fry the garlic, chiles, and pork for 2–3 minutes. Add the shrimp and stir-fry for an additional 2–3 minutes.

3 Add the chives and noodles, then cover and cook for 1–2 minutes. Add the fish sauce, lime juice, sugar, and eggs. Cook, stirring and tossing constantly to mix in the eggs.

4 Stir in the bean sprouts, cilantro, and peanuts, and serve with small dishes of crispy fried onions and extra chopped peanuts.

spicy fried ground pork

ingredients

SERVES 4

2 garlic cloves

3 shallots

1-inch/2.5-cm piece fresh
ginger

2 tbsp corn oil

1 lb 2 oz/500 g ground lean
pork

2 tbsp Thai fish sauce

1 tbsp dark soy sauce

1 tbsp Thai red curry paste

4 dried kaffir lime leaves,
crumbled

4 plum tomatoes, chopped

3 tbsp chopped cilantro

salt and pepper

freshly cooked fine egg
noodles, to serve

cilantro sprigs and scallion
tassels, to serve

method

1 Finely chop the garlic, shallots, and ginger. Heat the oil in a large skillet or preheated wok over medium heat. Add the garlic, shallots, and ginger and stir-fry for 2 minutes. Stir in the pork and continue stir-frying until golden brown.

2 Stir in the fish sauce, soy sauce, curry paste, and lime leaves and stir-fry for an additional 1–2 minutes over high heat.

3 Add the chopped tomatoes and cook for an additional 5–6 minutes, stirring occasionally. Stir in the chopped cilantro and season to taste with salt and pepper.

4 Serve hot, spooned onto freshly cooked fine egg noodles, garnished with cilantro sprigs and scallion tassels.

stir-fried pork with vegetables

ingredients

SERVES 4

8 tbsp vegetable or peanut oil

4 oz/115 g rice vermicelli
noodles

4 belly pork strips, sliced
thickly

1 red onion, sliced

2 garlic cloves, chopped

1-inch/2.5-cm piece fresh
ginger, sliced thinly

1 large fresh red chile, seeded
and chopped

4 oz/115 g baby corn, halved
lengthwise

1 red bell pepper, seeded and
sliced

6 oz/175 g broccoli, cut into
florets

5^1/$_2$-oz/150-g jar black bean
sauce

^{3}/$_4$ cup bean sprouts

method

1 Heat the oil in a wok and cook the rice
noodles, in batches, for 15–20 seconds, until
they puff up. Remove with a slotted spoon,
drain on paper towels, and set aside.

2 Pour off all but 2 tablespoons of the oil and
stir-fry the pork, onion, garlic, ginger, and chile
for 4–5 minutes, or until the meat has browned.

3 Add the corn, red bell pepper, and broccoli
and stir-fry for 3–4 minutes, until the vegetables
are just tender. Stir in the black bean sauce
and bean sprouts, then cook for an additional
2–3 minutes. Serve immediately, topped with
the crispy noodles.

pork with mixed green beans

ingredients

SERVES 4

2 tbsp vegetable or peanut oil

2 shallots, chopped

8 oz/225 g pork tenderloin, sliced thinly

1-inch/2.5-cm piece fresh galangal, sliced thinly

2 garlic cloves, chopped

1¼ cups chicken stock

4 tbsp chili sauce

4 tbsp crunchy peanut butter

4 oz/115 g fine green beans

generous 1 cup frozen fava beans

4 oz/115 g string beans, sliced

crispy noodles, to serve

method

1 Heat the oil in a wok and stir-fry the shallots, pork, galangal, and garlic until lightly browned.

2 Add the stock, chili sauce, and peanut butter, and stir until the peanut butter has melted. Add all the beans and let simmer for 3–4 minutes. Serve hot with crispy noodles.

spicy szechuan pork

ingredients

SERVES 4

10 oz/280 g pork belly, thinly
  sliced

1 tbsp vegetable or peanut oil

1 tbsp chili bean sauce

1 tbsp fermented black beans,
  rinsed and lightly mashed

1 tsp sweet red bean paste
  (optional)

1 green bell pepper, seeded
  and finely sliced

1 red bell pepper, seeded and
  finely sliced

1 tsp sugar

1 tsp dark soy sauce

pinch of white pepper

method

1 Bring a pan of water to a boil and place the pork slices in the pan, then cover and let simmer for about 20 minutes, skimming occasionally. Remove the pork with a slotted spoon and let cool.

2 In a preheated wok or deep pan, heat the oil and stir-fry the pork slices until they begin to shrink. Stir in the chili bean sauce, then add the black beans and the red bean paste, if using. Finally, toss in the bell peppers and the remaining ingredients and stir-fry for a couple of minutes.

szechuan-style pork with bell pepper

ingredients

SERVES 4

1 lb 2 oz/500 g pork
    tenderloin, cubed
2 tbsp cornstarch
3 tbsp soy sauce
1 tbsp white wine vinegar
generous 1 cup water
2 tbsp peanut oil
2 leeks, sliced thinly
1 red bell pepper, cut into thin
    strips
1 zucchini, cut into thin strips
1 carrot, cut into thin strips
pinch of salt
freshly cooked white and wild
    rice, to serve

marinade
1 tbsp soy sauce
pinch of chile flakes

method

1 To make the marinade, mix the soy sauce and chile flakes in a bowl. Add the pork cubes and toss to coat. Cover with plastic wrap and let stand for 30 minutes.

2 Combine the cornstarch, soy sauce, and white wine vinegar in a small bowl. Stir in the water gradually, then set aside.

3 Heat 1 tablespoon of the oil in a wok or skillet. Add the pork and marinade mixture and stir-fry for 2–3 minutes. Remove the pork from the skillet with a slotted spoon and set aside.

4 Heat the remaining oil in the skillet, add the leeks and red bell pepper, and stir-fry for 2 minutes. Add the zucchini, carrot, and salt and stir-fry for an additional 2 minutes.

5 Stir in the pork and the cornstarch mixture and bring to a boil, stirring constantly until the sauce thickens. Remove from the heat and serve immediately with freshly cooked white and wild rice.

five-spice crispy pork with egg-fried rice

ingredients

SERVES 4

1¼ cups long-grain white rice

2½ cups cold water

salt and pepper

12 oz/350 g pork tenderloin

2 tsp Chinese five-spice powder

4 tbsp cornstarch

3 extra-large eggs

2 tbsp raw brown sugar

2 tbsp corn oil

1 onion, chopped

2 garlic cloves, minced

1 large carrot, diced

1 red bell pepper, seeded and diced

scant 1 cup peas

1 tbsp butter

method

1 Rinse the rice in a strainer under cold running water. Place in a large pan and add the cold water and a pinch of salt. Bring to a boil, cover, then reduce the heat, and let simmer for about 9 minutes, or until all of the liquid has been absorbed and the rice is tender.

2 Meanwhile, slice the pork into very thin, even-size pieces, using a sharp knife or meat cleaver. Set aside.

3 Stir together the Chinese five-spice powder, cornstarch, 1 of the eggs, and the raw brown sugar. Toss the pork in the mixture until coated.

4 Heat the oil in a preheated wok or skillet. Add the pork and cook over high heat until the pork is cooked through and crispy. Remove the pork from the wok or skillet with a slotted spoon and keep warm.

5 Add the onion, garlic, carrot, bell pepper, and peas to the wok or skillet and stir-fry for 5 minutes. Return the pork to the wok, together with the cooked rice, and stir-fry for 5 minutes.

6 Heat the butter in a skillet. Beat the remaining eggs, add to the skillet, and cook until set. Turn out onto a clean board and slice thinly. Toss the strips of egg into the rice mixture and serve immediately.

hoisin pork with garlic noodles

ingredients

SERVES 4

9 oz/250 g dried thick Chinese egg noodles, or Chinese wholemeal egg noodles

1 lb/450 g pork tenderloin, thinly sliced

1 tsp sugar

1 tbsp peanut or corn oil

4 tbsp rice vinegar

4 tbsp white wine vinegar

4 tbsp bottled hoisin sauce

2 scallions, sliced on the diagonal

about 2 tbsp garlic-flavored corn oil

2 large garlic cloves, thinly sliced

chopped fresh cilantro, to garnish

method

1 Start by boiling the noodles for 3 minutes, until soft. Alternatively, cook according to the package instructions. Drain well, rinse under cold water to stop the cooking, and drain again, then set aside.

2 Meanwhile, sprinkle the pork slices with the sugar and use your hands to toss together. Heat a wok over high heat. Add the oil and heat until it shimmers. Add the pork and stir-fry for about 3 minutes, until the pork is cooked through and is no longer pink. Use a slotted spoon to remove the pork from the wok and keep warm. Add both vinegars to the wok and boil until they are reduced to about 5 tablespoons. Pour in the hoisin sauce with the scallions and let bubble until reduced by half. Add to the pork and stir together.

3 Quickly wipe out the wok and reheat. Add the garlic-flavored oil and heat until it shimmers. Add the garlic slices and stir around for about 30 seconds, until they are golden and crisp, then use a slotted spoon to scoop them out of the wok and set aside.

4 Add the noodles to the wok and stir them around to warm them through. Divide the noodles between 4 plates, top with the pork and onion mixture, and sprinkle over the garlic slices and cilantro.

sour & spicy pork

ingredients

SERVES 4

2 oz/55 g dried Chinese cloud
ear mushrooms

3½ oz/100 g baby corn,
halved lengthwise

2 tbsp honey

1 tbsp tamarind paste

4 tbsp boiling water

2 tbsp dark soy sauce

1 tbsp rice vinegar

2 tbsp peanut or corn oil

1 large garlic clove, very finely
chopped

½-inch/1-cm piece fresh
ginger, peeled and very
finely chopped

½ tsp dried red pepper flakes,
or to taste

12 oz/350 g pork tenderloin,
thinly sliced

4 scallions, thickly sliced on
the diagonal

1 green bell pepper, cored,
seeded, and sliced

9 oz/250 g fresh Hokkien
noodles

chopped fresh cilantro,
to garnish

method

1 Soak the mushrooms in enough boiling water to cover for 20 minutes, or until they are tender. Drain them well, then cut off and discard any thick stems, and slice the cups if they are large. Meanwhile, bring a large pan of lightly salted water to a boil, add the baby corn, and blanch for 3 minutes. Drain the corn and run it under cold running water to stop the cooking, then set aside. Put the honey and tamarind paste in a small bowl and stir in the water, stirring until the paste dissolves. Stir in the soy sauce and rice vinegar and set aside.

2 Heat a wok over high heat. Add 1 tablespoon of the oil and heat until it shimmers. Add the garlic, ginger, and red pepper flakes and stir-fry for about 30 seconds. Add the pork and continue stir-frying for 2 minutes.

3 Add the remaining oil to the wok and heat. Add the scallions, bell pepper, mushrooms, and baby corn, along with the tamarind mixture, and stir-fry for an additional 2–3 minutes, until the pork is cooked through and the vegetables are tender, but still firm to the bite. Add the noodles and use 2 forks to mix all the ingredients together. When the noodles and sauce are hot, sprinkle with cilantro.

spareribs in a sweet-&-sour sauce

ingredients

SERVES 4

1 lb/450 g spareribs, cut into bite-size pieces (you or your butcher can cut ribs into pieces with a cleaver)

vegetable or peanut oil, for deep-frying

marinade

2 tsp light soy sauce

1/2 tsp salt

pinch of white pepper

sauce

3 tbsp white rice vinegar

2 tbsp sugar

1 tbsp light soy sauce

1 tbsp ketchup

1 1/2 tbsp vegetable or peanut oil

1 green bell pepper, coarsely chopped

1 small onion, coarsely chopped

1 small carrot, finely sliced

1/2 tsp finely chopped garlic

1/2 tsp finely chopped ginger

3 1/2 oz/100 g pineapple chunks

method

1 Combine the marinade ingredients in a bowl with the spareribs and let marinate for at least 20 minutes.

2 Heat enough oil for deep-frying in a wok or deep-fat fryer until it reaches 350–375°F/ 180–190°C, or until a cube of bread browns in 30 seconds. Deep-fry the spareribs for 8 minutes. Drain and set aside.

3 To prepare the sauce, first mix together the vinegar, sugar, light soy sauce, and ketchup. Set aside.

4 In a preheated wok, heat 1 tablespoon of the oil and stir-fry the bell pepper, onion, and carrot for 2 minutes. Remove and set aside.

5 In the clean preheated wok, heat the remaining oil and stir-fry the garlic and ginger until fragrant. Add the vinegar mixture. Bring back to a boil and add the pineapple chunks. Finally add the spareribs and the bell pepper, onion, and carrot. Stir until warmed through and serve immediately.

paella with pork & chorizo

ingredients

SERVES 4–6

5 cups simmering fish stock

12 large raw shrimp, in their shells

1/2 tsp saffron threads

2 tbsp hot water

31/2 oz/100 g skinless, boneless chicken breast, cut into 11/2-inch/1-cm pieces

31/2 oz/100 g pork tenderloin, cut into 1/2-inch/1-cm pieces

salt and pepper

3 tbsp olive oil

31/2 oz/100 g Spanish chorizo sausage, casing removed, cut into 1/2-inch/1-cm slices

1 large red onion, chopped

2 garlic cloves, crushed

1/2 tsp cayenne pepper

1/2 tsp paprika

1 red bell pepper, seeded and sliced

1 green bell pepper, seeded and sliced

12 cherry tomatoes, halved

generous 11/2 cups paella rice

1 tbsp chopped fresh parsley

2 tsp chopped fresh tarragon

method

1 Add the shrimp to the simmering stock and cook for 2 minutes, then transfer to a bowl and set aside. Put the saffron threads and water in a small bowl and let infuse.

2 Season the chicken and pork with salt and pepper. Heat the oil in a paella pan and cook the chicken, pork, and chorizo over medium heat, stirring, until golden. Add the onion and cook, stirring, until softened. Add the garlic, cayenne pepper, paprika, and saffron and its soaking liquid and cook, stirring constantly, for 1 minute. Add the bell pepper slices and tomato halves and cook, stirring, for an additional 2 minutes.

3 Add the rice and herbs and cook, stirring constantly, for 1 minute. Pour in most of the hot stock, bring to a boil, then let simmer, uncovered, for 10 minutes. Do not stir during cooking, but shake the pan once or twice and when adding ingredients. Season, then cook for an additional 10 minutes, or until the rice is almost cooked, adding a little more hot stock if necessary. Add the shrimp and cook for an additional 2 minutes.

4 When all the liquid has been absorbed and you detect a faint toasty aroma coming from the rice, remove from the heat. Cover with foil and let stand for 5 minutes. Serve.

sausages with lentils

ingredients

SERVES 4-6

2 tbsp olive oil

12 merguez sausages

2 onions, chopped finely

2 red bell peppers, cored, seeded, and chopped

1 orange or yellow bell pepper, cored, seeded, and chopped

scant 1½ cups small green lentils, rinsed

1 tsp dried thyme or marjoram

2 cups vegetable stock

salt and pepper

4 tbsp chopped fresh parsley

red wine vinegar, to serve

method

1 Heat the oil in a large, preferably nonstick, lidded skillet over medium–high heat. Add the sausages and cook, stirring frequently, for about 10 minutes, until they are brown all over and cooked through. Remove from the skillet and set aside.

2 Pour off all but 2 tablespoons of oil from the skillet. Add the onions and bell peppers and cook for about 5 minutes, until softened, but not browned. Add the lentils and thyme and stir until coated with oil.

3 Stir in the stock and bring to a boil. Reduce the heat, cover, and let simmer for about 30 minutes, until the lentils are tender and the liquid is absorbed. If the lentils are tender, but too much liquid remains, uncover the skillet and let simmer until it evaporates. Season to taste with salt and pepper.

4 Return the sausages to the skillet and reheat. Stir in the parsley. Serve the sausages with lentils on the side, then splash a little red wine vinegar over each portion.

sausage & rosemary risotto

ingredients

SERVES 4–6

2 long fresh rosemary sprigs, plus extra to garnish

2 tbsp olive oil

4 tbsp butter

1 large onion, finely chopped

1 celery stalk, finely chopped

2 garlic cloves, finely chopped

1/2 tsp dried thyme leaves

1 lb/450 g pork sausage, such as luganega or cumberland, cut into 1/2-inch/1-cm pieces

1²/3 cups risotto rice

1/2 cup fruity red wine

generous 5¹/2 cups chicken stock

salt and pepper

3/4 cup freshly grated Parmesan cheese

method

1 Strip the long thin leaves from the rosemary sprigs and chop finely, then set aside.

2 Heat the oil and half the butter in a deep pan over medium heat. Add the onion and celery and cook, stirring occasionally, for 2 minutes. Stir in the garlic, thyme, sausage, and rosemary. Cook, stirring frequently, for 5 minutes, or until the sausage starts to brown. Transfer the sausage to a plate.

3 Reduce the heat, add the rice, and mix to coat in oil and butter. Cook, stirring constantly, for 2–3 minutes, or until the grains are translucent.

4 Add the wine and cook, stirring constantly, for 1 minute, until reduced. Gradually add the hot stock, a ladleful at a time. Stir constantly and add more liquid as the rice absorbs each addition. Increase the heat to medium so that the liquid bubbles. Cook for 20 minutes, or until all the liquid is absorbed and the rice is creamy.

5 Toward the end of cooking, return the sausage pieces to the risotto and heat through. Season to taste with salt and pepper. Remove from the heat and add the remaining butter. Mix well, then stir in the Parmesan until it melts. Spoon the risotto onto warmed plates, garnish with rosemary sprigs, and serve.

pork hash

ingredients

SERVES 4

14 oz/400 g canned chopped
   tomatoes
2¹/₂–3 cups beef stock
1 tbsp corn oil
1 lb/450 g fresh ground pork
1 large onion, chopped
1 red bell pepper, seeded and
   chopped
2 cups long-grain rice
1 tbsp chili powder
1 lb/450 g fresh or frozen
   green beans
salt and pepper

method

1 Preheat the oven to 350°F/180°C. Drain the tomatoes, reserving their juices, and reserve. Make the juices up to 3¹/₂ cups with the stock and reserve.

2 Heat the oil in a large, flameproof casserole. Add the pork, onion, and red bell pepper and cook over medium heat, stirring frequently, for 8–10 minutes, or until the onion is softened and the meat is broken up and golden brown. Add the rice and cook, stirring constantly, for 2 minutes.

3 Add the tomatoes, stock mixture, chili powder, and beans to the casserole and season to taste with salt and pepper. Bring to a boil, then cover and transfer to the preheated oven to bake for 40 minutes. Serve immediately.

fish & seafood

The ideal choice for busy people who care about food but have little time to cook, fish and seafood really benefit from quick cooking and simple recipes that don't disguise their natural flavors. What's more, they taste delicious and are low in fat and highly nutritious.

Fish that have a meaty texture, such as salmon, swordfish, and tuna, are perfect for pan-frying, broiling, and grilling—fillets and steaks take only about 5 minutes, and if you like your tuna rare the cooking time is even less. Gentle poaching is the perfect technique for more delicate fish fillets, while whole fish is superb when roasted. Fish stews will take less time to prepare and cook than those made with meat and are spectacular enough to impress the most discerning guests. Easiest of all is to bake fish in a foil or wax paper parcel.

Seafood is the ultimate fast food—most types must be cooked very rapidly or they become tough. Cooked shrimp need only be heated through and raw ones cook in a matter of minutes, depending on their size. Mollusks, such as clams and mussels, just need a good scrub and brief steaming. Scallops can be tricky and time-consuming to remove from their shells but they are available already shelled or you can ask your fish supplier to do it for you. Similarly, ready-prepared squid is widely available.

Fish combines well with an extensive range of other ingredients, whether the Mediterranean flavors of garlic, onion, and tomatoes or the Asian tang of ginger, chiles, and lime. Shellfish are equally versatile being just as delicious in curries, risottos, cream sauces, and even omelets.

roast salmon with lemon & herbs

ingredients

SERVES 4

6 tbsp extra virgin olive oil
1 onion, sliced
1 leek, sliced
juice of $1/2$ lemon
2 tbsp chopped fresh parsley
2 tbsp chopped fresh dill
salt and pepper
1 lb 2 oz/500 g salmon fillets
freshly cooked baby spinach
    leaves, to serve
lemon slices, to garnish

method

1 Preheat the oven to 400°F/200°C. Heat 1 tablespoon of the oil in a skillet over medium heat. Add the onion and leek and cook, stirring occasionally, for 4 minutes, or until slightly softened.

2 Meanwhile, place the remaining oil in a small bowl with the lemon juice and herbs and season with salt and pepper. Stir together well. Rinse the fish under cold running water, then pat dry with paper towels. Arrange the fish in a shallow ovenproof dish.

3 Remove the skillet from the heat and spread the onion and leek over the fish. Pour the oil mixture over the top, making sure that everything is well coated. Roast in the center of the preheated oven for 10 minutes, or until the fish is cooked through.

4 Arrange the cooked spinach on serving plates. Remove the fish and vegetables and serve next to the spinach with the vegetables arranged on top of the fish. Garnish with lemon slices and serve immediately.

pan-fried spiced salmon

ingredients

SERVES 4

1-inch/2.5-cm piece fresh
   ginger, grated

1 tsp coriander seeds,
   crushed

1/4 tsp chili powder

1 tbsp lime juice

1 tsp sesame oil

4 salmon fillet pieces with
   skin, about 5 1/2 oz/150 g
   each

2 tbsp vegetable oil

stir-fried vegetables and freshly
   cooked rice, to serve

cilantro leaves, to garnish

method

1 Mix the ginger, crushed coriander, chili powder, lime juice, and sesame oil together in a bowl.

2 Place the salmon on a wide, nonmetallic plate or dish and spoon the mixture over the flesh side of the fillets, spreading it to coat each piece of salmon evenly.

3 Cover the dish with plastic wrap and let chill in the refrigerator for 30 minutes.

4 Heat a wide, heavy-bottom skillet or ridged grill pan with the vegetable oil over high heat. Place the salmon in the hot skillet, skin-side down, and cook for 4–5 minutes, without turning, until the salmon is crusty underneath and the flesh flakes easily.

5 Serve the salmon immediately with freshly cooked rice and stir-fried vegetables, garnished with cilantro leaves.

salmon steaks with green sauce

ingredients

SERVES 4

green sauce

generous 4 tbsp sprigs fresh
    flat-leaf parsley

8 large fresh basil leaves

2 sprigs fresh oregano,
    or $1/2$ tsp dried

3–4 anchovy fillets in oil,
    drained and chopped

2 tsp capers in brine, rinsed

1 shallot, chopped

1 large garlic clove

2–3 tsp lemon juice, to taste

$1/2$ cup extra virgin olive oil

4 skinned salmon fillets, each
    about 5 oz/150 g

2 tbsp olive oil

salt and pepper

method

1 To make the green sauce, put the parsley, basil, oregano, anchovies, capers, shallot, garlic, and lemon juice in a food processor or blender and process until chopped. With the motor running, slowly add the oil through the feed tube. Taste and adjust the seasoning, if necessary, remembering that the anchovies and capers can be salty. Pour into a serving bowl, cover with plastic wrap, and let chill until required.

2 When ready to serve, brush the salmon fillets on both sides with the olive oil and season with salt and pepper to taste. Heat a large skillet until you can feel the heat rising from the surface. Add the salmon steaks and cook for 3 minutes. Flip the steaks over and continue cooking for 2–3 minutes, until they feel springy and the flesh flakes easily.

3 Serve the hot salmon steaks with a little of the chilled sauce spooned over.

salmon with red curry in banana leaves

ingredients

SERVES 4

4 salmon steaks, about
   6 oz/175 g each
2 banana leaves, halved
1 garlic clove, crushed
1 tsp grated fresh ginger
1 tbsp Thai red curry paste
1 tsp brown sugar
1 tbsp Thai fish sauce
2 tbsp lime juice

to garnish
lime wedges
whole fresh red chiles
finely chopped fresh red chile

method

1 Preheat the oven to 425°F/220°C. Place a salmon steak in the center of each half banana leaf. Mix the garlic, ginger, curry paste, sugar, and fish sauce together, then spread over the surface of the fish. Sprinkle with lime juice.

2 Carefully wrap the banana leaves around the fish, tucking in the sides as you go to make neat, compact pockets.

3 Place the pockets seam-side down on a baking sheet. Bake in the preheated oven for 15–20 minutes, or until the fish is cooked and the banana leaves are beginning to brown.

4 Serve garnished with lime wedges, whole chiles, and finely chopped chile.

linguine with smoked salmon & arugula

ingredients

SERVES 4

12 oz/350 g dried linguine
2 tbsp olive oil
1 garlic clove, finely chopped
4 oz/115 g smoked salmon,
    cut into thin strips
2 oz/55 g arugula
salt and pepper
1/2 lemon, to garnish

method

1 Bring a large, heavy-bottom pan of lightly salted water to a boil. Add the pasta, return to a boil, and cook for 8–10 minutes, or until tender but still firm to the bite.

2 Just before the end of the cooking time, heat the olive oil in a heavy-bottom skillet. Add the garlic and cook over low heat, stirring constantly, for 1 minute. Do not allow the garlic to brown or it will taste bitter. Add the salmon and arugula. Season to taste with salt and pepper and cook, stirring constantly, for 1 minute. Remove the skillet from the heat.

3 Drain the pasta and transfer to a warmed serving dish. Add the smoked salmon and arugula mixture, toss lightly, and serve, garnished with a lemon half.

spiced tuna in sweet-&-sour sauce

ingredients

SERVES 4

4 fresh tuna steaks, about
    1 lb 2 oz/500 g in total

1/4 tsp pepper

2 tbsp peanut oil

1 onion, diced

1 small yellow bell pepper,
    seeded and cut into short,
    thin sticks

1 garlic clove, crushed

1/2 cucumber, seeded and cut
    into short, thin sticks

2 pineapple slices, diced

1 tsp finely chopped fresh
    ginger

1 tbsp brown sugar

1 tbsp cornstarch

1 1/2 tbsp lime juice

1 tbsp Thai fish sauce

1 cup fish stock

lime slices and cucumber
    slices, to garnish

method

1 Sprinkle the tuna steaks with pepper on both sides. Heat a heavy-bottom skillet or ridged grill pan and brush with a little of the oil. Arrange the tuna steaks in the skillet and cook for 8 minutes, turning them over once.

2 Meanwhile, heat the remaining oil in a separate skillet. Add the onion, bell pepper, and garlic and cook gently for 3–4 minutes to soften.

3 Remove the skillet from the heat and stir in the cucumber, pineapple, ginger, and sugar.

4 Blend the cornstarch with the lime juice and fish sauce, then stir into the stock and add to the skillet. Stir over medium heat until boiling, then cook for 1–2 minutes, or until thickened and clear.

5 Spoon the sauce over the tuna and serve immediately, garnished with slices of lime and cucumber.

sicilian tuna

ingredients

SERVES 4

marinade

1/2 cup extra virgin olive oil

4 garlic cloves, chopped finely

4 fresh red chiles, seeded and
chopped finely

juice and finely grated rind
of 2 lemons

4 tbsp finely chopped fresh
flat-leaf parsley

salt and pepper

4 x 5-oz/150-g tuna steaks

2 fennel bulbs, sliced thickly
lengthwise

2 red onions, sliced

2 tbsp virgin olive oil

arugula salad and crusty
bread, to serve

method

1 First, make the marinade by whisking all the ingredients together in a bowl. Place the tuna steaks in a large shallow dish and spoon over 4 tablespoons of the marinade, turning to coat. Cover and set aside for 30 minutes. Set aside the remaining marinade.

2 Heat a ridged grill pan. Put the fennel and onions in a bowl, add the oil, and toss well to coat. Add to the grill pan and cook for 5 minutes on each side, until just starting to color. Transfer to 4 warmed serving plates, drizzle with the reserved marinade, and keep warm.

3 Add the tuna steaks to the grill pan and cook, turning once, for 4–5 minutes, until firm to the touch but still moist inside. Transfer the tuna to the plates and serve immediately with with the arugula salad and crusty bread.

broiled tuna & vegetable kebabs

ingredients

SERVES 4

4 tuna steaks, about
   5 oz/140 g each

2 red onions

12 cherry tomatoes

1 red bell pepper, seeded and
   cut into 1-inch/2.5-cm
   pieces

1 yellow bell pepper, seeded
   and cut into 1-inch/
   2.5-cm pieces

1 zucchini, sliced

1 tbsp chopped fresh oregano

4 tbsp olive oil

pepper

lime wedges, to garnish

method

1 Preheat the broiler to high. Cut the tuna into 1-inch/2.5-cm pieces. Peel the onions, leaving the root intact, and cut each onion lengthwise into 6 wedges.

2 Divide the fish and vegetables evenly among 8 wooden skewers (presoaked to avoid burning) and arrange on the broiler pan.

3 Mix the oregano and oil together in a small bowl. Season to taste with pepper. Lightly brush the kebabs with the oil and cook under the preheated broiler for 10–15 minutes, or until evenly cooked, turning occasionally. If you cannot fit all the kebabs on the broiler pan at once, cook them in batches, keeping the cooked kebabs warm while cooking the remainder. Alternatively, these kebabs can be cooked on a barbecue.

4 Garnish with lime wedges.

risotto with tuna & pine nuts

ingredients

SERVES 4

4 tbsp olive oil

3 tbsp butter

1 small onion, finely chopped

1¹/₂ cups risotto rice

5 cups fish or chicken stock

salt and pepper

8 oz/225 g tuna, canned and drained, or broiled fresh steaks

8–10 black olives, pitted and sliced

1 small pimiento, thinly sliced

1 tsp finely chopped fresh parsley

1 tsp finely chopped fresh marjoram

2 tbsp white wine vinegar

¹/₂ cup pine nuts

1 garlic clove, chopped

8 oz/225 g fresh tomatoes, peeled, seeded, and diced

³/₄ cup Parmesan or Grana Padano cheese

method

1 Melt 2 tablespoons of the butter with 1 tablespoon of the oil in a deep saucepan over medium heat. Add the onion and cook, stirring occasionally, until softened and starting to turn golden. Reduce the heat, add the rice, and mix to coat in oil and butter. Cook, stirring constantly, until the grains are translucent. Add the hot stock, a ladleful at a time, stirring constantly, until all the liquid is absorbed and the rice is creamy. Season to taste.

2 While the risotto is cooking, flake the tuna into a bowl and mix in the olives, pimiento, parsley, marjoram, and vinegar. Season with salt and pepper.

3 Heat the remaining oil in a small skillet over high heat. Add the pine nuts and garlic. Cook, stirring constantly, for 2 minutes, or until they just start to brown. Add the tomatoes and mix well. Continue cooking over medium heat for 3–4 minutes, or until they are thoroughly warmed. Pour the tomato mixture over the tuna mixture and mix. Fold into the risotto 5 minutes before the end of the cooking time.

4 Remove the risotto from the heat when all the liquid has been absorbed and add the remaining butter. Mix well, then stir in the Parmesan until it melts. Serve immediately.

spaghetti with tuna & parsley

ingredients

SERVES 4

1 lb 2 oz/500 g dried spaghetti

2 tbsp butter

fresh flat-leaf parsley sprigs, to garnish

black olives, to serve (optional)

s a u c e

7 oz/200 g canned tuna, drained

2 oz/55 g canned anchovies, drained

1 cup olive oil

generous 1 cup coarsely chopped fresh flat-leaf parsley

2/3 cup sour cream or yogurt

salt and pepper

method

1 Bring a large, heavy-bottom pan of lightly salted water to a boil. Add the spaghetti, return to a boil, and cook for 8–10 minutes, or until tender but still firm to the bite. Drain the spaghetti in a colander and return to the pan. Add the butter, toss thoroughly to coat, and keep warm until required.

2 Flake the tuna into smaller pieces using 2 forks. Place the tuna in a blender or food processor with the anchovies, olive oil, and parsley and process until the sauce is smooth. Pour in the sour cream and process for a few seconds to blend. Taste the sauce and season with salt and pepper, if necessary.

3 Shake the pan of spaghetti over medium heat for a few minutes, or until it is thoroughly warmed through.

4 Pour the sauce over the spaghetti and toss quickly, using 2 forks. Garnish with parsley sprigs and serve immediately with a small dish of black olives, if liked.

linguine with anchovies, olives & capers

ingredients

SERVES 4

3 tbsp olive oil

2 garlic cloves, chopped finely

10 anchovy fillets, drained and
　chopped

scant 1 cup black olives,
　pitted and chopped

1 tbsp capers, rinsed

1 lb/450 g plum tomatoes,
　peeled, seeded, and
　chopped

pinch of cayenne pepper

salt

14 oz/400 g dried linguine

2 tbsp chopped fresh flat-leaf
　parsley, to garnish

method

1 Heat the olive oil in a heavy-bottom pan. Add the garlic and cook over low heat, stirring frequently, for 2 minutes. Add the anchovies and mash them to a pulp with a fork. Add the olives, capers, and tomatoes and season to taste with cayenne pepper. Cover and let simmer for 25 minutes.

2 Meanwhile, bring a pan of lightly salted water to a boil. Add the pasta, bring back to a boil, and cook for 8–10 minutes, until tender but still firm to the bite. Drain and transfer to a warmed serving dish.

3 Spoon the anchovy sauce into the dish and toss the pasta, using 2 large forks. Garnish with the parsley and serve immediately.

broiled sardines with lemon sauce

ingredients

SERVES 4

1 large lemon
6 tbsp unsalted butter
salt and pepper
20 fresh sardines, cleaned
    and heads removed
1 tbsp chopped fresh fennel
    leaves

method

1 Peel the lemon. Remove all the bitter pith and discard. Using a small, serrated knife, cut between the membranes and ease out the flesh segments, discarding any seeds. Chop finely and set aside.

2 Melt 2 tablespoons of the butter in a small pan and season with salt and pepper. Brush the sardines all over with the melted butter and cook under a preheated broiler or on a barbecue, turning once, for 5–6 minutes, until cooked through.

3 Meanwhile, melt the remaining butter, then remove the pan from the heat. Stir in the chopped lemon and fennel.

4 Transfer the sardines to a warmed platter, pour over the sauce, and serve immediately.

fresh sardines baked with lemon & oregano

ingredients

SERVES 4

2 lemons, plus extra lemon
    wedges to garnish
12 large fresh sardines,
    cleaned
4 tbsp olive oil
4 tbsp chopped fresh oregano
salt and pepper

method

1 Preheat the oven to 375°F/190°C. Slice 1 of the lemons and grate the rind and squeeze the juice from the second lemon.

2 Cut the heads off the sardines. Put the fish in a shallow, ovenproof dish large enough to hold them in a single layer. Put the lemon slices between the fish. Drizzle the lemon juice and oil over the fish. Sprinkle over the lemon rind and oregano and season to taste with salt and pepper.

3 Bake in the the preheated oven for 20–30 minutes, until the fish are tender. Serve garnished with lemon wedges.

swordfish with olives & capers

ingredients

SERVES 4

2 tbsp all-purpose flour

salt and pepper

4 x 8-oz/225-g swordfish
    steaks

generous 1/2 cup olive oil

2 garlic cloves, halved

1 onion, chopped

4 anchovy fillets, drained and
    chopped

4 tomatoes, peeled, seeded,
    and chopped

12 green olives, pitted and
    sliced

1 tbsp capers, rinsed

fresh rosemary sprigs,
    to garnish

method

1 Spread out the flour on a plate and season with salt and pepper. Coat the fish in the seasoned flour, shaking off any excess.

2 Gently heat the olive oil in a large, heavy-bottom skillet. Add the garlic and cook over low heat for 2–3 minutes, until just golden. Do not let it turn brown or burn. Remove the garlic and discard.

3 Add the fish to the skillet and cook over medium heat for about 4 minutes on each side, until cooked through and golden brown. Remove the steaks from the skillet and set aside.

4 Add the onion and anchovies to the skillet and cook, mashing the anchovies with a wooden spoon until the anchovies have turned to a paste and the onion is golden. Add the tomatoes and cook over low heat, stirring occasionally, for about 20 minutes, until the mixture has thickened.

5 Stir in the olives and capers, then taste and adjust the seasoning. Return the steaks to the skillet and heat through gently. Serve garnished with rosemary.

spanish swordfish stew

ingredients

SERVES 4

4 tbsp olive oil

3 shallots, chopped

2 garlic cloves, chopped

8 oz/225 g canned chopped
    tomatoes

1 tbsp tomato paste

1 lb 7 oz/650 g potatoes,
    sliced

generous 1 cup vegetable
    stock

2 tbsp lemon juice

1 red bell pepper, seeded and
    chopped

1 orange bell pepper, seeded
    and chopped

20 black olives, pitted and
    halved

2 lb 4 oz/1 kg swordfish steak,
    skinned and cut into bite-
    size pieces

salt and pepper

fresh flat-leaf parsley sprigs
    and lemon slices,
    to garnish

method

1 Heat the oil in a pan over low heat, add the shallots, and cook, stirring frequently, for 4 minutes, or until softened. Add the garlic, tomatoes, and tomato paste, cover, and let simmer gently for 20 minutes.

2 Meanwhile, put the potatoes in an ovenproof casserole with the stock and lemon juice. Bring to a boil, then reduce the heat and add the bell peppers. Cover and cook for 15 minutes.

3 Add the olives, swordfish, and the tomato mixture to the potatoes. Season to taste with salt and pepper. Stir well, then cover and let simmer for 7–10 minutes, or until the swordfish is cooked to your taste.

4 Remove from the heat and serve, garnished with parsley sprigs and lemon slices.

roasted monkfish

ingredients

SERVES 4

1 lb 8 oz/675 g monkfish tail, skinned

4–5 large garlic cloves, peeled

salt and pepper

3 tbsp olive oil

1 onion, cut into wedges

1 small eggplant, about 10^1/$_2$ oz/300 g, cut into chunks

1 red bell pepper, seeded and cut into wedges

1 yellow bell pepper, seeded and cut into wedges

1 large zucchini, about 8 oz/225 g, cut into wedges

1 tbsp shredded fresh basil

method

1 Preheat the oven to 400°F/200°C. Remove the central bone from the fish, if not already removed, and make small slits down each fillet. Cut 2 of the garlic cloves into thin slivers and insert into the fish. Place the fish on a sheet of waxed paper, season with salt and pepper to taste, and drizzle over 1 tablespoon of the oil. Bring the top edges together. Form into a pleat and fold over, then fold the ends underneath, completely encasing the fish. Set aside.

2 Put the remaining garlic cloves and all the vegetables into a roasting pan and sprinkle with the remaining oil, turning the vegetables so that they are well coated in the oil.

3 Roast in the preheated oven for 20 minutes, turning occasionally. Put the fish parcel on top of the vegetables and cook for an additional 15–20 minutes, or until the vegetables are tender and the fish is cooked.

4 Remove from the oven and open up the parcel. Cut the monkfish into thick slices. Arrange the vegetables on warmed serving plates, top with the fish slices, and sprinkle with the basil. Serve immediately.

fusilli with monkfish & broccoli

ingredients

SERVES 4

4 oz/115 g broccoli, divided
   into florets

3 tbsp olive oil

12 oz/350 g monkfish fillet,
   skinned and cut into
   bite-size pieces

2 garlic cloves, crushed

salt and pepper

1/2 cup dry white wine

1 cup heavy cream

14 oz/400 g dried fusilli

3 oz/85 g Gorgonzola cheese,
   diced

method

1 Divide the broccoli florets into tiny sprigs. Bring a pan of lightly salted water to a boil, add the broccoli, and cook for 2 minutes. Drain and refresh under cold running water.

2 Heat the olive oil in a large, heavy-bottom skillet. Add the monkfish and garlic and season to taste with salt and pepper. Cook, stirring frequently, for 5 minutes, or until the fish is opaque. Pour in the white wine and cream and cook, stirring occasionally, for 5 minutes, or until the fish is cooked through and the sauce has thickened. Stir in the broccoli sprigs.

3 Meanwhile, bring a large, heavy-bottom pan of lightly salted water to a boil. Add the pasta, return to a boil, and cook for 8–10 minutes, or until tender but still firm to the bite. Drain and tip the pasta into the pan with the fish, add the cheese, and toss lightly. Serve immediately.

basque-style cod

ingredients

SERVES 4

3 tbsp olive oil

4 cod fillets, about 6 oz/175 g
   each, all skin and bones
   removed and patted dry

1 tbsp all-purpose flour

salt and pepper

1 large onion, finely chopped

4 large tomatoes, peeled,
   seeded, and chopped

2 large garlic cloves, crushed

2/3 cup dry white wine

1/2 tsp paprika, to taste

2 red bell peppers,
   charbroiled, peeled,
   and seeded, then
   cut into strips

2 green bell peppers,
   charbroiled, peeled, and
   seeded, then cut into strips

zest of 1 lemon, in broad strips

finely chopped fresh flat-leaf
   parsley, to garnish

method

1 Preheat the oven to 400°F/200°C. Heat 1 tablespoon of the oil in a flameproof casserole over medium–high heat. Very lightly dust 1 side of each cod fillet with the flour, seasoned to taste with salt and pepper.

2 Pan-fry, floured-side down, for 2 minutes, or until just golden. Set aside. Wipe out the casserole, then heat the remaining oil over medium–high heat. Add the onion and sauté for 5 minutes, or until softened, but not browned.

3 Stir in the tomatoes, garlic, wine, paprika, and salt and pepper to taste and bring to a boil. Reduce the heat and simmer for 5 minutes, stirring occasionally.

4 Stir the red and green bell peppers into the casserole with the lemon strips and bring to a boil. Lay the cod fillets on top, browned-side up, and season to taste with salt and pepper. Cover the casserole and bake in the preheated oven for 12–15 minutes, depending on the thickness of the cod, until it is cooked through and flakes easily.

5 Discard the lemon zest just before serving. Serve the cod on a bed of the vegetables and sprinkle with the chopped parsley.

cod with catalan spinach

ingredients

SERVES 4

catalan spinach

1/2 cup raisins

1/3 cup pine nuts

4 tbsp extra virgin olive oil

3 garlic cloves, crushed

11 1/4 cups baby spinach
leaves, rinsed and
shaken dry

4 cod fillets, each about
6 oz/175 g

olive oil

salt and pepper

lemon wedges, to serve

method

1 Put the raisins for the Catalan spinach in a small bowl, cover with hot water, and set aside to soak for 15 minutes. Drain well.

2 Meanwhile, put the pine nuts in a dry skillet over medium–high heat and dry-fry for 1–2 minutes, shaking frequently, until toasted and golden brown: watch closely because they burn quickly.

3 Heat the oil in a large, lidded skillet over medium–high heat. Add the garlic and cook for 2 minutes, or until golden but not browned. Remove with a slotted spoon and discard.

4 Add the spinach to the oil with only the rinsing water clinging to its leaves. Cover and cook for 4–5 minutes, until wilted. Uncover, stir in the drained raisins and pine nuts, and continue cooking until all the liquid evaporates. Season to taste and keep warm.

5 To cook the cod, brush the fillets lightly with oil and sprinkle with salt and pepper. Place under a preheated hot broiler about 4 inches/10 cm from the heat and broil for 8–10 minutes, until the flesh is opaque and flakes easily.

6 Divide the spinach among 4 plates and place the cod fillets on top. Serve with lemon wedges.

italian fish

ingredients

SERVES 4

2 tbsp butter

scant 1 cup fresh whole wheat
   bread crumbs

1 heaped tbsp chopped
   walnuts

grated rind and juice of
   2 lemons

2 fresh rosemary sprigs, stalks
   removed

2 tbsp chopped fresh parsley

4 cod fillets, about
   5¹/₂ oz/150 g each

1 garlic clove, crushed

1 small fresh red chile, diced

3 tbsp walnut oil

method

1 Preheat the oven to 400°F/200°C. Melt the butter in a large pan over low heat, stirring constantly. Remove the pan from the heat and add the bread crumbs, walnuts, the rind and juice of 1 lemon, half the rosemary, and half the parsley, stirring until mixed.

2 Press the bread crumb mixture over the top of the cod fillets. Place the cod fillets in a shallow foil-lined roasting pan and roast in the preheated oven for 25–30 minutes.

3 Mix the garlic, the remaining lemon rind and juice, rosemary, and parsley, and the chile together in a bowl. Beat in the oil and mix to combine. Drizzle the dressing over the cod steaks as soon as they are cooked.

4 Transfer the fish to warmed serving plates and serve immediately.

nut-crusted halibut

ingredients

SERVES 4

3 tbsp butter, melted

1 lb 10 oz/750 g halibut fillet

generous ⅓ cup pistachios,
    shelled and very finely
    chopped

method

1 Brush the melted butter over the halibut fillet. Spread the nuts out on a large, flat plate. Roll the fish in the nuts, pressing down gently.

2 Preheat a ridged stovetop grill pan over medium heat. Cook the halibut, turning once, for 10 minutes, or until firm but tender—the exact cooking time will depend on the thickness of the fillet.

3 Remove the fish and any loose pistachio pieces from the heat and transfer to a large, warmed serving platter. Serve immediately.

412 fish & seafood

fish parcels with fresh herbs

ingredients

SERVES 4

vegetable oil spray

4 flounder fillets, skinned

6 tbsp chopped fresh herbs,
    such as dill, parsley,
    chives, thyme, or marjoram

finely grated rind and juice of
    2 lemons

1 small onion, sliced thinly

1 tbsp capers, rinsed
    (optional)

salt and pepper

method

1 Preheat the oven to 375°F/190°C. Cut 4 large squares of aluminum foil, each large enough to hold a fish and form a parcel, and spray with oil.

2 Place each fish fillet on a foil sheet and sprinkle with the herbs, lemon rind and juice, onion, capers, if using, and salt and pepper to taste. Fold the foil to make a secure parcel and place on a cookie sheet.

3 Bake the parcels in the preheated oven for 15 minutes, or until tender. Serve the fish piping hot, in their loosely opened parcels.

hake in white wine

ingredients

SERVES 4

about 2 tbsp all-purpose flour

salt and pepper

4 hake fillets, about
    5$\frac{1}{2}$ oz/150 g each

4 tbsp extra virgin olive oil

$\frac{1}{2}$ cup dry white wine

2 large garlic cloves, chopped
    very finely

6 scallions, sliced finely

2 tbsp finely chopped fresh
    parsley

method

1 Preheat the oven to 450°F/230°C. Season the flour generously with salt and pepper on a flat plate. Dredge the skin side of the hake fillets in the seasoned flour, then shake off the excess. Set aside.

2 Heat a shallow, flameproof casserole over high heat until you can feel the heat rising. Add the oil and heat until a cube of day-old bread sizzles—it takes about 30 seconds. Add the hake fillets, skin-side down, and cook for 3 minutes, until the skin is golden brown.

3 Turn the fish over and season with salt and pepper to taste. Pour in the wine and add the garlic, scallions, and parsley. Transfer the casserole to the preheated oven, uncovered, and bake for 5 minutes, or until the flesh flakes easily. Serve straight from the casserole.

sole à la meunière

ingredients

SERVES 4

4 tbsp all-purpose flour

1 tsp salt

4 x 14-oz/400-g sole, cleaned
   and skinned

scant 3/4 cup butter

3 tbsp lemon juice

1 tbsp chopped fresh parsley

1/4 preserved lemon, finely
   chopped (optional)

fresh parsley sprigs, to garnish

lemon wedges, to serve

method

1 Mix the flour with the salt and place on a large plate. Drop the fish into the flour, one at a time, and shake well to remove any excess. Melt 3 tablespoons of the butter in a small pan and use to brush the fish liberally all over. Place the fish under a broiler preheated to medium and cook for 5 minutes on each side.

2 Meanwhile, melt the remaining butter in a pan. Pour cold water into a bowl that is large enough to take the bottom of the pan and keep nearby.

3 Heat the butter until it turns a golden brown and begins to smell nutty. Remove from the heat immediately and immerse the bottom of the pan in the cold water, to stop the cooking.

4 Place the fish fillets on individual plates, drizzle with the lemon juice, and sprinkle with the parsley and preserved lemon, if using. Pour over the browned butter, garnish with parsley sprigs, and serve immediately with lemon wedges for squeezing over.

skate in mustard & caper sauce

ingredients

SERVES 4

2 skate wings
lemon wedges, to serve

mustard & caper
sauce
2 tbsp olive oil
1 onion, chopped finely
1 garlic clove, chopped finely
2/3 cup strained plain yogurt
1 tsp lemon juice
1 tbsp chopped fresh flat-leaf
parsley
1 tbsp capers, chopped
coarsely
1 tbsp whole-grain mustard
salt and pepper
chopped fresh flat-leaf parsley,
to garnish

method

1 Cut each skate wing in half and place in a large skillet. Cover with salted water, bring to a boil, then simmer for 10–15 minutes, until tender.

2 Meanwhile, make the mustard and caper sauce. Heat the oil in a saucepan, add the onion and garlic, and cook for 5 minutes, until softened. Add the yogurt, lemon juice, parsley, and capers and cook for 1–2 minutes, until heated through. (Do not boil or the sauce will curdle.) Stir in the mustard and season with salt and pepper.

3 Drain the skate and put on 4 warmed serving plates. Pour over the mustard and caper sauce and sprinkle with chopped parsley.

4 Serve hot, with lemon wedges.

sweet-&-sour sea bass

ingredients

SERVES 2

scant 1 cup shredded bok
   choy

scant 1/2 cup bean sprouts

scant 1/3 cup sliced shiitake
   mushrooms

scant 1/3 cup torn oyster
   mushrooms

3 scallions, finely sliced

1 tsp finely grated ginger

1 tbsp finely sliced lemongrass

2 x 3 1/4-oz/90-g sea bass
   fillets, skinned and boned

1 tbsp sesame seeds, toasted

sweet-&-sour sauce

scant 1/2 cup unsweetened
   pineapple juice

1 tbsp sugar

1 tbsp red wine vinegar

2 star anise, crushed

1/3 cup tomato juice

1 tbsp cornstarch, blended
   with a little cold water

method

1 Preheat the oven to 400°F/200°C. Cut 2 x 15-inch/38-cm squares of parchment paper and 2 x 15-inch/38-cm squares of aluminum foil.

2 To make the sauce, heat the pineapple juice, sugar, red wine vinegar, star anise, and tomato juice. Let simmer for 1–2 minutes, then thicken with the cornstarch and water mixture, whisking continuously. Pass through a fine strainer into a small bowl to cool.

3 In a separate large bowl, mix together the bok choy, bean sprouts, mushrooms, and scallions, then add the ginger and lemongrass. Toss all the ingredients together.

4 Put a square of parchment paper on top of a square of foil and fold into a triangle. Open up and place half the vegetable mix in the center, pour half the sweet and sour sauce over the vegetables, and place the sea bass on top. Sprinkle with a few sesame seeds. Close the triangle over the mixture and crumple the edges together to form an airtight triangular parcel. Repeat to make another parcel.

5 Place on a cookie sheet and cook in the preheated oven for 10 minutes, until the foil parcels puff with steam. To serve, place on individual plates and snip open at the table.

roast sea bream with fennel

ingredients

SERVES 4

2¼ cups dried, uncolored
    bread crumbs

2 tbsp milk

1 fennel bulb, sliced thinly,
    fronds reserved for garnish

1 tbsp lemon juice

2 tbsp sambuca

1 tbsp chopped fresh thyme

1 bay leaf, crumbled

3 lb 5 oz/1.5 kg whole sea
    bream, cleaned, scaled,
    and boned

salt and pepper

3 tbsp olive oil, plus extra
    for brushing

1 red onion, chopped

1¼ cups dry white wine

method

1 Preheat the oven to 475°F/240°C. Place the bread crumbs in a bowl, add the milk, and set aside for 5 minutes to soak. Place the fennel in another bowl and add the lemon juice, sambuca, thyme, and bay leaf. Squeeze the bread crumbs and add them to the mixture, stirring well.

2 Rinse the fish inside and out under cold running water and pat dry with paper towels. Season with salt and pepper. Spoon the fennel mixture into the cavity, then bind the fish with trussing thread or kitchen string.

3 Brush a large, ovenproof dish with olive oil and sprinkle the onion over the bottom. Lay the fish on top and pour in the wine—it should reach about one third of the way up the fish. Drizzle the sea bream with the olive oil and cook the preheated oven for 25–30 minutes. Baste the fish occasionally with the cooking juices and, if it starts to brown, cover with a piece of foil to protect it.

4 Carefully lift out the fish, remove the string, and place on a warmed serving platter. Garnish with the reserved fennel fronds and serve immediately.

chiles stuffed with fish paste

ingredients

SERVES 4–6

8 oz/225 g white fish, minced

2 tbsp lightly beaten egg

4–6 mild red and green chiles

vegetable or peanut oil,
    for shallow-frying

2 garlic cloves, finely chopped

1/2 tsp fermented black beans,
    rinsed and lightly mashed

1 tbsp light soy sauce

pinch of sugar

1 tbsp water

marinade

1 tsp finely chopped fresh
    ginger

pinch of salt

pinch of white pepper

1/2 tsp vegetable or peanut oil

method

1 Combine all the ingredients for the marinade in a bowl and marinate the fish for 20 minutes. Add the egg and mix by hand to create a smooth paste.

2 To prepare the chiles, cut in half lengthwise and scoop out the seeds and loose flesh. Cut into bite-size pieces. Spread each piece of chile with about 1/2 teaspoon of the fish paste.

3 In a preheated wok or deep pan, heat plenty of the oil and cook the chile pieces on both sides until beginning to turn golden brown. Drain and set aside.

4 Heat 1 tablespoon of the oil in a wok or deep pan and stir-fry the garlic until aromatic. Stir in the black beans and mix well. Add the light soy sauce and sugar and stir, then add the chile pieces. Add the water, then cover and let simmer over low heat for 5 minutes. Serve immediately.

broiled red snapper with garlic

ingredients

SERVES 4

2 tbsp lemon juice

4 tbsp olive oil, plus extra
  for oiling

salt and pepper

4 red snapper or mullet,
  scaled and gutted

2 tbsp chopped fresh
  herbs, such as oregano,
  marjoram, flat-leaf parsley,
  or thyme

2 garlic cloves, chopped finely

2 tbsp chopped fresh flat-leaf
  parsley

lemon wedges

method

1 Preheat the broiler. Put the lemon juice, oil, and salt and pepper to taste in a bowl and whisk together. Brush the mixture inside and on both sides of the fish and sprinkle over the chopped herb of your choice. Place on a greased broiler pan.

2 Broil the fish for about 10 minutes, basting frequently and turning once, until golden brown.

3 Meanwhile, mix together the chopped garlic and chopped parsley. Sprinkle the garlic mixture on top of the cooked fish and serve hot or cold with lemon wedges.

spiced steamed fish

ingredients

SERVES 4–6

1-inch/2.5-cm piece fresh
  ginger, finely grated
1 lemongrass stem (base
  only), thinly sliced
6 fresh red chiles, seeded and
  coarsely chopped
1 small red onion, finely
  chopped
1 tbsp Thai fish sauce
2 lb/900 g whole fish, cleaned
2 fresh kaffir lime leaves,
  thinly sliced
2 fresh basil sprigs
freshly cooked rice and thin
  cucumber sticks, to serve

method

1 Place the ginger, lemongrass, chiles, onion, and fish sauce in a food processor. Process to a coarse paste, adding a little water, if needed.

2 Cut 3–4 deep slits crosswise on each side of the fish. Spread over the spice paste, rubbing it well into the slits. Place the fish in a dish deep enough to hold the liquid that collects during steaming. Sprinkle over the lime leaves and basil.

3 Set up a steamer or place a rack into a wok or deep pan. Bring about 2 inches/5 cm of water to a boil in the steamer or wok.

4 Place the dish of fish into the steamer or onto the rack. Reduce the heat to a simmer, then cover tightly and steam the fish for 15–20 minutes, or until the fish is cooked through. Serve with freshly cooked rice and cucumber sticks.

trout in lemon & red wine sauce

ingredients

SERVES 4

4 trout, cleaned and heads
   removed
1 cup red wine vinegar
1¼ cups red wine
⅔ cup water
2 bay leaves
4 sprigs fresh thyme
4 sprigs fresh flat-leaf parsley,
   plus extra to garnish
thinly pared rind of 1 lemon
3 shallots, sliced thinly
1 carrot, sliced thinly
12 black peppercorns
8 cloves
salt and pepper
6 tbsp unsalted butter, diced
1 tbsp chopped fresh flat-leaf
   parsley
1 tbsp snipped fresh dill

method

1 Rinse the fish inside and out under cold running water and pat dry on paper towels. Place them in a single layer in a nonmetallic dish. Pour the vinegar into a small pan and bring to a boil, then pour it over the fish. Set aside to marinate for 30 minutes.

2 Pour the wine and water into a pan, add the bay leaves, thyme sprigs, parsley sprigs, lemon rind, shallots, carrots, peppercorns, and cloves, and season with salt. Bring to a boil over low heat.

3 Meanwhile, drain the trout and discard the vinegar. Place the fish in a single layer in a large skillet and strain the wine mixture over them. Cover and let simmer over low heat for 15 minutes, until cooked through and tender. There is no need to turn them.

4 Using a spatula, transfer the trout to individual serving plates and keep warm. Bring the cooking liquid back to a boil and cook until reduced by about three quarters. Gradually beat in the butter, a little at a time, until fully incorporated. Stir in the chopped parsley and dill and adjust the seasoning if necessary. Pour the sauce over the fish, garnish with parsley sprigs, and serve immediately.

marseilles-style fish stew

ingredients

SERVES 4–6

large pinch of saffron threads
2 tbsp olive oil
1 large onion, finely chopped
1 bulb of fennel, thinly sliced,
    with the feathery green
    fronds reserved
2 large garlic cloves, crushed
4 tbsp pastis
4 cups fish stock
2 large sun-ripened tomatoes,
    peeled, seeded, and diced,
    or 14 oz/400 g chopped
    tomatoes, drained
1 tbsp tomato paste
1 bay leaf
pinch of sugar
pinch of dried chile flakes
    (optional)
salt and pepper
24 large raw shrimp, peeled
1 squid, cleaned and cut
    into 1/4-inch/5-mm rings,
    tentacles reserved
2 lb/900 g fresh, skinned
    and boned Mediterranean
    fish, such as sea bass,
    monkfish, red snapper,
    or halibut, cut into large
    chunks

method

1 Put the saffron threads in a small dry skillet over high heat and toast, stirring constantly, for 1 minute, or until you can smell the aroma. Immediately tip the saffron threads out of the skillet and set aside.

2 Heat the oil in a large flameproof casserole over medium heat. Add the onion and fennel and sauté for 3 minutes, then add the garlic and sauté for an additional 5 minutes, or until the onion and fennel are soft but not colored.

3 Remove the casserole from the heat. Warm the pastis in a ladle or small pan, then ignite and pour it over the onion and fennel to flambé. When the flames die down, return the casserole to the heat and stir in the stock, tomatoes, tomato paste, bay leaf, sugar, chile flakes, if using, and salt and pepper to taste. Slowly bring to a boil, skimming the surface if necessary, then reduce the heat to low and let simmer, uncovered, for 15 minutes. Adjust the seasoning if necessary.

4 Add the prepared shrimp and squid rings and simmer until the shrimp turn pink and the squid rings are opaque. Do not overcook, or they will be tough. Use a slotted spoon to transfer to serving bowls. Add the fish chunks to the broth and simmer just until the flesh flakes easily. Transfer the seafood and broth to the serving bowls and garnish with the reserved fennel fronds.

catalan fish stew

ingredients

SERVES 4–6

large pinch of saffron threads
6 tbsp olive oil
1 large onion, chopped
2 garlic cloves, chopped finely
1 1/2 tbsp chopped fresh thyme
	leaves
2 bay leaves
2 red bell peppers, cored,
	seeded, and chopped
	coarsely
1 lb 12 oz/800 g canned
	chopped tomatoes
1 tsp sweet smoked paprika
scant 1 1/4 cups fish stock
1 cup blanched almonds,
	toasted and ground finely
salt and pepper
12–16 live mussels with tightly
	closed shells
12–16 live clams with tightly
	closed shells
1 lb 5 oz/600 g thick, boned
	hake or cod fillets, skinned
	and cut into 2-inch/5-cm
	chunks
12–16 uncooked shrimp,
	heads and tails removed
	and deveined
crusty bread, to serve

method

1 Infuse the saffron threads in 4 tablespoons of boiling water in a heatproof bowl.

2 Heat the oil in a large, heavy-bottom flameproof casserole over medium–high heat. Reduce the heat to low, add the onion, and cook for 10 minutes, or until golden, but not browned. Stir in the garlic, thyme, bay leaves, and red bell peppers and continue cooking for an additional 5 minutes, or until the bell peppers are soft and the onions have softened further.Add the tomatoes and paprika and continue to simmer for 5 minutes, stirring frequently.

3 Stir in the fish stock, reserved saffron water, and ground almonds, and bring to a boil, stirring frequently. Reduce the heat and simmer for 5–10 minutes, until the sauce reduces and thickens. Add salt and pepper to taste.

4 Meanwhile, prepare the mussels and clams, discarding any with broken shells and any that do not close when tapped. Cut off and discard any beards from the mussels, then scrub any dirty shells.

5 Gently stir the hake into the casserole and add the shrimp, mussels, and clams. Reduce the heat to very low, cover the casserole, and simmer for about 5 minutes, until the hake is cooked through, the shrimp turn pink, and the mussels and clams open; discard any that remain closed. Serve immediately with the bread.

fish curry with rice noodles

ingredients

SERVES 4

2 tbsp vegetable or peanut oil

1 large onion, chopped

2 garlic cloves, chopped

3 oz/75 g white mushrooms

8 oz/225 g monkfish, cut into 1-inch/2.5-cm cubes

8 oz/225 g salmon fillets, cut into 1-inch/2.5-cm cubes

8 oz/225 g cod, cut into 1-inch/2.5-cm cubes

2 tbsp Thai red curry paste

1³/₄ cups canned coconut milk

handful of fresh cilantro, chopped

1 tsp jaggery or light brown sugar

1 tsp fish sauce

4 oz/115 g rice noodles

3 scallions, chopped

¹/₂ cup bean sprouts

a few Thai basil leaves

method

1 Heat the oil in a wok or large skillet and gently sauté the onion, garlic, and mushrooms until softened but not browned.

2 Add the fish, curry paste, and coconut milk and bring gently to a boil. Let simmer for 2–3 minutes before adding half the the cilantro, the sugar, and fish sauce. Keep warm.

3 Meanwhile, soak the noodles for 3–4 minutes, (check the package instructions) or until tender, and drain well through a colander. Put the colander and noodles over a pan of simmering water. Add the scallions, bean sprouts, and most of the basil and steam on top of the noodles for 1–2 minutes, or until just wilted.

4 Pile the noodles onto warmed serving plates and top with the fish curry. Sprinkle over the remaining cilantro and basil and serve immediately.

fish in coconut

ingredients

SERVES 4

2 tbsp vegetable or peanut oil

6 scallions, chopped coarsely

1-inch/2.5-cm piece fresh
    ginger, grated

2–3 tbsp Thai red curry paste

1³/₄ cups coconut milk

²/₃ cup fish stock

4 kaffir lime leaves

1 lemongrass stalk, halved

12 oz/350 g whitefish fillets,
    skinned and cut into
    chunks

8 oz/225 g squid rings and
    tentacles

8 oz/225 g large cooked
    peeled shrimp

1 tbsp fish sauce

2 tbsp Thai soy sauce

4 tbsp chopped fresh Chinese
    chives

boiled jasmine rice with
    chopped fresh cilantro,
    to serve

method

1 Heat the oil in a wok or large skillet and stir-fry the scallions and ginger for 1–2 minutes. Add the curry paste and stir-fry for 1–2 minutes.

2 Add the coconut milk, fish stock, lime leaves, and lemongrass. Bring to a boil, then reduce the heat and let simmer for 1 minute.

3 Add the fish, squid, and shrimp and let simmer for 2–3 minutes, until the fish is cooked. Add the fish and soy sauces and stir in the chives. Serve immediately with jasmine rice with fresh cilantro stirred through it.

seafood paella with lemon & herbs

ingredients

SERVES 4–6

1/2 tsp saffron threads

2 tbsp hot water

51/2 oz/150 g cod fillet,
    skinned and rinsed under
    cold running water

51/2 cups simmering fish stock

12 large raw shrimp, peeled
    and deveined

1 lb/450 g raw squid, cleaned
    and cut into rings or
    bite-size pieces (or use the
    same quantity of shelled
    scallops)

3 tbsp olive oil

1 large red onion, chopped

2 garlic cloves, crushed

1 small fresh red chile, seeded
    and finely chopped

8 oz/225 g tomatoes, peeled
    and cut into wedges

generous 11/2 cups
    medium-grain paella rice

1 tbsp chopped fresh parsley

2 tsp chopped fresh dill

salt and pepper

method

1 Put the saffron threads and water in a small bowl for a few minutes to infuse.

2 Add the cod to the pan of simmering stock and cook for 5 minutes, then transfer to a colander, rinse under cold running water, and drain. Add the shrimp and squid to the stock and cook for 2 minutes. Cut the cod into chunks, then transfer, with the other seafood, to a bowl and set aside. Let the stock simmer.

3 Heat the oil in a paella pan and stir the onion over medium heat until softened. Add the garlic, chile, and saffron and its soaking liquid and cook, stirring, for 1 minute. Add the tomato wedges and cook, stirring, for 2 minutes. Add the rice and herbs and cook, stirring, for 1 minute. Add most of the stock and bring to a boil. Simmer, uncovered, for 10 minutes. Do not stir during cooking, but shake the pan once or twice, and when adding ingredients. Season and cook for 10 minutes, until the rice is almost cooked. Add more stock if necessary. Add the seafood and cook for 2 minutes.

4 When all the liquid has been absorbed and you detect a faint toasty aroma coming from the rice, remove from the heat immediately. Cover with foil and let stand for 5 minutes.

rice with seafood & squid

ingredients

SERVES 4

2 tbsp vegetable or peanut oil

3 shallots, chopped finely

2 garlic cloves, chopped finely

generous 1 cup jasmine rice

1¼ cups fish stock

4 scallions, chopped

2 tbsp Thai red curry paste

8 oz/225 g baby squid,
    cleaned and sliced thickly

8 oz/225 g whitefish fillets,
    skinned and cut into cubes

8 oz/225 g salmon fillets,
    skinned and cut into cubes

4 tbsp chopped fresh cilantro

method

1 Heat 1 tablespoon of the oil in a wok and stir-fry the shallots and garlic for 2–3 minutes, until softened. Add the rice and stir-fry for 2–3 minutes.

2 Add a ladleful of the stock and simmer, adding more stock as needed, for 12–15 minutes, until tender. Transfer to a dish, let cool, and chill overnight.

3 Heat the remaining oil in a wok and stir-fry the scallions and curry paste for 2–3 minutes. Add the squid and fish and stir-fry gently to avoid breaking up the fish. Stir in the rice and cilantro, heat through gently, and serve.

spaghetti with shrimp

ingredients

SERVES 4

1 lb/450 g dried spaghetti

1/2 cup olive oil

6 garlic cloves, sliced thinly

1 lb/450 g medium raw
 shrimp, peeled and
 deveined

2 tbsp finely chopped
 fresh parsley, plus extra
 to garnish

1/2 cup dry white wine

4 tbsp freshly squeezed lemon
 juice

salt and pepper

method

1 Bring a large pan of salted water to a boil over high heat. Add the spaghetti, return the water to a boil, and continue boiling for 10 minutes (check the package instructions), or until tender.

2 Meanwhile, heat the oil in another large pan over medium heat. Add the garlic and cook until just golden brown. Add the shrimp and chopped parsley and stir. Add the wine and let simmer for 2 minutes. Stir in the lemon juice and continue simmering until the shrimp turn pink and curl.

3 Drain the spaghetti. Tip into the pan with the shrimp and toss. Add salt and pepper to taste.

4 Transfer to a large serving platter and sprinkle with parsley. Serve immediately.

fusilli with hot cajun seafood sauce

ingredients

SERVES 4

scant 2 cups heavy cream

8 scallions, sliced thinly

2 oz/55 g chopped fresh
flat-leaf parsley

1 tbsp chopped fresh thyme

1/2 tbsp pepper

1/2–1 tsp dried chile flakes

1 tsp salt

1 lb/450 g dried fusilli or
tagliatelle

1/3 cup freshly grated Gruyère
cheese

2 tbsp freshly grated
Parmesan cheese

2 tbsp olive oil

8 oz/225 g raw peeled shrimp

8 oz/225 g scallops, sliced

1 tbsp shredded fresh basil,
to serve

method

1 Heat the cream in a large saucepan over medium heat, stirring constantly. When almost boiling, reduce the heat and add the scallions, parsley, thyme, pepper, chile flakes, and salt. Simmer for 7–8 minutes, stirring, until thickened. Remove from the heat.

2 Cook the pasta in plenty of boiling salted water until tender but still firm to the bite. Drain and return to the saucepan. Add the cream mixture and the cheeses to the pasta. Toss over low heat until the cheeses have melted. Transfer to a warmed serving dish.

3 Heat the oil in a large skillet over medium–high heat. Add the shrimp and scallops. Stir-fry for 2–3 minutes, until the shrimp have just turned pink.

4 Pour the seafood over the pasta and toss well to mix. Sprinkle with the basil and serve immediately.

seafood omelet

ingredients

SERVES 3

2 tbsp unsalted butter

1 tbsp olive oil

1 onion, chopped very finely

6 oz/175 g zucchini, halved
lengthwise and sliced

1 celery stalk, chopped very
finely

3 oz/85 g white mushrooms,
sliced

2 oz/55 g green beans,
cut into 2-inch/5-cm
lengths

4 eggs

scant 1/2 cup mascarpone
cheese

1 tbsp chopped fresh thyme

1 tbsp shredded fresh basil

salt and pepper

7 oz/200 g canned tuna,
drained and flaked

4 oz/115 g cooked peeled
shrimp

method

1 Melt the butter with the olive oil in a heavy-bottom skillet with a flameproof handle. If the skillet has a wooden handle, protect it with foil because it needs to go under the broiler. Add the onion and cook over low heat, stirring occasionally, for 5 minutes, until softened.

2 Add the zucchini, celery, mushrooms, and beans and cook, stirring occasionally, for an additional 8–10 minutes, until starting to brown.

3 Beat the eggs with the mascarpone, thyme, basil, and salt and pepper to taste.

4 Add the tuna to the skillet and stir it into the mixture with a wooden spoon. Add the shrimp last.

5 Pour the egg mixture into the skillet and cook for 5 minutes, until it is just starting to set. Draw the egg from the sides of the skillet toward the center to let the uncooked egg run underneath.

6 Put the skillet under a preheated broiler and cook until the egg is just set and the surface is starting to brown. Cut the omelet into wedges and serve.

paprika shrimp

ingredients

SERVES 4–6

16–24 large, raw jumbo
    shrimp
6 tbsp extra virgin olive oil
1 large garlic clove, crushed
1/2 tsp mild paprika, or to taste
salt
lemon wedges, to serve

method

1 Remove the shell from the center of the shrimp, leaving the heads and tails intact. Devein the shrimp.

2 Mix together the oil, garlic, paprika, and salt in a shallow dish large enough to hold the shrimp in a single layer. Stir together, then add the shrimp and turn so they are coated. Cover with plastic wrap and let marinate in the refrigerator for at least 1 hour.

3 When ready to cook, heat a large, ridged, cast-iron grill pan over medium–high heat until you can feel the heat rising. Add as many shrimp as will fit without overcrowding the grill pan. Cook for about 1 minute, until the shrimp curl and turn pink. Turn over and continue cooking for an additional minute, or until cooked through. Drain well on paper towels and keep hot while you continue to cook the remainder.

4 Serve immediately with lemon wedges for squeezing over the shrimp.

ginger shrimp with oyster mushrooms

ingredients

SERVES 4

about 3 tbsp vegetable oil

3 carrots, sliced thinly

12 oz/350 g oyster
    mushrooms, sliced thinly

1 large red bell pepper, sliced
    thinly

1 lb/450g large shrimp, peeled

2 garlic cloves, crushed

fresh cilantro leaves,
    to garnish

s a u c e

2/3 cup chicken stock

2 tsp sesame seeds

3 tsp grated fresh ginger

1 tbsp soy sauce

1/4 tsp hot pepper sauce

1 tsp cornstarch

method

1 In a small bowl, stir together the chicken stock, sesame seeds, ginger, soy sauce, hot pepper sauce, and cornstarch until well blended. Set aside.

2 In a large skillet or wok, heat 2 tablespoons of the oil. Stir-fry the carrots for 3 minutes, then remove from the skillet and set aside.

3 Add another 1 tablespoon of the oil to the skillet and fry the mushrooms for 2 minutes. Remove from the skillet and set aside.

4 Add more oil if needed and stir-fry the bell pepper with the shrimp and garlic for 3 minutes, until the shrimp turn pink and opaque.

5 Stir the sauce again and pour it into the skillet. Cook until the mixture bubbles, then return the carrots and mushrooms to the skillet. Cover and cook for an additional 2 minutes, until heated through. Serve garnished with cilantro.

stir-fried shrimp, snow peas & cashews

ingredients

SERVES 4

$^1/_2$ cup cashews

3 tbsp peanut oil

4 scallions, slivered

2 celery stalks, sliced thinly

3 carrots, sliced finely

$3^1/_2$ oz/100 g baby corn,
    halved

6 oz/175 g mushrooms,
    sliced finely

1 garlic clove, chopped
    coarsely

1 lb/450 g raw shrimp, peeled

1 tsp cornstarch

2 tbsp soy sauce

$^1/_4$ cup chicken stock

8 oz/225 g savoy cabbage,
    shredded

6 oz/175 g snow peas

method

1 Put a skillet or wok over medium heat, add the cashews, and toast them until they begin to brown. Remove with a slotted spoon and set aside.

2 Add the oil to the skillet and heat. Add the scallions, celery, carrots, and baby corn and cook, stirring occasionally, over medium–high heat for 3–4 minutes.

3 Add the mushrooms and cook until they become brown. Mix in the garlic and shrimp, stirring until the shrimp turn pink.

4 Mix the cornstarch with the soy sauce and chicken stock until smooth. Add the liquid to the shrimp mixture and stir. Add the savoy cabbage, snow peas, and all but a few of the cashews and cook for 2 minutes.

5 Garnish with the reserved cashews and serve.

curried noodles with shrimp & straw mushrooms

ingredients

SERVES 4

1 tbsp vegetable or peanut oil

3 shallots, chopped

1 fresh red chile, seeded and
chopped

1 tbsp Thai red curry paste

1 lemongrass stalk (white part
only), chopped finely

8 oz/225 g cooked peeled
shrimp

14 oz/225 g canned straw
mushrooms, drained

2 tbsp fish sauce

2 tbsp Thai soy sauce

8 oz/225 g fresh egg noodles

chopped fresh cilantro,
to garnish

method

1 Heat the oil in a wok and stir-fry the shallots and chile for 2–3 minutes. Add the curry paste and lemongrass and stir-fry for 2–3 minutes.

2 Add the shrimp, mushrooms, fish sauce, and soy sauce, and stir well to mix.

3 Meanwhile, cook the noodles in boiling water for 3–4 minutes, drain, and transfer to warmed plates. Top with the shrimp mixture, sprinkle over the cilantro, and serve immediately.

shrimp pilaf

ingredients

SERVES 4

3 tbsp olive oil

1 onion, chopped finely

1 red bell pepper, cored,
   seeded, and sliced thinly

1 garlic clove, crushed

1$\frac{1}{3}$ cups long-grain white rice

3 cups fish, chicken,
   or vegetable stock

1 bay leaf

salt and pepper

14 oz/400 g peeled cooked
   shrimp, thawed and
   drained if frozen

grated kefalotiri or pecorino
   cheese and cubes of feta
   cheese, to serve

to garnish

whole cooked shrimp

lemon wedges

Greek black olives

method

1 Heat the oil in a large, lidded skillet, add the onion, red bell pepper, and garlic, and fry for 5 minutes, until softened. Add the rice and cook for 2–3 minutes, stirring all the time, until the grains look transparent.

2 Add the stock, bay leaf, and salt and pepper to taste. Bring to a boil, cover the skillet with a tightly fitting lid, and simmer for about 15 minutes, until the rice is tender and the liquid has been absorbed. Do not stir during cooking. When cooked, very gently stir in the shrimp.

3 Remove the lid, cover the skillet with a clean dish towel, replace the lid, and let stand in a warm place for 10 minutes to dry out. Stir with a fork to separate the grains.

4 Serve garnished with whole shrimp, lemon wedges, and black olives. Accompany with kefalotiri or pecorino cheese for sprinkling on top and a bowl of feta cubes.

shrimp & asparagus risotto

ingredients

SERVES 4

5 cups vegetable stock
12 oz/375 g fresh asparagus
  spears, cut into 2-inch/
  5-cm lengths
2 tbsp olive oil
1 onion, finely chopped
1 garlic clove, finely chopped
1²/₃ cups risotto rice
1 lb/450 g raw jumbo shrimp,
  peeled and deveined
2 tbsp olive paste or tapenade
2 tbsp chopped fresh basil
salt and pepper
freshly grated Parmesan
  cheese, to serve
fresh basil sprigs, to garnish

method

1 Bring the stock to a boil in a large pan. Add the asparagus and cook for 3 minutes, until just tender. Strain, reserving the stock, and refresh the asparagus under cold running water. Drain and set aside.

2 Return the stock to the pan and keep simmering gently over low heat while you are cooking the risotto.

3 Heat the olive oil in a large, heavy-bottom pan. Add the onion and cook over medium heat, stirring occasionally, for 5 minutes, until softened. Add the garlic and cook for an additional 30 seconds.

4 Reduce the heat, add the rice, and mix to coat in oil. Cook, stirring constantly, for 2–3 minutes, or until the grains are translucent.

5 Gradually add the hot stock, a ladleful at a time. Stir constantly and add more liquid as the rice absorbs each addition. Increase the heat to medium so that the liquid bubbles. Cook for 20 minutes, until all the liquid is absorbed and the rice is creamy. Add the shrimp and asparagus with the last ladleful of stock.

6 Remove the pan from the heat, stir in the olive paste and basil, and season to taste with salt and pepper. Spoon the risotto onto warmed plates and serve immediately, garnished with parmesan cheese and basil sprigs.

spaghetti with clams

ingredients

SERVES 4

2 lb 4 oz/1 kg live clams

3/4 cup water

3/4 cup dry white wine

12 oz/350 g dried spaghetti

5 tbsp olive oil

2 garlic cloves, chopped finely

4 tbsp chopped fresh flat-leaf
    parsley

salt and pepper

method

1 Scrub the clams under cold running water and discard any with broken shells and any that do not close when tapped. Place the clams in a large, heavy-bottom pan, add the water and wine, cover, and cook over high heat, shaking the pan occasionally, for 5 minutes, until the shells have opened.

2 Remove the clams with a slotted spoon and set aside to cool slightly. Strain the cooking liquid through a cheesecloth-lined strainer into a small pan. Bring to a boil and cook until reduced by about half, then remove from heat. Meanwhile, discard any clams that remain closed, remove the remainder from their shells, and set aside.

3 Bring a large pan of lightly salted water to a boil. Add the pasta, bring back to a boil, and cook for 8–10 minutes, until tender but still firm to the bite.

4 Meanwhile, heat the olive oil in a large, heavy-bottom skillet. Add the garlic and cook, stirring frequently, for 2 minutes. Add the parsley and the reduced cooking liquid and let simmer gently.

5 Drain the pasta and add it to the skillet with the clams. Season to taste with salt and pepper and cook, stirring constantly, for 4 minutes, until the pasta is coated and the clams have heated through. Transfer to a warmed serving dish and serve immediately.

fettuccine with scallops & porcini

ingredients

SERVES 4

1 1/3 cups dried porcini
    mushrooms
generous 2 cups hot water
3 tbsp olive oil
3 tbsp butter
1 1/2 cups scallops, sliced
2 garlic cloves, chopped very
    finely
2 tbsp lemon juice
1 cup heavy cream
salt and pepper
12 oz/350 g dried fettuccine
    or pappardelle
2 tbsp chopped fresh flat-leaf
    parsley, to serve

method

1 Put the porcini and hot water in a bowl. Let soak for 20 minutes. Strain the mushrooms, reserving the soaking water, and chop coarsely. Line a strainer with paper towels and strain the mushroom water into a bowl.

2 Heat the oil and butter in a large skillet over medium heat. Add the scallops and cook for 2 minutes, or until just golden. Add the garlic and mushrooms, then stir-fry for another minute.

3 Stir in the lemon juice, cream, and 1/2 cup of the mushroom water. Bring to a boil, then simmer over medium heat for 2–3 minutes, stirring constantly, until the liquid is reduced by half. Season with salt and pepper. Remove from the heat.

4 Cook the pasta in plenty of boiling salted water until al dente. Drain and transfer to a warmed serving dish. Briefly reheat the sauce and pour over the pasta. Sprinkle with the parsley and toss well to mix. Serve immediately.

saffron & lemon risotto with scallops

ingredients

SERVES 4

16 live scallops, shucked

juice of 1 lemon, plus extra for
    seasoning

3 tbsp butter

1 tbsp olive oil, plus extra for
    brushing

1 small onion, finely chopped

1 1/2 cups risotto rice

1 tsp crumbled saffron threads

5 cups fish or vegetable stock

salt and pepper

2 tbsp vegetable oil

1 cup freshly grated
    Parmesan cheese

1 lemon, cut into wedges

2 tsp grated lemon zest,
    to garnish

method

1 Place the scallops in a nonmetallic bowl and mix with the lemon juice. Cover the bowl with plastic wrap and let chill for 15 minutes.

2 Melt 2 tablespoons of the butter with the oil in a deep pan over medium heat. Add the onion and cook, stirring occasionally, until softened and starting to turn golden. Add the rice and mix to coat in oil and butter. Cook, stirring, until the grains are translucent. Dissolve the saffron in 4 tablespoons of hot stock and add to the rice. Gradually add the remaining stock a ladleful at a time, stirring constantly, until all the liquid is absorbed and the rice is creamy. Season with salt and pepper.

3 When the risotto is nearly cooked, heat a grill pan over high heat. Brush the scallops with oil and sear on the grill pan for 3–4 minutes on each side, depending on their thickness. Take care not to overcook or they will be rubbery.

4 Remove the risotto from the heat and add the remaining butter. Mix well, then stir in the Parmesan until it melts. Season with lemon juice, adding just 1 teaspoon at a time and tasting as you go. Serve the risotto immediately with the scallops and lemon wedges arranged on top, sprinkled with lemon zest.

simple stir-fried scallops

ingredients

SERVES 4

1 lb/450 g scallops
2 tbsp sesame oil
1 tbsp chopped fresh cilantro
1 tbsp chopped flat-leaf
    parsley
rice noodles, to serve

s a u c e
2 tbsp lemon juice
2 tbsp soy sauce
1 tbsp honey
1 tbsp minced fresh ginger
1 tbsp fish sauce
1 garlic clove, peeled and
    flattened

method

1 Combine the lemon juice, soy sauce, honey, ginger, fish sauce, and garlic in a bowl and stir well to dissolve the honey. Add the scallops and toss to coat.

2 Heat a heavy skillet or wok over the highest heat for 3 minutes. Add the oil and heat for 30 seconds.

3 Add the scallops with their sauce and the cilantro and parsley to the skillet. Stir constantly, cooking for about 3 minutes (less time if the scallops are small). Serve immediately with rice noodles.

spicy scallops with lime & chile

ingredients

SERVES 4

16 large scallops, shelled

1 tbsp butter

1 tbsp vegetable oil

1 tsp crushed garlic

1 tsp grated fresh ginger

1 bunch of scallions, finely sliced

finely grated rind of 1 lime

1 small fresh red chile, seeded and very finely chopped

3 tbsp lime juice

lime wedges, to garnish

freshly cooked rice, to serve

method

1 Using a sharp knife, trim the scallops to remove any black intestine, then wash and pat dry with paper towels. Separate the corals from the white parts, then slice each white part in half horizontally, making 2 circles.

2 Heat the butter and oil in a skillet or preheated wok. Add the garlic and ginger and stir-fry for 1 minute without browning. Add the scallions and stir-fry for an additional 1 minute.

3 Add the scallops and continue stir-frying over high heat for 4–5 minutes. Stir in the lime rind, chile, and lime juice and cook for an additional 1 minute.

4 Transfer the scallops to serving plates, then spoon over the pan juices and garnish with lime wedges. Serve hot with freshly cooked rice.

scallops with bread crumbs & parsley

ingredients

SERVES 4

20 large fresh scallops, shucked, about 1½ inches/4 cm thick

salt and pepper

scant 1 cup clarified butter

3 oz/85 g day-old French bread, made into fine bread crumbs

4 garlic cloves, finely chopped

5 tbsp finely chopped fresh flat-leaf parsley

lemon wedges, to serve

method

1 Preheat the oven to its lowest temperature. Use a small knife to remove the dark vein that runs around each scallop, then rinse and pat dry. Season to taste with salt and pepper and set aside.

2 Melt half the butter in a large sauté pan or skillet over high heat. Add the bread crumbs, then reduce the heat to medium and cook, stirring, for 5–6 minutes, or until they are golden brown and crisp. Remove the bread crumbs from the pan and drain well on paper towels, then keep warm in the oven. Wipe out the pan.

3 Use 2 large sauté pans or skillets to cook all the scallops at the same time without overcrowding the pans. Divide the remaining butter between the pans and melt over high heat. Reduce the heat to medium. Divide the scallops between the 2 pans in single layers and cook for 2 minutes.

4 Turn the scallops over and continue pan-frying for an additional 2–3 minutes, or until they are golden and cooked through.

5 Divide the scallops among 4 warmed plates and sprinkle with the bread crumbs, garlic, and parsley mixed together. Serve with lemon wedges for squeezing over.

penne with squid & tomatoes

ingredients

SERVES 4

8 oz/225 g dried penne

12 oz/350 g prepared squid

6 tbsp olive oil

2 onions, sliced

1 cup fish or chicken stock

2/3 cup full-bodied red wine

14 oz/400 g canned chopped
    tomatoes

2 tbsp tomato paste

1 tbsp chopped fresh
    marjoram

1 bay leaf

salt and pepper

2 tbsp chopped fresh parsley

method

1 Bring a large, heavy-bottom pan of lightly salted water to a boil. Add the pasta, return to a boil, and cook for 3 minutes, then drain and set aside until required. With a sharp knife, cut the squid into strips.

2 Heat the olive oil in a large, flameproof dish or casserole. Add the onions and cook over low heat, stirring occasionally, for 5 minutes, or until softened. Add the squid and fish stock, bring to a boil, and let simmer for 3 minutes. Stir in the wine, chopped tomatoes and their can juices, tomato paste, marjoram, and bay leaf. Season to taste with salt and pepper. Bring to a boil and cook for 5 minutes, or until slightly reduced.

3 Add the pasta, return to a boil, and let simmer for 5–7 minutes, or until tender but still firm to the bite. Remove and discard the bay leaf, stir in the parsley, and serve immediately, straight from the dish.

sweet chile squid

ingredients

SERVES 4

1 tbsp sesame seeds, toasted

2$\frac{1}{2}$ tbsp sesame oil

10 oz/280 g squid, cut into strips

2 red bell peppers, sliced thinly

3 shallots, sliced thinly

3 oz/85 g mushrooms, sliced thinly

1 tbsp dry sherry

4 tbsp soy sauce

1 tsp sugar

1 tsp hot chile flakes, or to taste

1 garlic clove, crushed

freshly cooked rice, to serve

method

1 Place the sesame seeds on a cookie sheet, toast under a hot broiler, and set aside.

2 Heat 1 tablespoon of the oil in a skillet or wok over medium heat. Add the squid and cook for 2 minutes, then remove and set aside.

3 Add the 1 tablespoon of the remaining oil to the skillet and fry the bell peppers and shallots over medium heat for 1 minute. Add the mushrooms and fry for an additional 2 minutes.

4 Return the squid to the skillet and add the sherry, soy sauce, sugar, chile flakes, and garlic, stirring thoroughly. Cook for an additional 2 minutes.

5 Sprinkle with the toasted sesame seeds, drizzle over the remaining oil, and mix. Serve on a bed of rice.

stir-fried squid with hot black bean sauce

ingredients

SERVES 4

1 lb 10 oz/750 g squid, cleaned and tentacles discarded

1 large red bell pepper, seeded

scant 1 cup snow peas

1 head bok choy

3 tbsp black bean sauce

1 tbsp Thai fish sauce

1 tbsp rice wine or dry sherry

1 tbsp dark soy sauce

1 tsp brown sugar

1 tsp cornstarch

1 tbsp water

1 tbsp corn oil

1 tsp sesame oil

1 small fresh red Thai chile, chopped

1 garlic clove, finely chopped

1 tsp grated fresh ginger

2 scallions, chopped

method

1 Cut the squid body cavities into quarters lengthwise. Use the tip of a small, sharp knife to score a diamond pattern into the flesh, without cutting all the way through. Pat dry with paper towels.

2 Cut the bell pepper into long, thin slices. Cut the snow peas in half diagonally. Coarsely shred the bok choy.

3 Mix the black bean sauce, fish sauce, rice wine, soy sauce, and sugar together in a bowl. Blend the cornstarch with the water and stir into the other sauce ingredients. Reserve until required.

4 Heat the oils in a preheated wok. Add the chile, garlic, ginger, and scallions and stir-fry for 1 minute. Add the bell pepper slices and stir-fry for 2 minutes.

5 Add the squid and stir-fry over high heat for an additional 1 minute. Stir in the snow peas and bok choy and stir for an additional 1 minute, or until wilted.

6 Stir in the sauce ingredients and cook, stirring constantly, for 2 minutes, or until the sauce thickens and clears. Serve immediately.

black rice

ingredients

SERVES 4–6

scant 2 cups Spanish short-
    grain rice
6 tbsp olive oil
1 large onion, sliced finely
2 large garlic cloves, crushed
2 tomatoes, broiled, peeled,
    seeded, and chopped
    finely
1 prepared squid body, cut
    into ¼-inch/5-mm rings
    (tentacles set aside,
    if available)
4 cups fish stock
ink sac from squid, or an
    envelope of squid ink
salt and pepper
12 large raw shrimp, peeled
    and deveined
2 red bell peppers, broiled,
    peeled, seeded, and sliced
garlic mayonnaise, to serve

method

1 Put the rice in a strainer and rinse until the water runs clear. Set aside.

2 Heat the oil in a large, shallow casserole or skillet over medium–high heat. Add the onion and cook for 3 minutes, then add the garlic and cook for an additional 2 minutes, until the onion is softened, but not browned.

3 Add the tomatoes and let simmer until they are very soft. Add the squid rings and cook quickly until they turn opaque.

4 Add the rice and stir until it is coated in oil. Pour in the stock, squid ink, and salt and pepper to taste and bring to a boil. Reduce the heat and let simmer for 15 minutes, uncovered and without stirring, but shaking the skillet frequently, until most of the stock is absorbed and small holes appear on the surface.

5 Lightly stir in the shrimp, squid tentacles, if using, and bell peppers. Cover the skillet and continue simmering for about 5 minutes, until the shrimp turn pink and the tentacles turn opaque and curl.

6 Taste and adjust the seasoning. Serve with garlic mayonnaise.

vegetarian

Almost all common vegetarian ingredients benefit from quick cooking. For example, stir-frying is perfect for retaining the texture and goodness of vegetables, while eggs are generally ready in minutes, whatever cooking method you use. Dried beans are the most notable exception because they require prolonged soaking and lengthy cooking but you can skip these stages by using drained and rinsed canned beans. Lentils do not need to be soaked and, depending on the type, are usually cooked within 30 minutes.

There is a huge range of vegetables to choose from and most are suited to many different kinds of dishes—from curries to gratins and from pasta sauces to kebabs. They go well with rice, whether in European risotto or paella or in Chinese dishes. Cheese is a good source of protein in the vegetarian diet and is extremely versatile, partnering many vegetables and rice, as well as being a classic accompaniment to pasta dishes. Chinese and Southeast Asian cooks have created an array of superb vegetarian dishes with a wonderful balance of flavors, textures, and colors, yet, like most Eastern food, they are characteristically simple and very quick to cook.

With the global increase in food prices plus a growing awareness about

healthy eating, it makes sense for meat-eating families to include at least one vegetarian meal in the weekly menu. There is such a variety of delicious, nutritious, inexpensive dishes that are also easy and quick to prepare and cook that you simply can't go wrong.

sweet-&-sour vegetables with cashews

ingredients

SERVES 4

1 tbsp vegetable or peanut oil

1 tsp chili oil

2 onions, sliced

2 carrots, thinly sliced

2 zucchini, thinly sliced

4 oz/115 g broccoli, cut into florets

4 oz/115 g white mushrooms, sliced

4 oz/115 g small bok choy, halved

2 tbsp jaggery or brown sugar

2 tbsp Thai soy sauce

1 tbsp rice vinegar

generous 1/3 cup cashews

method

1 Heat both the oils in a preheated wok or skillet, add the onions, and stir-fry for 1–2 minutes, until beginning to soften.

2 Add the carrots, zucchini, and broccoli and stir-fry for 2–3 minutes. Add the mushrooms, bok choy, sugar, soy sauce, and vinegar and stir-fry for 1–2 minutes.

3 Meanwhile, heat a dry, heavy-bottom skillet over high heat, add the cashews, and cook, shaking the skillet frequently, until lightly toasted. Sprinkle the cashews over the stir-fry and serve immediately.

crisp noodle & vegetable stir-fry

ingredients

SERVES 4

peanut or sunflower-seed oil,
   for deep-frying
4 oz/115 g rice vermicelli,
   broken into 3-inch/7.5-cm
   lengths
4 oz/115 g green beans,
   cut into short lengths
2 carrots, cut into thin sticks
2 zucchini, cut into thin sticks
4 oz/115 g shiitake
   mushrooms, sliced
1-inch/2.5-cm piece fresh
   ginger, shredded
$1/2$ small head Chinese
   cabbage, shredded
4 scalllions, shredded
$1/2$ cup bean sprouts
2 tbsp dark soy sauce
2 tbsp Chinese rice wine
large pinch of sugar
2 tbsp coarsely chopped fresh
   cilantro

method

1 Half-fill a wok or deep, heavy-bottom skillet with oil. Heat to 350–375°F/180–190°C, or until a cube of bread browns in 30 seconds.

2 Add the noodles, in batches, and cook for $1^1/_2$–2 minutes, or until crisp and puffed up. Remove and drain on paper towels. Pour off all but 2 tablespoons of oil from the wok.

3 Heat the remaining oil over high heat. Add the green beans and stir-fry for 2 minutes. Add the carrot and zucchini sticks, sliced mushrooms, and ginger and stir-fry for an additional 2 minutes.

4 Add the shredded cabbage, scallions, and bean sprouts and stir-fry for an additional 1 minute. Add the soy sauce, rice wine, and sugar and cook, stirring constantly, for 1 minute.

5 Add the noodles and chopped cilantro and toss well. Serve immediately.

chinese vegetables & bean sprouts with noodles

ingredients

SERVES 4

5 cups vegetable stock

1 garlic clove, crushed

1/2-inch/1-cm piece fresh ginger, finely chopped

8 oz/225 g dried medium egg noodles

1 red bell pepper, seeded and sliced

3/4 cup frozen peas

4 oz/115 g broccoli florets

3 oz/85 g shiitake mushrooms, sliced

2 tbsp sesame seeds

8 oz/225 g canned water chestnuts, drained and halved

8 oz/225 g canned bamboo shoots, drained

10 oz/280 g Chinese cabbage, sliced

scant 1 cup bean sprouts

3 scallions, sliced

1 tbsp dark soy sauce

freshly ground black pepper

method

1 Bring the stock, garlic, and ginger to a boil in a large pan. Stir in the noodles, red bell pepper, peas, broccoli, and mushrooms and return to a boil. Reduce the heat, cover, and let simmer for 5–6 minutes, or until the noodles are tender.

2 Meanwhile, preheat the broiler to medium. Spread the sesame seeds out in a single layer on a baking sheet and toast under the preheated broiler, turning to brown evenly— watch constantly because they brown very quickly. Tip the sesame seeds into a small dish and set aside.

3 Once the noodles are tender, add the water chestnuts, bamboo shoots, cabbage, bean sprouts, and scallions to the pan. Return the stock to a boil, stir to mix the ingredients, and let simmer for an additional 2–3 minutes to heat through thoroughly.

4 Carefully drain off 1 1/4 cups of the stock into a small heatproof pitcher and set aside. Drain and discard any remaining stock and turn the noodles and vegetables into a warmed serving dish. Quickly mix the soy sauce with the reserved stock and pour over the noodles and vegetables. Season to taste with pepper and serve immediately.

stir-fried rice with green vegetables

ingredients

SERVES 4

generous 1 cup jasmine rice

2 tbsp vegetable or peanut oil

1 tbsp Thai green curry paste

6 scallions, sliced

2 garlic cloves, crushed

1 zucchini, cut into thin sticks

4 oz/115 g yard-long beans,
    cut into short lengths

6 oz/175 g asparagus,
    trimmed

3–4 fresh Thai basil leaves

method

1 Cook the rice in lightly salted boiling water for 12–15 minutes, drain well, then cool thoroughly and chill overnight.

2 Heat the oil in a wok and stir-fry the curry paste for 1 minute. Add the scallions and garlic and stir-fry for 1 minute.

3 Add the zucchini, beans, and asparagus, and stir-fry for 3–4 minutes, until just tender. Break up the rice and add it to the wok. Cook, stirring constantly for 2–3 minutes, until the rice is hot. Stir in the basil leaves. Serve hot.

classic stir-fried vegetables

ingredients

SERVES 4

3 tbsp sesame oil

6 scallions, chopped finely, plus extra to garnish

1 garlic clove, crushed

1 tbsp grated fresh ginger

1 head of broccoli, cut into florets

1 orange or yellow bell pepper, chopped coarsely

4$\frac{1}{2}$ oz/125 g red cabbage, shredded

4$\frac{1}{2}$ oz/125 g baby corn

6 oz/175 g portobello or large cup mushrooms, sliced thinly

1$\frac{1}{3}$ cups fresh bean sprouts

9 oz/250 g canned water chestnuts, drained

4 tsp soy sauce, or to taste

cooked wild rice, to serve

method

1 Heat 2 tablespoons of the oil in a large skillet or wok over high heat. Stir-fry the 6 chopped scallions with the garlic and ginger for 30 seconds.

2 Add the broccoli, bell pepper, and red cabbage and stir-fry for 1–2 minutes. Mix in the baby corn and mushrooms and stir-fry for an additional 1–2 minutes.

3 Finally, add the bean sprouts and water chestnuts and cook for 2 minutes. Pour in the soy sauce and stir well.

4 Serve immediately over cooked wild rice, garnished with scallions.

oyster mushrooms & vegetables with peanut sauce

ingredients

SERVES 4

1 tbsp sesame oil

4 scallions, sliced finely

1 carrot, cut into sticks

1 zucchini, cut into sticks

$1/2$ head of broccoli, cut into
    florets

1 lb/450 g oyster mushrooms,
    sliced thinly

2 tbsp coarse peanut butter

1 tsp chili powder, or to taste

3 tbsp water

cooked rice or noodles,
    to serve

lime wedges, to garnish

method

1 Heat the oil in a skillet or wok until almost smoking. Stir-fry the scallions for 1 minute. Add the carrot and zucchini and stir-fry for an additional 1 minute. Add the broccoli and cook for 1 minute more.

2 Stir in the mushrooms and cook until they are softened and at least half the liquid they produce has evaporated. Add the peanut butter and stir well. Season with the chili powder. Finally, add the water and cook for an additional 1 minute.

3 Serve over rice or noodles and garnish with lime wedges.

thai potato stir-fry

ingredients

SERVES 4

2 lb/900 g waxy potatoes

2 tbsp vegetable oil

1 yellow bell pepper, seeded and diced

1 red bell pepper, seeded and diced

1 carrot, cut into thin strips

1 zucchini, cut into thin strips

2 garlic cloves, crushed

1 fresh red chile, sliced

1 bunch scallions, halved lengthwise

1/2 cup coconut milk

1 tsp chopped lemongrass

2 tsp lime juice

finely grated zest of 1 lime

1 tbsp chopped fresh cilantro

method

1 Using a sharp knife, cut the potatoes into small dice. Bring a large pan of water to the boil and cook the diced potatoes for 5 minutes. Drain thoroughly.

2 Heat the vegetable oil in a wok or large skillet, swirling the oil around the base of the wok until it is really hot.

3 Add the potatoes, diced bell peppers, carrot, zucchini, garlic, and chile to the wok and stir-fry the vegetables for 2–3 minutes.

4 Stir in the scallions, coconut milk, lemongrass, and lime juice and stir-fry the mixture for a further 2 minutes. Add the lime zest and cilantro and stir-fry for 1 minute. Serve hot.

tofu & green vegetable curry

ingredients

SERVES 4

vegetable or peanut oil,
   for deep-frying
8 oz/225 g firm tofu, drained
   and cut into cubes
2 tbsp vegetable or peanut oil
1 tbsp chili oil
2 fresh green chiles, seeded
   and sliced
2 garlic cloves, crushed
6 scallions, sliced
2 medium zucchini, cut into
   sticks
1/2 cucumber, peeled, seeded,
   and sliced
1 green bell pepper, seeded
   and sliced
1 small head broccoli, cut into
   florets
2 oz/55 g fine green beans,
   halved
scant 1/2 cup frozen peas,
   thawed
1 1/2 cups coconut milk
2 tbsp Thai soy sauce
1 tsp jaggery or light
   brown sugar
4 tbsp chopped fresh parsley

method

1 Heat the oil for deep-frying in a skillet and carefully lower in the tofu cubes, in batches, and cook for 2–3 minutes, until golden brown. Remove with a slotted spoon and drain on paper towels.

2 Heat the other oils in a wok and stir-fry the chiles, garlic, and scallions for 2–3 minutes. Add the zucchini, cucumber, green bell pepper, broccoli, and green beans, and stir-fry for an additional 2–3 minutes.

3 Add the peas, coconut milk, soy sauce, and sugar. Cover and let simmer for 2–3 minutes, until all the vegetables are tender.

4 Stir in the tofu and serve immediately, sprinkled with the parsley.

spicy tofu

ingredients

SERVES 4

9 oz/250 g firm tofu, rinsed and drained thoroughly and cut into $1/2$-inch/1-cm cubes

4 tbsp peanut oil

1 tbsp grated fresh ginger

3 garlic cloves, crushed

4 scallions, sliced thinly

1 head of broccoli, cut into florets

1 carrot, cut into sticks

1 yellow bell pepper, sliced thinly

9 oz/250 g shiitake mushrooms, sliced thinly

steamed rice, to serve

marinade

5 tbsp vegetable stock

2 tsp cornstarch

2 tbsp soy sauce

1 tbsp superfine sugar

pinch of chile flakes

method

1 Combine all the ingredients for the marinade in a large bowl. Add the tofu and toss well to cover in the marinade. Set aside to marinate for 20 minutes.

2 In a large skillet or wok, heat 2 tablespoons of the peanut oil and stir-fry the tofu with its marinade until brown and crispy. Remove from the skillet and set aside.

3 Heat the remaining 2 tablespoons of peanut oil in the skillet and stir-fry the ginger, garlic, and scallions for 30 seconds. Add the broccoli, carrot, yellow bell pepper, and mushrooms to the skillet and cook for 5–6 minutes. Return the tofu to the skillet and stir-fry to reheat. Serve immediately over steamed rice.

mixed vegetables with quick-fried basil

ingredients

SERVES 4

2 tbsp vegetable or peanut oil

2 garlic cloves, chopped

1 onion, sliced

4 oz/115 g baby corn, cut in half diagonally

1/2 cucumber, peeled, halved, seeded, and sliced

8 oz/225 g canned water chestnuts, drained and rinsed

2 1/4 oz/60 g snow peas, trimmed

4 oz/115 g shiitake mushrooms

1 red bell pepper, seeded and sliced thinly

1 tbsp jaggery or light brown sugar

3 tbsp Thai soy sauce

1 tbsp rice vinegar

boiled rice, to serve

quick-fried basil

vegetable or peanut oil, for cooking

8–12 sprigs fresh Thai basil

method

1 Heat the oil in a wok and stir-fry the garlic and onion for 1–2 minutes. Add the corn, cucumber, water chestnuts, snow peas, mushrooms, and red bell pepper and stir-fry for 2–3 minutes, until starting to soften.

2 Add the sugar, soy sauce, and vinegar and gradually bring to a boil. Let simmer for 1–2 minutes.

3 Meanwhile, heat the oil for the basil in a wok or skillet and add the basil sprigs. Cook for 20–30 seconds, until crisp. Remove with a slotted spoon and drain on paper towels.

4 Garnish the vegetable stir-fry with the crispy basil and serve immediately with the boiled rice.

cauliflower & beans with cashews

ingredients

SERVES 4

1 tbsp vegetable or peanut oil

1 tbsp chili oil

1 onion, chopped

2 garlic cloves, chopped

2 tbsp Thai red curry paste

1 small cauliflower, cut into florets

6 oz/175 g yard-long beans, cut into 3-inch/7.5-cm lengths

$2/3$ cup vegetable stock

2 tbsp Thai soy sauce

scant $1/3$ cup toasted cashews, to garnish

method

1 Heat both the oils in a wok and stir-fry the onion and garlic until softened. Add the curry paste and stir-fry for 1–2 minutes.

2 Add the cauliflower and beans and stir-fry for 3–4 minutes, until softened. Pour in the stock and soy sauce and let simmer for 1–2 minutes. Serve immediately, garnished with the cashews.

eggplant & bean curry

ingredients

SERVES 4

2 tbsp vegetable or peanut oil

1 onion, chopped

2 garlic cloves, crushed

2 fresh red chiles, seeded and
   chopped

1 tbsp Thai red curry paste

1 large eggplant, cut into
   chunks

4 oz/115 g pea or small
   eggplants

generous 1 cup baby fava
   beans

4 oz/115 g fine green beans

1¹/₂ cups coconut milk

3 tbsp Thai soy sauce

1 tsp jaggery or light
   brown sugar

3 kaffir lime leaves, torn
   coarsely

4 tbsp chopped fresh cilantro

method

1 Heat the oil in a wok or large skillet and sauté the onion, garlic, and chiles for 1–2 minutes. Stir in the curry paste and cook for 1–2 minutes.

2 Add the eggplants and cook for 3–4 minutes, until starting to soften. (You may need to add a little more oil as eggplants soak it up quickly.) Add all the beans and stir-fry for 2 minutes.

3 Pour in the coconut milk and add the soy sauce, sugar, and lime leaves. Bring gently to a boil and cook until the coconut has dissolved. Stir in the cilantro and serve hot.

vegetable & coconut curry

ingredients

SERVES 4

1 onion, coarsely chopped

3 garlic cloves, thinly sliced

1-inch/2.5-cm piece fresh
    ginger, thinly sliced

2 fresh green chiles, seeded
    and finely chopped

1 tbsp vegetable oil

1 tsp ground turmeric

1 tsp ground coriander

1 tsp ground cumin

2 lb 4 oz/1 kg mixed
    vegetables, such as
    cauliflower, zucchini,
    potatoes, carrots, and
    green beans, cut into
    chunks

scant 1 cup coconut cream or
    coconut milk

salt and pepper

2 tbsp chopped fresh cilantro,
    to garnish

freshly cooked rice, to serve

method

1 Put the onion, garlic, ginger, and chiles in a food processor and process until almost smooth.

2 Heat the oil in a large, heavy-bottom pan over medium–low heat, add the onion mixture, and cook, stirring constantly, for 5 minutes.

3 Add the turmeric, ground coriander, and cumin and cook, stirring frequently, for 3–4 minutes. Add the vegetables and stir to coat in the spice paste.

4 Add the coconut cream to the vegetables, cover, and let simmer for 30–40 minutes, until the vegetables are tender.

5 Season with salt and pepper, garnish with the chopped fresh cilantro, and serve with rice.

spinach with chickpeas

ingredients

SERVES 4–6

2 tbsp olive oil

1 large garlic clove, cut in half

1 medium onion, chopped
   finely

1/2 tsp cumin

pinch of cayenne pepper

pinch of ground turmeric

1 lb 12 oz/800 g canned
   chickpeas, drained and
   rinsed

1 lb 2 oz/500 g baby spinach
   leaves, rinsed and shaken
   dry

2 pimientos del piquillo,
   drained and sliced

salt and pepper

method

1 Heat the oil in a large, lidded skillet over medium–high heat. Add the garlic and cook for 2 minutes, or until golden, but not browned. Remove with a slotted spoon and discard.

2 Add the onion, cumin, cayenne, and turmeric and cook, stirring, for about 5 minutes, until softened. Add the chickpeas and stir around until they are lightly colored with the turmeric and cayenne.

3 Stir in the spinach with just the water clinging to its leaves. Cover and cook for 4–5 minutes, until wilted. Uncover, stir in the pimientos del piquillo and continue cooking, stirring gently, until all the liquid evaporates. Season to taste and serve.

chickpea curry

ingredients

SERVES 4

6 tbsp vegetable oil

2 onions, sliced

1 tsp finely chopped fresh
    ginger

1 tsp ground cumin

1 tsp ground coriander

1 tsp fresh garlic, crushed

1 tsp chili powder

2 fresh green chiles

2–3 tbsp fresh cilantro leaves

$^2/_3$ cup water

1 large potato

14 oz/400 g canned
    chickpeas, drained

1 tbsp lemon juice

method

1 Heat the vegetable oil in a large, heavy-bottom pan. Add the onions and cook, stirring occasionally, until golden. Reduce the heat, add the ginger, ground cumin, ground coriander, garlic, chili powder, fresh green chiles, and fresh cilantro leaves and stir-fry for 2 minutes.

2 Add the water to the mixture in the pan and stir to mix.

3 Using a sharp knife, cut the potato into dice, then add with the chickpeas to the pan. Cover and let simmer, stirring occasionally, for 5–7 minutes.

4 Sprinkle the lemon juice over the curry. Transfer the chickpea curry to serving dishes and serve hot.

potato & spinach yellow curry

ingredients

SERVES 4

2 garlic cloves, finely chopped

1¼-inch/3-cm piece fresh
   galangal, finely chopped

1 lemongrass stem, finely
   chopped

1 tsp coriander seeds

3 tbsp vegetable oil

2 tsp Thai red curry paste

½ tsp ground turmeric

generous ¾ cup coconut milk

9 oz/250 g potatoes, cut into
   ¾-inch/2-cm cubes

scant ½ cup vegetable stock

7 oz/200 g fresh young
   spinach leaves

1 small onion, thinly sliced

method

1 Place the garlic, galangal, lemongrass, and coriander seeds in a mortar and, using a pestle, grind to a smooth paste.

2 Heat 2 tablespoons of the oil in a skillet or preheated wok. Stir in the garlic paste mixture and stir-fry for 30 seconds. Stir in the curry paste and turmeric, then add the coconut milk and bring to a boil.

3 Add the potatoes and stock. Return to a boil, then reduce the heat and simmer, uncovered, for 10–12 minutes, or until the potatoes are almost tender.

4 Stir in the spinach and simmer until the leaves are wilted.

5 Meanwhile, heat the remaining oil in a separate skillet. Add the onion and cook until crisp and golden brown. Place the fried onions on top of the curry just before serving.

carrot & pumpkin curry

ingredients

SERVES 4

$2/3$ cup vegetable stock

1-inch/2.5-cm piece fresh
  galangal, sliced

2 garlic cloves, chopped

1 lemongrass stalk (white part
  only), chopped finely

2 fresh red chiles, seeded and
  chopped

4 carrots, peeled and cut into
  chunks

8 oz/225 g pumpkin, peeled,
  seeded, and cut into cubes

2 tbsp vegetable or peanut oil

2 shallots, chopped finely

3 tbsp Thai yellow curry paste

$1^3/4$ cups coconut milk

4–6 sprigs fresh Thai basil

2 tbsp toasted pumpkin seeds,
  to garnish

method

1 Pour the stock into a large pan and bring to a boil. Add the galangal, half the garlic, the lemongrass, and chiles, and let simmer for 5 minutes. Add the carrots and pumpkin and let simmer for 5–6 minutes, until tender.

2 Meanwhile, heat the oil in a wok or skillet and stir-fry the shallots and the remaining garlic for 2–3 minutes. Add the curry paste and stir-fry for 1–2 minutes.

3 Stir the shallot mixture into the pan and add the coconut milk and basil. Let simmer for 2–3 minutes. Serve hot, sprinkled with the toasted pumpkin seeds.

baby corn with dal

ingredients

SERVES 4

generous 1 cup red split lentils

2 tbsp vegetable oil

1 tsp cumin seeds

1 tsp ground coriander

$1/2$ tsp asafetida

1 fresh red chile, seeded and
    finely chopped

4 oz/115 g green beans,
    chopped, blanched, and
    drained

1 green bell pepper, seeded
    and chopped

4 oz/115 g baby corn,
    diagonally sliced

$2/3$ cup vegetable stock

2 tomatoes, seeded and
    chopped

1 tbsp chopped fresh cilantro

1 tbsp poppy seeds

method

1 Rinse the lentils 2–3 times in cold water. Put into a large pan and cover with cold water. Bring to a boil, then reduce the heat and let simmer for 15–20 minutes, or until tender. Drain, return to the pan, and keep warm.

2 Meanwhile, heat the oil in a separate pan over low heat, add the spices and chile, and cook for 2 minutes, stirring constantly. Add the beans, green bell pepper, and baby corn and cook for 2 minutes, stirring constantly.

3 Stir in the stock and bring to a boil, then reduce the heat and let simmer for 5 minutes, or until the vegetables are just tender.

4 Stir the vegetables and their liquid into the cooked lentils with the tomatoes and heat through for 5–8 minutes, or until piping hot.

5 Serve immediately sprinkled with the fresh cilantro and poppy seeds.

lentil & rice casserole

ingredients

SERVES 4

generous 1 cup red split
   lentils, rinsed

1/4 cup long-grain rice

5 cups vegetable stock

1 leek, cut into chunks

3 garlic cloves, crushed

14 oz/400 g canned chopped
   tomatoes

1 tsp each of ground cumin,
   chili powder, and garam
   masala

1 red bell pepper, seeded and
   sliced

31/2 oz/100 g small broccoli
   florets

8 baby corn cobs, halved
   lengthwise

2 oz/55 g green beans, halved

1 tbsp shredded fresh basil

salt and pepper

fresh basil sprigs, to garnish

method

1 Place the lentils, rice, and vegetable stock in a flameproof casserole and cook over low heat, stirring occasionally, for 20 minutes.

2 Add the leek and garlic to the pan with the tomatoes and their juices, ground spices, bell pepper, broccoli, baby corn, and green beans and stir well to mix.

3 Bring the mixture to a boil, then reduce the heat, cover, and simmer for an additional 10–15 minutes, until the vegetables are tender. Add the shredded basil and season to taste with salt and pepper. Garnish with basil sprigs and serve.

celeriac, chestnut, spinach & feta filo pies

ingredients

SERVES 4

4 tbsp olive oil

2 garlic cloves, crushed

1/2 large or 1 whole small head celeriac, cut into short thin sticks

5 2/3 cups baby spinach leaves

scant 1/2 cup cooked, peeled chestnuts, coarsely chopped

7 oz/200 g feta cheese (drained weight), crumbled

1 egg

2 tbsp pesto sauce

1 tbsp finely chopped fresh parsley

pepper

4 sheets filo pastry, about 13 x 7 inches/33 x 18 cm each

method

1 Preheat the oven to 375°F/190°C. Heat 1 tablespoon of the oil in a large skillet over medium heat, add the garlic, and cook for 1 minute, stirring constantly. Add the celeriac and cook for 5 minutes, or until softened, but not browned. Remove from the skillet and keep warm.

2 Add 1 tablespoon of the remaining oil to the skillet, then add the spinach, cover, and cook for 2–3 minutes, or until the spinach has wilted. Uncover and cook until any liquid has evaporated.

3 Mix the garlic and celeriac, spinach, chestnuts, cheese, egg, pesto, parsley, and pepper to taste in a large bowl. Divide the mixture among 4 individual gratin dishes or put it all into 1 medium gratin dish.

4 Brush each sheet of filo with the remaining oil and arrange on top of the celeriac mixture. Bake in the preheated oven for 15–20 minutes, or until browned. Serve immediately.

eggplant gratin

ingredients

SERVES 4

4 tbsp olive oil

2 onions, finely chopped

2 garlic cloves, very finely
    chopped

2 eggplants, thickly sliced

3 tbsp chopped fresh flat-leaf
    parsley

$^1/_2$ tsp dried thyme

salt and pepper

14 oz/400 g canned chopped
    tomatoes

6 oz/175 g mozzarella cheese,
    coarsely grated

6 tbsp freshly grated
    Parmesan cheese

method

1 Preheat the oven to 400°F/200°C. Heat the oil in a skillet over medium heat. Add the onion and cook for 5 minutes, or until softened. Add the garlic and cook for a few seconds, or until just beginning to color. Using a slotted spoon, transfer the onion mixture to a plate. Cook the eggplant slices in batches in the same skillet until they are just lightly browned.

2 Arrange a layer of eggplant slices in the bottom of a shallow ovenproof dish. Sprinkle with some of the parsley, thyme, and salt and pepper to taste. Add a layer of onion, tomatoes, and mozzarella, sprinkling with parsley, thyme, and salt and pepper to taste.

3 Continue layering, finishing with a layer of eggplant slices. Sprinkle with the Parmesan cheese. Bake, uncovered, in the preheated oven for 20–30 minutes, or until the top is golden and the eggplants are tender.
Serve hot.

roasted summer vegetables

ingredients

SERVES 4

2 tbsp olive oil

1 fennel bulb

2 red onions

2 beefsteak tomatoes

1 eggplant

2 zucchini

1 yellow bell pepper

1 red bell pepper

1 orange bell pepper

4 garlic cloves

4 fresh rosemary sprigs

pepper

crusty bread, to serve
    (optional)

method

1 Preheat the oven to 400°F/200°C. Brush a large, ovenproof dish with a little of the oil. Prepare the vegetables. Cut the fennel, red onions, and tomatoes into wedges. Slice the eggplant and zucchini thickly, then seed all the bell peppers and cut into chunks. Arrange the vegetables in the dish and tuck the garlic cloves and rosemary sprigs among them. Drizzle with the remaining oil and season to taste with pepper.

2 Roast the vegetables in the preheated oven for 10 minutes. Remove the dish from the oven and turn the vegetables over with a slotted spoon. Return to the oven and roast for an additional 10–15 minutes, until tender and beginning to turn golden brown.

3 Serve the vegetables straight from the dish or transfer to a warmed serving plate. Serve with crusty bread, if liked.

roasted red bell peppers

ingredients

SERVES 6

6 small red bell peppers
2 tbsp olive oil
3 garlic cloves, sliced thinly
9 oz/250 g provolone or feta
  cheese, sliced thinly
12 fresh mint leaves
grated rind and juice of
  1 lemon
1 tbsp chopped fresh thyme
3 tbsp pine nuts
pepper

method

1 Preheat the oven to 400°F/200°C. Cut the bell peppers in half lengthwise and remove the core and seeds. Rub the skins of the bell peppers with a little of the oil then arrange the bell peppers, skin-side down, on a large greased baking sheet.

2 Scatter half the garlic over the bell peppers. Add the cheese, then the mint leaves, lemon rind, the remaining garlic, the thyme, pine nuts, and pepper to taste. Drizzle over the remaining oil and the lemon juice.

3 Roast the bell peppers in the preheated oven for 30 minutes, until tender and beginning to char around the edges. Serve warm.

stuffed zucchini with walnuts & feta

ingredients

SERVES 4

4 fat, medium zucchini

3 tbsp olive oil

1 onion, chopped finely

1 garlic clove, chopped finely

2 oz/55 g authentic Greek feta cheese, crumbled

1/4 cup chopped walnut pieces

1 cup fresh white bread crumbs

1 egg, beaten

1 tsp chopped fresh dill

salt and pepper

method

1 Preheat the oven to 375°F/190°C. Put the zucchini in a saucepan of boiling water, return to a boil and then boil for 3 minutes. Drain, rinse under cold water, and drain again. Let cool.

2 When the zucchini are cool enough to handle, cut a thin strip off the top side of each one with a sharp knife and gently score around the inside edges to help scoop out the flesh. Using a teaspoon, scoop out the flesh, leaving a shell to hold the stuffing. Chop the zucchini flesh.

3 Heat 2 tablespoons of the oil in a saucepan. Add the onion and garlic and fry for 5 minutes, until softened. Add the zucchini flesh and fry for 5 minutes, until the onion is golden brown. Remove from the heat and let cool slightly. Stir in the cheese then the walnuts, bread crumbs, egg, dill, and salt and pepper to taste.

4 Use the stuffing to fill the zucchini shells and place side by side in an ovenproof dish. Drizzle over the remaining oil.

5 Cover the dish with foil and bake in the preheated oven for 30 minutes. Remove the foil and bake for an additional 10–15 minutes, or until golden brown. Serve hot.

stuffed portobello mushrooms

ingredients

SERVES 4

12 large portobello
    mushrooms, wiped over
    and stems removed
2 tbsp corn oil, plus extra for
    oiling
1 fennel bulb, stalks removed,
    finely chopped
scant 1/2 cup sun-dried
    tomatoes, finely chopped
2 garlic cloves, crushed
generous 1 cup grated fontina
    cheese
scant 1/2 cup freshly grated
    Parmesan cheese
3 tbsp chopped fresh basil
salt and pepper
1 tbsp olive oil
fresh Parmesan cheese
    shavings and chopped
    fresh parsley, to serve

method

1 Preheat the oven to 350°F/180°C. Place 8 of the mushrooms, cup-side up, in the dish and chop the remaining 4 mushrooms finely.

2 Heat the corn oil in a nonstick skillet, add the chopped mushrooms, fennel, sun-dried tomatoes, and garlic, and cook over low heat until the vegetables are softened, but not browned. Remove from the heat and let cool.

3 When cool, add the cheeses, basil, and salt and pepper to taste. Mix well. Brush the mushrooms lightly with the olive oil and fill each cavity with a spoonful of the vegetable filling. Bake in the preheated oven for 20–25 minutes, or until the mushrooms are tender and the filling is heated through.

4 Top with Parmesan shavings and parsley and serve immediately, allowing 2 mushrooms for each person.

provolone cheese & vegetable kebabs

ingredients

SERVES 4

kebabs

8 oz/225 g provolone cheese
12 button mushrooms
8 pearl onions
12 cherry tomatoes
2 zucchini, cut into small
    chunks
1 red bell pepper, seeded and
    cut into small chunks
chopped fresh cilantro,
    to garnish
freshly cooked rice or fresh
    mixed salad leaves and
    fresh crusty bread, to serve

marinade

4 tbsp extra virgin olive oil
2 tbsp balsamic vinegar
2 garlic cloves, finely chopped
1 tbsp chopped fresh cilantro
salt and pepper

method

1 If using wooden skewers, soak them in cold water for 30 minutes before use.

2 Put the oil, vinegar, garlic, and cilantro into a large bowl. Season with salt and pepper and mix until well combined.

3 Cut the provolone cheese into bite-size cubes. Thread the cubes onto skewers, alternating them with whole button mushrooms, pearl onions, and cherry tomatoes, and chunks of zucchini and bell pepper. When the skewers are full (leave a small space at either end), transfer them to the bowl and turn them in the marinade until they are well coated. Cover with plastic wrap and place in the refrigerator to marinate for at least 2 hours.

4 When the skewers are thoroughly marinated, barbecue them over hot coals for 5–10 minutes, or until they are cooked to your taste, turning frequently, and basting with the remaining marinade. Arrange the skewers on a bed of freshly cooked rice or fresh mixed salad leaves, garnish with cilantro leaves, and serve with fresh crusty bread.

lentil bolognese

ingredients

SERVES 4

1 tsp vegetable oil

1 tsp crushed garlic

2 tbsp finely chopped onion

2 tbsp finely chopped leek

1/4 cup finely chopped celery

2 tbsp finely chopped green
    bell pepper

2 tbsp finely chopped carrot

2 tbsp finely chopped zucchini

1 1/4 cups diced flat
    mushrooms

4 tbsp red wine

pinch of dried thyme

14 oz/400 g canned tomatoes,
    chopped, strained through
    a colander, and the
    juice and pulp reserved
    separately

4 tbsp dried Puy lentils,
    cooked

freshly ground black pepper,
    to taste

2 tsp lemon juice

1 tsp sugar

3 tbsp chopped fresh basil,
    plus extra sprigs to garnish

freshly cooked spaghetti,
    to serve

method

1 Heat a saucepan over low heat, add the oil and garlic, and cook, stirring, until golden brown. Add all the vegetables, except the mushrooms, increase the heat to medium, and cook, stirring occasionally, for 10–12 minutes, or until softened and there is no liquid from the vegetables left in the pan.

2 Add the mushrooms. Increase the heat to high, add the wine, and cook for 2 minutes. Add the thyme and juice from the tomatoes and cook until reduced by half.

3 Add the lentils and pepper, stir in the tomatoes, and cook for an additional 3–4 minutes. Remove the pan from the heat and stir in the lemon juice, sugar, and basil.

4 Serve the sauce with the cooked spaghetti, garnished with basil sprigs.

mushroom stroganoff

ingredients

SERVES 4

1 lb 4 oz/550 g mixed fresh
    mushrooms, such as
    cremini, chanterelles,
    porcini, and oyster
1 red onion, diced
2 garlic cloves, crushed
scant 2 cups vegetable stock
1 tbsp tomato paste
2 tbsp lemon juice
scant 1 tbsp cornstarch
2 tbsp cold water
$1/2$ cup low-fat plain yogurt
3 tbsp chopped fresh parsley
freshly ground black pepper
boiled brown or white rice and
    crisp green salad, to serve

method

1 Put the mushrooms, onion, garlic, stock, tomato paste, and lemon juice into a pan and bring to a boil. Reduce the heat, cover, and let simmer for 15 minutes, or until the onion is tender.

2 Blend the cornstarch with the water in a small bowl and stir into the mushroom mixture. Return to a boil, stirring constantly, and cook until the sauce thickens. Reduce the heat and let simmer for an additional 2–3 minutes, stirring occasionally.

3 Just before serving, remove the pan from the heat, and stir in the yogurt, making sure that the stroganoff is not boiling or it may separate and curdle. Stir in 2 tablespoons of the parsley and season to taste with pepper. Transfer the stroganoff to a warmed serving dish, sprinkle over the remaining parsley, and serve immediately with boiled brown or white rice and a crisp green salad.

spaghetti olio e aglio

ingredients

SERVES 4

1 lb/450 g dried spaghetti

1/2 cup extra virgin olive oil

3 garlic cloves, finely chopped

salt and pepper

3 tbsp chopped fresh flat-leaf
     parsley

method

1 Bring a large, heavy-bottom pan of lightly salted water to a boil. Add the spaghetti, return to a boil, and cook for 8–10 minutes, or until tender but still firm to the bite.

2 Meanwhile, heat the olive oil in a heavy-bottom skillet. Add the garlic and a pinch of salt and cook over low heat, stirring constantly, for 3–4 minutes, or until golden. Do not allow the garlic to brown or it will taste bitter. Remove the skillet from the heat.

3 Drain the pasta and transfer to a warmed serving dish. Pour in the garlic-flavored olive oil, then add the chopped parsley and season to taste with salt and pepper. Toss well and serve immediately.

fettuccine alfredo

ingredients

SERVES 4

2 tbsp butter

1 cup heavy cream

1 lb/450 g dried fettuccine

1 tbsp olive oil

1 cup freshly grated Parmesan
   cheese, plus extra to serve

pinch of freshly grated nutmeg

salt and pepper

fresh flat-leaf parsley sprigs,
   to garnish

method

1 Place the butter and $2/3$ cup of the cream in a large saucepan and bring the mixture to a boil over medium heat. Reduce the heat and simmer gently for about $1^1/2$ minutes, or until slightly thickened.

2 Meanwhile, bring a large saucepan of lightly salted water to a boil. Add the fettuccine and oil, return to a boil, and cook for 2–3 minutes, until tender but still firm to the bite. Drain the fettuccine, return it to the pan, and pour the sauce over it. Return the pan to low heat and toss the fettuccine in the sauce until coated.

3 Add the remaining cream, the Parmesan cheese, and nutmeg to the fettuccine mixture and season with salt and pepper. Toss thoroughly to coat while gently heating through.

4 Transfer the fettuccine mixture to a warmed serving plate and garnish with parsley sprigs. Serve immediately, with extra grated Parmesan cheese.

spaghetti with tomato, garlic & basil sauce

ingredients

SERVES 4

5 tbsp extra virgin olive oil
1 onion, chopped finely
1 lb 12 oz/800 g canned
    chopped tomatoes
4 garlic cloves, quartered
salt and pepper
1 lb/450 g dried spaghetti
large handful fresh basil
    leaves, shredded
fresh Parmesan cheese
    shavings, to serve

method

1 Heat the oil in a large saucepan over medium heat. Add the onion and fry gently for 5 minutes, until softened. Add the tomatoes and garlic. Bring to a boil, then simmer over medium–low heat for 25–30 minutes, until the oil separates from the tomato. Season with salt and pepper.

2 Cook the pasta in plenty of boiling salted water until al dente. Drain and transfer to a warmed serving dish.

3 Pour the sauce over the pasta. Add the basil and toss well to mix. Serve with the Parmesan cheese shavings.

tagliatelle with asparagus & gorgonzola sauce

ingredients

SERVES 4

1 lb/450 g asparagus tips

olive oil

salt and pepper

8 oz/225 g Gorgonzola, crumbled

3/4 cup heavy cream

12 oz/350 g dried tagliatelle

method

1 Preheat the oven to 450°F/230°C. Place the asparagus tips in a single layer in a shallow ovenproof dish. Sprinkle with a little olive oil. Season with salt and pepper. Turn to coat in the oil and seasoning. Roast in the preheated oven for 10–12 minutes, until slightly browned and just tender. Set aside and keep warm.

2 Combine the crumbled cheese with the cream in a bowl. Season with salt and pepper.

3 Cook the pasta in plenty of boiling salted water until al dente. Drain and transfer to a warmed serving dish.

4 Immediately add the asparagus and the cheese mixture. Toss well until the cheese has melted and the pasta is coated with the sauce. Serve immediately.

chile broccoli pasta

ingredients

SERVES 4

8 oz/225 g dried penne or
macaroni

8 oz/225 g broccoli, cut into
florets

1/4 cup extra virgin olive oil

2 large garlic cloves, chopped

2 fresh red chiles, seeded and
diced

8 cherry tomatoes (optional)

fresh basil leaves, to garnish

method

1 Bring a large pan of salted boiling water to a
boil. Add the pasta, return to a boil, and cook
for 8–10 minutes, until tender but still firm to
the bite. Drain the pasta, refresh under cold
running water, and drain again. Set aside.

2 Bring a separate pan of salted water to a
boil, add the broccoli, and cook for 5 minutes.
Drain, refresh under cold running water, and
drain again.

3 Heat the oil in a large pan over high heat. Add
the garlic, chiles, and tomatoes, if using, and
cook, stirring, for 1 minute.

4 Add the broccoli and mix well. Cook for
2 minutes, stirring, to heat through. Add the
pasta and mix well again. Cook for an additional
minute. Transfer the pasta to a large, warmed
serving bowl and serve garnished with
basil leaves.

pasta with pesto

ingredients

SERVES 4

1 lb/450 g dried tagliatelle
fresh basil sprigs, to garnish

pesto
2 garlic cloves
$^{1}/_{4}$ cup pine nuts
salt
4 oz/115 g fresh basil leaves
$^{1}/_{2}$ cup freshly grated
    Parmesan cheese
$^{1}/_{2}$ cup olive oil

method

1 To make the pesto, put the garlic, pine nuts, a large pinch of salt, and the basil into a mortar and pound to a paste with a pestle. Transfer to a bowl and gradually work in the Parmesan cheese with a wooden spoon, followed by the olive oil, to make a thick, creamy sauce. Taste and adjust the seasoning if necessary.

2 Alternatively, put the garlic, pine nuts, and a large pinch of salt into a food processor or blender and process briefly. Add the basil leaves and process to a paste. With the motor still running, gradually add the olive oil. Scrape into a bowl and beat in the Parmesan cheese.

3 Bring a large pan of lightly salted water to a boil. Add the pasta, return to a boil, and cook for 8–10 minutes, or until tender but still firm to the bite. Drain the pasta well, return to the pan, and toss with half the pesto, then divide among warmed serving plates and top with the remaining pesto. Garnish with basil sprigs and serve immediately.

creamy spinach & mushroom pasta

ingredients

SERVES 4

10¹/₂ oz/300 g dried penne or
    pasta of your choice
2 tbsp olive oil
9 oz/250 g mushrooms, sliced
1 tsp dried oregano
scant 1¹/₄ cups vegetable
    stock
1 tbsp lemon juice
6 tbsp cream cheese
generous 1 cup frozen
    spinach leaves
salt and pepper

method

1 Cook the pasta in a large pan of lightly salted boiling water according to the package instructions. Drain, reserving 3/4 cup of the cooking liquid.

2 Meanwhile, heat the oil in a large, heavy-bottom skillet over medium heat, add the mushrooms, and cook, stirring frequently, for 8 minutes, or until almost crisp. Stir in the oregano, stock, and lemon juice and cook for 10–12 minutes, or until the sauce is reduced by half.

3 Stir in the cream cheese and spinach and cook over low–medium heat for 3–5 minutes. Add the reserved cooking liquid, then the cooked pasta. Stir well, season to taste with salt and pepper, and heat through before serving.

penne in a creamy mushroom sauce

ingredients

SERVES 4

4 tbsp butter

1 tbsp olive oil

6 shallots, sliced

1 lb/450 g cremini
    mushrooms, sliced

salt and pepper

1 tsp all-purpose flour

2/3 cup heavy cream or panna
    da cucina

2 tbsp port

4 oz/115 g sun-dried tomatoes
    in oil, drained and
    chopped

pinch of freshly grated nutmeg

12 oz/350 g dried penne

2 tbsp chopped fresh flat-leaf
    parsley

method

1 Melt the butter with the olive oil in a large, heavy-bottom skillet. Add the shallots and cook over low heat, stirring occasionally, for 4–5 minutes, or until softened. Add the mushrooms and cook over low heat for an additional 2 minutes. Season to taste with salt and pepper, sprinkle in the flour, and cook, stirring, for 1 minute.

2 Remove the skillet from the heat and gradually stir in the cream and port. Return to the heat, add the sun-dried tomatoes and grated nutmeg, and cook over low heat, stirring occasionally, for 8 minutes.

3 Meanwhile, bring a large, heavy-bottom pan of lightly salted water to a boil. Add the pasta, return to a boil, and cook for 8–10 minutes, or until tender but still firm to the bite. Drain the pasta well and add to the mushroom sauce. Cook for 3 minutes, then transfer to a warmed serving dish. Sprinkle with the chopped parsley and serve immediately.

penne with bell pepper & goat cheese sauce

ingredients

SERVES 4

2 tbsp olive oil

1 tbsp butter

1 small onion, chopped finely

4 bell peppers, yellow and red, seeded and cut into ³/₄-inch/2-cm squares

3 garlic cloves, sliced thinly

salt and pepper

1 lb/450 g dried rigatoni or penne

4¹/₂ oz/125 g goat cheese, crumbled

15 fresh basil leaves, shredded

10 black olives, pitted and sliced

method

1 Heat the oil and butter in a large skillet over medium heat. Add the onion and cook until softened. Raise the heat to medium–high and add the bell peppers and garlic. Cook for 12–15 minutes, stirring, until the peppers are tender but not mushy. Season with salt and pepper. Remove from the heat.

2 Cook the pasta in plenty of boiling salted water until al dente. Drain and transfer to a warmed serving dish. Add the goat cheese and toss to mix.

3 Briefly reheat the sauce. Add the basil and olives. Pour over the pasta and toss well to mix. Serve immediately.

spaghetti with roasted garlic & bell pepper sauce

ingredients

SERVES 4

6 large garlic cloves, unpeeled

14 oz/400 g bottled roasted red bell peppers, drained and sliced

7 oz/200 g canned chopped tomatoes

3 tbsp olive oil

1/4 tsp dried chile flakes

1 tsp chopped fresh thyme or oregano

salt and pepper

12 oz/350 g dried spaghetti, bucatini, or linguine

freshly grated Parmesan cheese, to serve

method

1 Preheat the oven to 400°F/200°C. Place the unpeeled garlic cloves in a shallow, ovenproof dish. Roast in the preheated oven for 7–10 minutes, or until the garlic cloves feel soft.

2 Put the bell peppers, tomatoes, and oil in a food processor or blender, then process until smooth. Squeeze in the garlic flesh. Add the chile flakes and oregano. Season with salt and pepper. Blend again, then scrape into a pan and set aside.

3 Cook the pasta in plenty of boiling salted water until al dente. Drain and transfer to a warmed serving dish.

4 Reheat the sauce and pour over the pasta. Toss well to mix. Serve immediately with Parmesan.

fusilli with zucchini, lemon & rosemary

ingredients

SERVES 4

6 tbsp olive oil

1 small onion, sliced very
  thinly

2 garlic cloves, chopped very
  finely

2 tbsp chopped fresh
  rosemary

1 tbsp chopped fresh flat-leaf
  parsley

1 lb/450 g small zucchini,
  cut into 1½-inch/4-cm
  lengths

finely grated rind of 1 lemon

salt and pepper

1 lb/450 g fusilli

4 tbsp freshly grated
  Parmesan cheese

method

1 Heat the olive oil in a large skillet over medium–low heat. Add the onion and gently fry, stirring occasionally, for about 10 minutes until golden.

2 Raise the heat to medium–high. Add the garlic, rosemary, and parsley. Cook for a few seconds, stirring. Add the zucchini and lemon rind. Cook for 5–7 minutes, stirring occasionally, until the zucchini are just tender. Season with salt and pepper. Remove from the heat.

3 Cook the pasta in plenty of boiling salted water until al dente. Drain and transfer to a warmed serving dish.

4 Briefly reheat the zucchini. Pour over the pasta and toss well to mix. Sprinkle with the Parmesan and serve immediately.

pasta with green vegetables

ingredients

SERVES 4

8 oz/225 g dried gemelli or
     other pasta shapes
2 tbsp chopped fresh parsley
2 tbsp freshly grated
     Parmesan cheese

s a u c e
1 head green broccoli,
     cut into florets
2 zucchini, sliced
8 oz/225 g asparagus spears,
     trimmed
4½ oz/125 g snow peas
4½ oz/125 g frozen peas
2 tbsp butter
3 tbsp vegetable stock
5 tbsp heavy cream
salt and pepper
large pinch of freshly grated
     nutmeg

method

1 Bring a large, heavy-bottom saucepan of lightly salted water to a boil. Add the pasta, return to a boil, and cook for 8–10 minutes, or until tender but still firm to the bite. Drain the pasta in a colander, return to the saucepan, cover, and keep warm.

2 Steam the broccoli, zucchini, asparagus spears, and snow peas over a saucepan of boiling, salted water until just beginning to soften. Remove from the heat and plunge into cold water to prevent further cooking. Drain and reserve. Cook the peas in boiling, salted water for 3 minutes, then drain. Refresh in cold water and drain again.

3 Place the butter and vegetable stock in a saucepan over medium heat. Add all the vegetables, except for the asparagus spears, and toss carefully with a wooden spoon to heat through, taking care not to break them up. Stir in the cream, allow the sauce to heat through, and season to taste with salt, pepper, and nutmeg.

4 Transfer the pasta to a warmed serving dish and stir in the chopped parsley. Spoon over the sauce and sprinkle over the freshly grated Parmesan. Arrange the asparagus spears in a pattern on top. Serve immediately.

potato & spinach gnocchi

ingredients

SERVES 4

1²/₃ cups diced mealy
    potatoes
6 oz/175 g spinach
1 egg yolk
1 tsp olive oil
1 cup all-purpose flour
salt and pepper
spinach leaves, to garnish

s a u c e
1 tbsp olive oil
2 shallots, chopped
1 garlic clove, crushed
1¼ cups bottled strained
    tomatoes
2 tsp light brown sugar

method

1 Cook the diced potatoes in a pan of boiling water for 10 minutes, or until cooked through. Drain and mash the potatoes.

2 Meanwhile, in a separate pan, blanch the spinach in a little boiling water for 1–2 minutes. Drain the spinach and shred the leaves.

3 Transfer the mashed potato to a lightly floured cutting board and make a well in the center. Add the egg yolk, olive oil, spinach, and a little of the flour. Quickly mix the ingredients into the potato, adding more flour as you go, until you have a smooth, firm dough. Divide the mixture into very small dumplings.

4 Cook the gnocchi, in batches, in a pan of lightly salted, boiling water for about 5 minutes, or until they rise to the surface.

5 Meanwhile, make the sauce. Put the oil, shallots, garlic, bottled strained tomatoes, and sugar into a pan and cook over low heat for 10–15 minutes, or until the sauce has thickened and reduced.

6 Drain the gnocchi using a slotted spoon and transfer to warmed serving dishes. Spoon the sauce over the gnocchi and garnish with the fresh spinach leaves.

risotto primavera

ingredients

SERVES 6–8

8 oz/225 g fresh thin
    asparagus spears
4 tbsp olive oil
6 oz/175 g young green
    beans, cut into 1-inch/
    2.5-cm lengths
6 oz/175 g young zucchini,
    quartered and cut into
    1-inch/2.5-cm lengths
generous 1^1/$_2$ cups shelled
    fresh peas
1 onion, finely chopped
1–2 garlic cloves, finely
    chopped
1^2/$_3$ cups risotto rice
generous 6^1/$_3$ cups chicken or
    vegetable stock
4 scallions, cut into
    1-inch/2.5-cm lengths
salt and pepper
4 tbsp butter
1 cup freshly grated Parmesan
    cheese
2 tbsp snipped fresh chives
2 tbsp shredded fresh basil
scallions, to garnish (optional)

method

1 Trim the woody ends of the asparagus and cut off the tips. Cut the stems into 1-inch/2.5-cm pieces and set aside with the tips.

2 Heat 2 tablespoons of the oil in a large skillet over high heat until very hot. Add the asparagus, beans, zucchini, and peas and stir-fry for 3–4 minutes, until they are bright green and just starting to soften. Set aside.

3 Heat the remaining oil in a large, heavy-bottom pan over medium heat. Add the onion and cook, stirring occasionally, for 3 minutes, or until it starts to soften. Stir in the garlic and cook, while stirring, for 30 seconds. Reduce the heat, add the rice, and mix to coat in oil. Cook, stirring constantly, for 2–3 minutes, or until the grains are translucent.

4 Gradually add the hot stock, a ladleful at a time. Stir constantly and add more liquid as the rice absorbs each addition. Increase the heat to medium so that the liquid bubbles. Cook for 20 minutes, or until all but 2 tablespoons of the liquid is absorbed and the rice is creamy.

5 Stir in the stir-fried vegetables and scallions with the remaining stock. Cook for 2 minutes, stirring frequently, then season to taste with salt and pepper. Stir in the butter, Parmesan, chives, and basil. Remove the pan from the heat. Transfer the risotto to a warmed serving dish and garnish with scallions, if using.

wild mushroom risotto

ingredients

SERVES 6

$^1/_2$ cup dried porcini or morel mushrooms

about 1 lb 2 oz/500 g mixed fresh wild mushrooms, such as porcini, cremini mushrooms, and chanterelles, halved if large

4 tbsp olive oil

3–4 garlic cloves, finely chopped

4 tbsp butter

1 onion, finely chopped

1$^2/_3$ cups risotto rice

$^1/_4$ cup dry white vermouth

5 cups chicken or vegetable stock

salt and pepper

1 cup freshly grated Parmesan cheese

4 tbsp chopped fresh flat-leaf parsley

method

1 Place the dried mushrooms in a heatproof bowl and add boiling water to cover. Set aside to soak for 30 minutes, then carefully lift out and pat dry. Strain the soaking liquid through a strainer lined with paper towels and set aside.

2 Trim the fresh mushrooms and gently brush clean. Heat 3 tablespoons of the oil in a large skillet. Add the fresh mushrooms and stir-fry for 1–2 minutes. Add the garlic and the soaked mushrooms and cook, stirring frequently, for 2 minutes. Transfer to a plate.

3 Heat the remaining oil and half the butter in a large, heavy-bottom pan. Add the onion and cook over medium heat, stirring occasionally, for 2 minutes, until softened.

4 Reduce the heat, add the rice, and mix to coat in oil and butter. Cook, stirring constantly, for 2–3 minutes, or until the grains are translucent. Add the vermouth and cook, stirring constantly, until it has reduced.

5 Gradually add the hot stock, a ladleful at a time. Stir constantly and add more liquid as the rice absorbs each addition. Increase the heat to medium so that the liquid bubbles. Cook for 20 minutes, or until all the liquid is absorbed and the rice is creamy.

6 Remove the pan from the heat and stir in the remaining butter, the grated Parmesan, and chopped parsley. Serve immediately.

minted green risotto

ingredients

SERVES 6

2 tbsp butter

shelled generous 1½ cups fresh peas or thawed frozen peas

5⅔ cups fresh young spinach leaves, washed and drained

1 bunch of fresh mint, leaves stripped from stalks

2 tbsp chopped fresh basil

2 tbsp chopped fresh oregano

pinch of freshly grated nutmeg

4 tbsp mascarpone cheese

2 tbsp vegetable oil

1 onion, finely chopped

2 celery stalks, including leaves, finely chopped

2 garlic cloves, finely chopped

½ tsp dried thyme

scant 1½ cups risotto rice

¼ cup dry white vermouth

4 cups chicken or vegetable stock

¾ cup freshly grated Parmesan cheese

method

1 Heat half the butter in a deep skillet over medium–high heat until sizzling. Add the peas, spinach, mint leaves, basil, and oregano and season with the nutmeg. Cook, stirring frequently, for 3 minutes, or until the spinach and mint leaves are wilted. Let cool slightly.

2 Pour the spinach mixture into a food processor and process for 15 seconds. Add the mascarpone and process again for 1 minute. Transfer to a bowl and set aside.

3 Heat the oil and remaining butter in a large, heavy-bottom pan over medium heat. Add the onion, celery, garlic, and thyme and cook, stirring occasionally, for 2 minutes, or until the vegetables are softened.

4 Reduce the heat, add the rice, and mix to coat in oil and butter. Cook, stirring constantly, for 2–3 minutes, or until the grains are translucent. Add the vermouth and cook, stirring constantly, until it has reduced.

5 Gradually add the hot stock, a ladleful at a time. Stir constantly and add more liquid as the rice absorbs each addition. Increase the heat to medium so that the liquid bubbles. Cook for 20 minutes, or until the liquid is absorbed and the rice is creamy.

6 Stir in the spinach-mascarpone mixture and the Parmesan. Transfer to warmed plates and serve immediately.

risotto with four cheeses

ingredients

SERVES 6

3 tbsp unsalted butter

1 onion, chopped finely

generous 1½ cups risotto rice

scant 1 cup dry white wine

4 cups vegetable stock

½ cup Gorgonzola cheese,
   crumbled

½ cup freshly grated Taleggio
   cheese

½ cup freshly grated fontina
   cheese

½ cup freshly grated
   Parmesan cheese

salt and pepper

2 tbsp chopped fresh flat-leaf
   parsley, to garnish

method

1 Melt the butter in a large, heavy-bottom pan. Add the onion and cook over low heat, stirring occasionally, for 5 minutes, until softened. Add the rice and cook, stirring constantly, for 2–3 minutes, or until the grains are translucent.

2 Add the wine and cook, stirring constantly, until it has almost completely evaporated. Add a ladleful of the hot stock and cook, stirring constantly, until all the stock has been absorbed. Continue cooking, stirring and adding the stock, a ladleful at a time, for about 20 minutes, or until the rice is tender and the liquid has been absorbed.

3 Remove the pan from the heat and stir in the Gorgonzola, Taleggio, fontina, and about one quarter of the Parmesan until melted. Season to taste with salt and pepper. Transfer the risotto to a warmed serving dish, sprinkle with the remaining Parmesan, garnish with the parsley, and serve immediately.

crunchy walnut risotto

ingredients

SERVES 4

1 tbsp olive oil

5 tbsp butter

1 small onion, finely chopped

1^1/$_2$ cups risotto rice

5 cups vegetable or chicken
   stock

salt and pepper

1 cup walnut halves

^{3}/$_4$ cup freshly grated
   Parmesan or Grana
   Padano cheese

^{1}/$_4$ cup mascarpone cheese

2 oz/55 g Gorgonzola cheese,
   diced

method

1 Heat the oil with 2 tablespoons of the butter in a deep pan over medium heat until the butter has melted. Add the onion and cook, stirring occasionally, for 5–7 minutes, or until softened and starting to turn golden. Do not brown.

2 Reduce the heat, add the rice, and mix to coat in oil and butter. Cook, stirring constantly, for 2–3 minutes, or until the grains are translucent.

3 Gradually add the hot stock, a ladleful at a time. Stir constantly and add more liquid as the rice absorbs each addition. Increase the heat to medium so that the liquid bubbles. Cook for 20 minutes, or until all the liquid is absorbed and the rice is creamy. Season with salt and pepper.

4 Melt 2 tablespoons of the remaining butter in a skillet over medium heat. Add the walnuts and toss for 2–3 minutes, or until just starting to brown.

5 Remove the risotto from the heat and add the remaining butter. Mix well, then stir in the Parmesan, mascarpone, and Gorgonzola until they melt, along with most of the walnuts. Spoon the risotto onto warmed plates, sprinkle with the remaining walnuts, and serve.

kidney bean risotto

ingredients

SERVES 4

4 tbsp olive oil

1 onion, chopped

2 garlic cloves, finely chopped

generous 3/4 cup brown rice

2 1/2 cups vegetable stock

salt and pepper

1 red bell pepper, seeded and
    chopped

2 celery stalks, sliced

8 oz/225 g cremini
    mushrooms, thinly sliced

15 oz/425 g canned red
    kidney beans, drained and
    rinsed

3 tbsp chopped fresh parsley,
    plus extra to garnish

1/3 cup cashews

method

1 Heat half the oil in a large, heavy-bottom pan. Add the onion and cook, stirring occasionally, for 5 minutes, or until softened. Add half the garlic and cook, stirring frequently, for 2 minutes, then add the rice and stir for 1 minute, or until the grains are thoroughly coated with the oil.

2 Add the stock and a pinch of salt and bring to a boil, stirring constantly. Reduce the heat, cover, and let simmer for 35–40 minutes, or until all the liquid has been absorbed.

3 Meanwhile, heat the remaining oil in a heavy-bottom skillet. Add the bell pepper and celery and cook, stirring frequently, for 5 minutes. Add the sliced mushrooms and the remaining garlic and cook, stirring frequently, for 4–5 minutes.

4 Stir the rice into the skillet. Add the beans, parsley, and cashews. Season to taste with salt and pepper and cook, stirring constantly, until hot. Transfer to a warmed serving dish, sprinkle with extra parsley, and serve immediately.

red wine, herb & sun-dried tomato risotto

ingredients

SERVES 4

4 cups vegetable stock

4 cups strong Italian red wine

1 tbsp olive oil

3 tbsp butter

1 small onion, finely chopped

1 lb/450 g Arborio rice

6 sun-dried tomatoes in olive oil, drained and finely chopped

1 tbsp chopped fresh thyme, plus extra sprigs to garnish

1 tbsp chopped fresh parsley

salt and pepper

1/2 cup freshly grated Parmesan or Grana Padano cheese, plus extra shavings to garnish

10–12 fresh basil leaves, shredded, to garnish

method

1 Bring the stock and wine to a boil in a pan, then reduce the heat and let simmer gently over low heat while you are cooking the risotto.

2 Heat the oil with 2 tablespoons of the butter in a deep pan over medium heat until the butter is melted. Add the onion and cook, stirring frequently, for 5 minutes, or until softened but not browned.

3 Add the rice, stir to coat in the butter and oil, and cook, stirring constantly, for 2–3 minutes, until the grains are translucent. Gradually add the hot stock, a ladleful at a time, stirring constantly. Stir in the sun-dried tomatoes, then continue to add the stock, a ladleful at a time. Cook for 20 minutes, or until all the stock has been absorbed, carefully folding in the chopped thyme and parsley 5 minutes before the end of cooking time. When the risotto is creamy but still with a little bite to the rice, season to taste.

4 Remove the risotto from the heat and add the remaining butter. Mix well, then stir in the Parmesan cheese until it has melted. Taste and adjust the seasoning, if necessary, and serve immediately, garnished with Parmesan cheese shavings, shredded basil leaves, and thyme sprigs.

vegetarian paella

ingredients

SERVES 4–6

1/2 tsp saffron threads

2 tbsp hot water

6 tbsp olive oil

1 Spanish onion, sliced

3 garlic cloves, minced

1 red bell pepper, seeded and
    sliced

1 orange bell pepper, seeded
    and sliced

1 large eggplant, cubed

1 cup medium-grain paella
    rice

2 1/2 cups vegetable stock

1 lb/450 g tomatoes, peeled
    and chopped

salt and pepper

4 oz/115 g mushrooms, sliced

4 oz/115 g green beans,
    halved

14 oz/400 g canned pinto
    beans

method

1 Put the saffron threads and water in a small bowl or cup and let infuse for a few minutes.

2 Meanwhile, heat the oil in a paella pan or wide, shallow skillet and cook the onion over medium heat, stirring, for 2–3 minutes, or until softened. Add the garlic, bell peppers, and eggplant and cook, stirring frequently, for 5 minutes.

3 Add the rice and cook, stirring constantly, for 1 minute, or until glossy and coated. Pour in the stock and add the tomatoes, saffron and its soaking water, and salt and pepper to taste. Bring to a boil, then reduce the heat and let simmer, shaking the skillet frequently and stirring occasionally, for 15 minutes.

4 Stir in the mushrooms, green beans, and pinto beans with their can juices. Cook for an additional 10 minutes, then serve immediately.

artichoke paella

ingredients

SERVES 4–6

1/2 tsp saffron threads

2 tbsp hot water

3 tbsp olive oil

1 large onion, chopped

1 zucchini, coarsely chopped

2 garlic cloves, crushed

1/4 tsp cayenne pepper

8 oz/225 g tomatoes, peeled
    and cut into wedges

15 oz/425 g canned
    chickpeas, drained

15 oz/425 g canned
    artichokes hearts, drained
    and coarsely sliced

generous 1 1/2 cups medium-
    grain paella rice

5 1/2 cups simmering vegetable
    stock

5 1/2 oz/150 g green beans,
    blanched

salt and pepper

1 lemon, cut into wedges,
    to serve

method

1 Put the saffron threads and water in a small bowl or cup and let infuse for a few minutes.

2 Meanwhile, heat the oil in a paella pan or wide, shallow skillet and cook the onion and zucchini over medium heat, stirring, for 2–3 minutes, or until softened. Add the garlic, cayenne pepper, and saffron and its soaking liquid and cook, stirring constantly, for 1 minute. Add the tomato wedges, chickpeas, and artichokes and cook, stirring, for an additional 2 minutes.

3 Add the rice and cook, stirring constantly, for 1 minute, or until the rice is glossy and coated. Pour in about 5 cups of the hot stock and bring to a boil. Reduce the heat and let simmer, uncovered, for 10 minutes. Do not stir during cooking, but shake the pan once or twice. Add the green beans and season to taste with salt and pepper. Shake the pan and cook for an additional 10–15 minutes, or until the rice grains are plump and cooked. If the liquid is absorbed too quickly, pour in a little more hot stock, then shake the pan to spread the liquid through the paella.

4 When all the liquid has been absorbed and you detect a faint toasty aroma coming from the rice, remove from the heat immediately to prevent burning. Cover the pan with a clean dish towel or foil and let stand for 5 minutes. Serve direct from the pan with the lemon wedges to squeeze over the rice.

brown rice vegetable pilaf

ingredients

SERVES 4

4 tbsp vegetable oil

1 red onion, finely chopped

2 tender celery stalks, leaves included, quartered lengthwise, and diced

2 carrots, coarsely grated

1 fresh green chile, seeded and finely chopped

3 scallions, green part included, finely chopped

generous $1/4$ cup whole almonds, sliced lengthwise

$13/4$ cups cooked brown basmati rice

$3/4$ cup cooked split red lentils

$3/4$ cup chicken or vegetable stock

5 tbsp fresh orange juice

salt and pepper

fresh celery leaves, to garnish

method

1 Heat 2 tablespoons of the oil in a deep skillet with a lid over medium heat. Add the onion. Cook for 5 minutes, or until softened.

2 Add the celery, carrots, chile, scallions, and almonds. Stir-fry for 2 minutes, or until the vegetables are al dente but still brightly colored. Transfer to a bowl and set aside until required.

3 Add the remaining oil to the skillet. Stir in the rice and lentils. Cook over medium–high heat, stirring, for 1–2 minutes, or until heated through. Reduce the heat. Stir in the stock and orange juice. Season to taste with salt and pepper.

4 Return the vegetables to the skillet. Toss with the rice for a few minutes until heated through. Transfer to a warmed dish, garnish with celery leaves, and serve.

egg fu yung

ingredients

SERVES 4–6

2 eggs

1/2 tsp salt

pinch of white pepper

1 tsp melted butter

2 tbsp vegetable or peanut oil

1 tsp finely chopped garlic

1 small onion, finely sliced

1 green bell pepper,
    finely sliced

3 cups cooked rice, chilled

1 tbsp light soy sauce

1 tbsp finely chopped scallions

1 cup bean sprouts, trimmed

1 tsp sesame oil

method

1 Beat the eggs with the salt and pepper. Heat the butter in a pan and pour in the eggs. Cook as an omelet, until set, then remove from the pan and cut into slivers.

2 In a preheated wok or deep pan, heat the oil and stir-fry the garlic until fragrant. Add the onion and stir-fry for 1 minute, then add the green bell pepper and stir-fry for an additional 1 minute. Stir in the rice and when the grains are separated, stir in the light soy sauce and cook for 1 minute.

3 Add the scallions and egg strips and stir well, then finally add the bean sprouts and sesame oil. Stir-fry for 1 minute and serve.

egg-fried rice with peas

ingredients

SERVES 4

5$^1/_2$ oz/150 g long-grain rice

3 eggs, beaten

2 tbsp vegetable oil

2 garlic cloves, crushed

4 scallions, chopped

4$^1/_2$ oz/125 g cooked peas

1 tbsp light soy sauce

pinch of salt

shredded scallions, to garnish

method

1 Cook the rice in a pan of boiling water for 10–12 minutes, until almost cooked but not soft. Drain well, rinse under cold running water, and drain thoroughly.

2 Place the beaten eggs in a pan and cook over low heat, stirring constantly, until softly scrambled. Remove the pan from the heat and set aside.

3 Preheat a wok over medium heat. Add the oil and swirl it around to coat the sides of the wok. When the oil is hot, add the garlic, scallions, and peas and sauté, stirring occasionally, for 1–2 minutes.

4 Stir the rice into the mixture in the wok, mixing to combine. Add the eggs, soy sauce, and salt to the wok and stir to mix in the eggs thoroughly.

5 Transfer to serving dishes and serve garnished with the shredded scallions.

egg-fried rice with vegetables & crispy onions

ingredients

SERVES 4

4 tbsp vegetable or peanut oil

2 garlic cloves, chopped finely

2 fresh red chiles, seeded and
    chopped

4 oz/115 g mushrooms, sliced

2 oz/55 g snow peas, halved

2 oz/55 g baby corn, halved

3 tbsp Thai soy sauce

1 tbsp jaggery or light
    brown sugar

a few Thai basil leaves

12 oz/350 g rice, cooked and
    cooled

2 eggs, beaten

2 onions, sliced

method

1 Heat half the oil in a wok or large skillet and sauté the garlic and chiles for 2–3 minutes.

2 Add the mushrooms, snow peas, and corn, and stir-fry for 2–3 minutes, before adding the soy sauce, sugar, and basil. Stir in the rice.

3 Push the mixture to one side of the wok and add the eggs to the bottom. Stir until lightly set before combining into the rice mixture.

4 Heat the remaining oil in another skillet and sauté the onions until crispy and brown. Serve the rice topped with the onions.

baked portobello mushrooms

ingredients

SERVES 4

4 large portobello mushrooms

7 oz/200 g canned red kidney beans, drained and rinsed

4 scallions, chopped

1 fresh red jalapeño chile, seeded and finely chopped

1 tbsp finely grated lemon rind

1 tbsp chopped fresh flat-leaf parsley, plus extra sprigs to garnish

salt and pepper

3 oz/85 g zucchini, coarsely grated

3 oz/85 g carrots, coarsely grated

scant $1/2$ cup pine nuts, toasted

generous $1/4$ cup raisins

$1^1/4$ cups vegetable stock

sauce

$2/3$ cup strained plain yogurt

1 tbsp chopped fresh parsley, plus extra to garnish

1 tbsp grated lemon rind

salt and pepper

method

1 Preheat the oven to 350°F/180°C. Peel the mushrooms and carefully remove the stalks. Trim and rinse the stalks.

2 Put the beans, mushroom stalks, scallions, chile, lemon rind, parsley, and salt and pepper to taste into a food processor and process for 2 minutes.

3 Scrape the mixture into a bowl and add the zucchini, carrots, pine nuts, and raisins. Mix well and use to stuff the mushroom cups.

4 Arrange the stuffed mushrooms in an ovenproof dish, pour around the stock, and cover with foil. Bake in the preheated oven for 30 minutes, removing the foil for the last 10 minutes of the cooking time.

5 Meanwhile, to make the sauce, blend all the ingredients together in a small serving dish.

6 Serve the mushrooms hot with the sauce, garnished with parsley sprigs.

spinach & mushroom tortilla

ingredients

SERVES 4

2 tbsp olive oil

3 shallots, finely chopped

12 oz/350 g mushrooms, sliced

10 oz/280 g fresh spinach leaves, coarse stems removed

2 oz/55 g toasted slivered almonds

5 eggs

2 tbsp chopped fresh parsley

2 tbsp cold water

3 oz/85 g mature Mahon, Manchego, or Parmesan cheese, grated

salt and pepper

method

1 Heat the olive oil in an ovenproof skillet. Add the shallots and cook over low heat, stirring occasionally, for 5 minutes, or until softened. Add the mushrooms and cook, stirring frequently, for an additional 4 minutes. Add the spinach, then increase the heat to medium and cook, stirring frequently, for 3–4 minutes, or until wilted. Reduce the heat, then season to taste with salt and pepper and stir in the slivered almonds.

2 Beat the eggs with the parsley, water, and salt and pepper to taste in a bowl. Pour the mixture into the skillet and cook for 5–8 minutes, or until the underside is set. Lift the edge of the tortilla occasionally to let the uncooked egg run underneath. Meanwhile, preheat the broiler to high.

3 Sprinkle the grated cheese over the tortilla and cook under the preheated hot broiler for 3 minutes, or until the top is set and the cheese has melted. Serve, lukewarm or cold, cut into thin wedges.

sweet treats

When you're cooking family meals and time is tight, making dessert can seem like one chore too many. Fresh fruit or pots of yogurt are convenient and healthy options but will quickly become boring, so it's worth pushing the boat out occasionally—perhaps at weekends—to give the family a sweet treat. Equally, when you're entertaining you don't have to struggle for hours in the kitchen or be a professional pastry cook to produce an impressive dessert as the crowning glory of the meal.

The hot desserts in this chapter include family favorites, such as fruit crumble, as well as baked and broiled fruit and delicious filled crepes. Pies and tarts are easy to prepare in advance and can then be popped into the oven while the main course is cooking. Cold desserts, even luxurious mousses and cheesecakes, are surprisingly straightforward to make and the only time-consuming part is leaving them to chill and set—perfect for a special occasion or a dinner party when you want to do as much as possible in advance.

Home baking is incredibly easy and you may be surprised to discover that it takes only minutes to rustle up a batch of muffins, cupcakes, brownies, or cookies. This is fortunate because it will take the family only minutes to demolish them if they get the chance! All these small bites are ideal

for adding to lunch bags, as after-school snacks, as a pick-me-up with morning coffee, or even, in some cases, serving with store-bought ice cream to make it a more special dessert.

cappuccino soufflés

ingredients

SERVES 4

butter, for greasing

2 tbsp superfine sugar,
    plus extra for coating

6 tbsp heavy cream

2 tsp instant espresso coffee
    granules

2 tbsp Kahlua

3 large eggs, separated,
    plus 1 extra egg white

5^{1}/$_{2}$ oz/150 g semisweet
    chocolate, melted and
    cooled

unsweetened cocoa,
    for dusting

vanilla ice cream, to serve

method

1 Preheat the oven to 375°F/190°C. Lightly grease the sides of 6 x ^{3}/$_{4}$-cup ramekins with butter and coat with superfine sugar. Place the ramekins on a baking sheet.

2 Place the cream in a small, heavy-bottom pan and heat gently. Stir in the coffee until it has dissolved, then stir in the Kahlua. Divide the coffee mixture among the prepared ramekins.

3 Place the egg whites in a clean, grease-free bowl and whisk until soft peaks form, then gradually whisk in the sugar until stiff but not dry. Stir the egg yolks and melted chocolate together in a separate bowl, then stir in a little of the whisked egg whites. Gradually fold in the remaining egg whites.

4 Divide the mixture among the dishes. Bake in the preheated oven for 15 minutes, or until just set. Dust with unsweetened cocoa and serve immediately with vanilla ice cream.

sticky coffee & walnut sponges

ingredients

SERVES 6

scant 1½ cups self-rising flour

1 tsp ground cinnamon

4 tbsp butter, softened, plus extra for greasing

½ cup light brown sugar

2 large eggs, beaten

1 tbsp instant coffee powder, dissolved

½ cup walnuts, finely chopped

butterscotch sauce

¼ cup coarsely chopped walnuts

4 tbsp butter

¼ cup light brown sugar

⅔ cup heavy cream

method

1 Preheat the oven to 375°F/190°C. Grease 6 individual heatproof metal bowls. Sift the flour and cinnamon into a bowl. Put the butter and sugar in a bowl and beat together until light and fluffy. Gradually beat in the eggs. Add a little flour if the mixture shows signs of curdling. Fold in half of the flour then fold in the remaining flour, alternately with the coffee. Gently stir in the walnuts.

2 Divide the mixture among the prepared bowls. Place a piece of buttered foil over each bowl and secure with a rubber band. Stand the bowls in a roasting pan and pour in boiling water to come halfway up the sides of the bowls. Cover the whole roasting pan with foil, folding it under the rim. Bake in the oven for 30–40 minutes, until well risen and firm to the touch.

3 Meanwhile, prepare the sauce. Put the walnuts, butter, sugar, and cream in a pan and heat gently, stirring, until the ingredients melt and blend together. Bring to a simmer then remove from the heat. Turn the sponges out onto a serving plate, spoon over the hot sauce, and serve.

individual molten chocolate cakes

ingredients

SERVES 4

scant 1/2 cup butter, plus extra
    for greasing
31/2 oz/100 g semisweet
    chocolate, broken into
    pieces
2 large eggs
1 tsp vanilla extract
1/2 cup superfine sugar,
    plus extra for coating
2 tbsp all-purpose flour
confectioners' sugar, for
    dusting
vanilla ice cream, to serve

method

1 Preheat the oven to 400°F/200°C. Grease 4 x 3/4-cup ovenproof bowls or ramekins and coat with superfine sugar. Place the butter and chocolate in a heatproof bowl and set over a pan of gently simmering water until melted. Stir until smooth. Let cool.

2 Place the eggs, vanilla extract, superfine sugar, and flour in a bowl and whisk together. Stir in the melted chocolate. Pour the mixture into the prepared molds and place on a baking sheet. Bake in the oven for 12–15 minutes, or until well risen and set on the outside but still molten inside.

3 Let stand for 1 minute, then turn out onto 4 serving plates. Dust with confectioners' sugar and serve immediately with vanilla ice cream.

zabaglione

ingredients

SERVES 4

4 egg yolks

1/3 cup superfine sugar

5 tbsp marsala

amaretti cookies, to serve

method

1 Whisk the egg yolks with the sugar in a heatproof bowl or, if you have one, the top of a double boiler for about 1 minute.

2 Gently whisk in the marsala. Set the bowl over a pan of barely simmering water or put the top of the double boiler on its bottom filled with barely simmering water, and whisk vigorously for 10–15 minutes, until thick, creamy, and foamy.

3 Immediately pour into serving glasses and serve with amaretti cookies.

peach cobbler

ingredients

SERVES 4–6

filling

6 peaches, peeled and sliced

4 tbsp superfine sugar

1/2 tbsp lemon juice

1 1/2 tsp cornstarch

1/2 tsp almond or vanilla
   extract

vanilla or pecan ice cream,
   to serve

topping

scant 1 1/4 cups all-purpose
   flour

generous 1/2 cup superfine
   sugar

1 1/2 tsp baking powder

1/2 tsp salt

6 tbsp butter, diced

1 egg

6 tbsp milk

method

1 Preheat the oven to 425°F/220°C. Place the peaches in a 9-inch/23-cm square ovenproof dish that is also suitable for serving. Add the sugar, lemon juice, cornstarch, and almond extract and toss together. Bake the peaches in the oven for 20 minutes.

2 Meanwhile, to make the topping, sift the flour, all but 2 tablespoons of the sugar, the baking powder, and salt into a bowl. Rub in the butter with the fingertips until the mixture resembles bread crumbs. Mix the egg and 5 tablespoons of the milk in a pitcher, then mix into the dry ingredients with a fork until a soft, sticky dough forms. If the dough seems too dry, stir in the extra tablespoon of milk.

3 Reduce the oven temperature to 400°F/ 200°C. Remove the peaches from the oven and drop spoonfuls of the topping over the surface, without smoothing. Sprinkle with the remaining sugar, return to the oven, and bake for an additional 15 minutes, or until the topping is golden brown and firm—the topping will spread as it cooks. Serve hot or at room temperature with ice cream.

apple & blackberry crumble

ingredients

SERVES 4

2 lb/900 g tart cooking apples

2 cups blackberries

1/2 cup light brown sugar

1 tsp ground cinnamon

custard or light cream,
     to serve

topping

2/3 cup self-rising flour

2/3 cup all-purpose whole
     wheat flour

1/2 cup butter

scant 1/2 cup raw sugar

method

1 Preheat the oven to 400°F/200°C. Peel and core the apples and cut into chunks. Place in a bowl with the blackberries, sugar, and cinnamon, mix together, and place in an ovenproof dish.

2 To make the topping, sift the self-rising flour into a bowl and stir in the whole wheat flour. Add the butter and rub in until the mixture resembles coarse bread crumbs. Stir in the sugar.

3 Spread the topping over the apples and bake in the oven for 40–45 minutes, until the apples are soft and the topping is golden brown and crisp.

4 Serve with custard or light cream.

peach & preserved ginger tarte tatin

ingredients

SERVES 6

9 oz/250 g prepared puff
   pastry
flour, for dusting

filling

6–8 just-ripe peaches
scant 1/2 cup superfine sugar
3 heaping tbsp unsalted butter
3 pieces preserved ginger in
   syrup, chopped
1 tbsp ginger syrup from the
   preserved ginger jar
1 egg, beaten
thick cream or ice cream,
   to serve

method

1 Preheat the oven to 375°F/190°C. Plunge the peaches into boiling water, then let drain and peel. Cut each in half. Put the sugar in a 10-inch/25-cm heavy, ovenproof skillet and heat it gently until it caramelizes. Don't stir, just shake the skillet if necessary. Once the sugar turns a dark caramel color, remove from the heat, and drop 2 tablespoons of the butter into it.

2 Place the peaches cut-side up on top of the caramel, packing them as close together as possible, and tucking the preserved ginger pieces into any gaps. Dot with the remaining butter and drizzle with the ginger syrup.

3 Return to gentle heat while you roll out the dough in a circle larger than the skillet you are using. Drape the dough over the peaches and tuck it in well round the edges, brush with the beaten egg, and bake in the preheated oven for 20–25 minutes, until the pastry is browned and puffed up. Remove from the oven and let rest for 5 minutes, then invert onto a serving plate and serve with thick cream or ice cream.

paper-thin fruit pies

ingredients

MAKES 4

1 apple

1 ripe pear

2 tbsp lemon juice

4 sheets filo pastry,
    thawed if frozen

4 tbsp melted butter

2 tbsp apricot jelly

1 tbsp unsweetened orange
    juice

1 tbsp finely chopped
    pistachios

2 tsp confectioners' sugar,
    for dusting

method

1 Preheat the oven to 400°F/200°C. Core and thinly slice the apple and pear and immediately toss them in the lemon juice to prevent them from turning brown.

2 Cut each sheet of pastry into 4 and cover with a clean, damp dish towel. Brush a 4-cup nonstick muffin pan (cup size 4 inches/10 cm in diameter) with a little of the butter.

3 Brush 4 small sheets of pastry with melted butter. Press a sheet of pastry into the base of 1 cup. Arrange the other sheets of pastry on top at slightly different angles. Repeat with the other sheets of pastry to make another 3 pies.

4 Arrange alternate slices of apple and pear in the center of each pie shell and lightly crimp the edges of the pastry.

5 Stir the jelly and orange juice together until smooth and brush over the fruit. Bake in the preheated oven for 12–15 minutes. Sprinkle with the pistachios, dust lightly with confectioners' sugar, and serve hot straight from the oven.

warm fruit nests

ingredients

MAKES 4

2–3 tbsp lemon-infused
    olive oil
8 sheets of frozen filo pastry,
    thawed
9 oz/250 g blueberries
9 oz/250 g raspberries
9 oz/250 g blackberries
3 tbsp superfine sugar
1 tsp ground allspice
sprigs of fresh mint,
    to decorate
heavy cream, to serve

method

1 Preheat the oven to 350°F/180°C. Brush 4 small muffin pans with oil. Cut the filo pastry into 16 squares measuring about 4$\frac{1}{2}$ inches/ 12 cm across. Brush each square with oil and use to line the muffin pans. Place 4 sheets in each pan, staggering them so that the overhanging corners make a decorative star shape. Transfer to a cookie sheet and bake in the preheated oven for 7–8 minutes, until golden. Remove from the oven and set aside.

2 Meanwhile, warm the fruit in a pan with the superfine sugar and allspice over medium heat until simmering. Lower the heat and continue simmering, stirring, for 10 minutes. Remove from the heat and drain. Using a slotted spoon, divide the warm fruit among the tartlet shells. Garnish with sprigs of fresh mint and serve warm with heavy cream.

walnut pastries

ingredients

MAKES 12

scant ¹/₂ cup butter
2¹/₂ cups walnut pieces,
     chopped finely
¹/₃ cup superfine sugar
1 tsp ground cinnamon
¹/₂ tsp ground cloves
8 oz/225 g authentic
     Greek filo pastry
³/₄ cup Greek honey
2 tsp lemon juice
²/₃ cup water

method

1 Preheat the oven to 425°F/220°C. Melt the butter and use a little to lightly grease a deep 10 x 7-inch/25 x 18-cm metal baking pan.

2 To make the filling, put the walnuts, sugar, cinnamon, and cloves in a bowl and mix well together.

3 Cut the pastry sheets in half widthwise. Take one sheet of pastry and use to line the pan. Cover the remaining sheets with a damp dish towel. Brush the sheet with a little of the melted butter. Repeat with half of the pastry sheets, then sprinkle with the walnut filling. Top with the remaining pastry sheets, brushing each with butter and tucking down the edges. Using a sharp knife, cut the top layers of the pastry into 12 diamond or square shapes.

4 Bake in the preheated oven for 10 minutes, then reduce the oven temperature to 350°F/180°C and bake for another 20 minutes, until golden brown.

5 Just before the pastries have cooked, make the honey syrup. Put the honey, lemon juice, and the water in a saucepan and simmer for about 5 minutes, until combined. Set aside.

6 When the pastries are cooked, remove from the oven and evenly pour over the honey syrup. Let cool. Before serving, cut along the marked lines again to divide into pieces.

chocolate tartlets

ingredients

MAKES 4

10 oz/280 g prepared sweet
  pie dough
5$^{1}/_{2}$ oz/150 g bittersweet
  chocolate, broken into
  pieces
4 tbsp butter
scant $^{1}/_{2}$ cup heavy cream
1 large egg
2 tbsp superfine sugar
unsweetened cocoa and
  chocolate curls, to decorate
whipped cream, to serve

method

1 Preheat the oven to 400°F/200°C. Roll out the pie dough and use to line 4 x 4$^{1}/_{2}$-inch/12-cm fluted tart pans with removable bases. Line the pastry shells with waxed paper, then fill with baking beans. Place on a preheated baking sheet and bake in the preheated oven for 5 minutes or until the pastry shells look set. Remove the paper and beans and return the pastry shells to the oven for 5 minutes or until the bases look dry. Remove from the oven, then set aside on the baking sheet. Reduce the oven temperature to 350°F/180°C.

2 Meanwhile, place the chocolate in a heatproof bowl set over a pan of simmering water so that the bowl does not touch the water. Add the butter and cream and leave until the chocolate and butter melt.

3 Beat the egg and sugar together until light and fluffy. Remove the melted chocolate mixture from the heat and stir until smooth, then stir it into the egg mixture. Carefully pour the filling into the pastry shells, then transfer to the oven and bake for 15 minutes, or until the filling is set and the pastry is golden brown. If the pie dough looks as though it is becoming too brown, cover it with a sheet of foil.

4 Transfer the tartlets to a wire rack to cool completely. Dust with cocoa powder, decorate with chocolate curls, and serve with the whipped cream.

creamy mango brûlée

ingredients

SERVES 4

2 mangoes

generous 1 cup mascarpone
    cheese

generous 3/4 cup strained plain
    yogurt

1 tsp ground ginger

grated rind and juice of 1 lime

2 tbsp light brown sugar

8 tbsp raw sugar

method

1 Slice the mangoes on either side of the
pit. Discard the pit and peel the fruit. Slice and
then chop the fruit and divide it among
4 ramekins.

2 Beat the mascarpone cheese with the yogurt.
Fold in the ginger, lime rind and juice, and
light brown sugar. Divide the mixture among the
ramekins and level off the tops. Chill for
2 hours.

3 Sprinkle 2 tablespoons of raw sugar over the
top of each dish, covering the creamy mixture.
Place under a hot broiler for 2–3 minutes, until
melted and browned. Cool completely, then
chill in the refrigerator.

spanish-style rice pudding

ingredients

SERVES 4

1 large orange

1 lemon

4 cups milk

generous 1 cup Spanish short-
    grain rice

1/2 cup superfine sugar

1 vanilla bean, split

pinch of salt

1/2 cup heavy cream

brown sugar, to serve
    (optional)

method

1 Finely grate the rinds from the orange and lemon; set aside. Rinse a heavy-bottom pan with cold water and do not dry it.

2 Put the milk and rice in the pan over medium–high heat and bring to a boil. Reduce the heat, stir in the superfine sugar, vanilla bean, orange and lemon rinds, and salt, and let simmer, stirring frequently, until the pudding is thick and creamy and the rice grains are tender: this can take up to 30 minutes, depending on how wide the pan is.

3 Remove the vanilla bean and stir in the cream. Serve immediately, sprinkled with brown sugar, if using, or let cool completely, cover, and let chill until required. (The pudding will thicken as it cools, so stir in extra milk, if necessary.)

white chocolate mousse

ingredients

SERVES 6

9 oz/250 g white chocolate,
    broken into pieces
generous 1/3 cup milk
1 1/4 cups heavy cream
1 tsp rose water
2 egg whites
4 oz/115 g semisweet
    chocolate, broken into
    pieces
candied rose petals,
    to decorate

method

1 Place the white chocolate and milk in a pan and heat gently until the chocolate has melted, then stir. Transfer to a large bowl and let cool.

2 Whip the cream and rose water in a separate bowl until soft peaks form. Whisk the egg whites in a separate large, spotlessly clean, grease-free bowl until stiff but not dry. Gently fold the whipped cream into the white chocolate mixture, then fold in the egg whites. Spoon the mixture into 6 small dishes or glasses, cover with plastic wrap, and let chill for 8 hours, or overnight, to set.

3 Melt the semisweet chocolate and let cool, then pour evenly over the mousses. Let stand until the chocolate has hardened, then decorate with rose petals and serve.

chocolate mousse

ingredients

SERVES 4–6

8 oz/225 g bittersweet
   chocolate, chopped
2 tbsp brandy, Grand Marnier,
   or Cointreau
4 tbsp water
2 tbsp unsalted butter, diced
3 large eggs, separated
1/4 tsp cream of tartar
1/4 cup sugar
1/2 cup heavy cream

method

1 Place the chocolate, brandy, and water in a small pan over low heat and melt, stirring, until smooth. Remove the pan from the heat and beat in the butter. Beat the egg yolks into the chocolate mixture, one after another, until blended, then let cool slightly.

2 Meanwhile, using an electric mixer on low speed, beat the egg whites in a spotlessly clean bowl until frothy, then gradually increase the mixer's speed and beat until soft peaks form. Sprinkle the cream of tartar over the surface, then add the sugar, tablespoon by tablespoon, and continue beating until stiff peaks form. Beat several tablespoons of the egg whites into the chocolate mixture to loosen.

3 In another bowl, whip the cream until soft peaks form. Spoon the cream over the chocolate mixture, then spoon the remaining whites over the cream. Use a large metal spoon or rubber spatula to fold the chocolate into the cream and egg whites.

4 Either spoon the chocolate mousse into a large serving bowl or divide among 4–6 individual bowls. Cover with plastic wrap and chill for at least 3 hours before serving.

chocolate trifle

ingredients

SERVES 4

10 oz/280 g store-bought
chocolate loaf cake
3–4 tbsp seeded raspberry
jelly
4 tbsp amaretto liqueur
9 oz/250 g frozen mixed
berries, thawed

custard
6 egg yolks
generous 1/4 cup superfine
sugar
1 tbsp cornstarch
2 cups milk
2 oz/55 g semisweet
chocolate, melted

topping
1 cup heavy cream
1 tbsp superfine sugar
1/2 tsp vanilla extract

to decorate
ready-made chocolate truffles
fresh fruit, such as cherries
and strawberries

method

1 Cut the cake into slices and make "sandwiches" with the raspberry jelly. Cut the sandwiches into cubes and place in a large serving bowl. Sprinkle with the amaretto liqueur. Spread the berries over the cake.

2 To make the custard, place the egg yolks and sugar in a heatproof bowl and whisk until thick and pale, then stir in the cornstarch. Place the milk in a pan and heat until almost boiling. Pour onto the egg yolk mixture, stirring. Return the mixture to the pan and bring just to a boil, stirring constantly, until it thickens. Remove from the heat and let cool slightly. Stir in the melted chocolate. Pour the custard over the cake and berries. Let cool, then cover and let chill in the refrigerator for 2 hours, or until set.

3 To make the topping, whip the cream until soft peaks form, then beat in the sugar and vanilla extract. Spoon over the trifle. Decorate with truffles and fruit and let chill until ready to serve.

tiramisu

ingredients

SERVES 4

scant 1 cup strong black
    coffee, cooled to room
    temperature
4 tbsp orange liqueur, such as
    Cointreau
3 tbsp orange juice
16 Italian ladyfingers
generous 1 cup mascarpone
    cheese
1¼ cups heavy cream, lightly
    whipped
3 tbsp confectioners' sugar
grated rind of 1 orange
2¼ oz/60 g semisweet
    chocolate, grated

to decorate
chopped toasted almonds
crystallized orange peel
chocolate shavings

method

1 Pour the cooled coffee into a pitcher and stir in the orange liqueur and orange juice. Place 8 of the ladyfingers in the bottom of a serving dish, then pour over half of the coffee mixture.

2 Place the mascarpone in a separate bowl together with the cream, confectioners' sugar, and orange rind and mix well. Spread half of the mascarpone mixture over the coffee-soaked ladyfingers, then arrange the remaining ladyfingers on top. Pour over the remaining coffee mixture then spread over the remaining mascarpone mixture. Sprinkle over the grated chocolate and let chill in the refrigerator for at least 2 hours.

3 Serve decorated with the chopped toasted almonds, crystallized orange peel, and chocolate shavings.

mascarpone creams

ingredients

SERVES 4

4 oz/115 g amaretti cookies,
    crushed
4 tbsp amaretto or
    Maraschino liqueur
4 eggs, separated
generous $\frac{1}{2}$ cup superfine
    sugar
1 cup mascarpone cheese
toasted slivered almonds,
    to decorate

method

1 Place the amaretti crumbs in a bowl, add the amaretto, and let soak.

2 Meanwhile, beat the egg yolks with the superfine sugar until pale and thick. Fold in the mascarpone and soaked cookie crumbs.

3 Whisk the egg whites in a separate, spotlessly clean, greasefree bowl until stiff, then gently fold into the cheese mixture. Divide among 4 serving dishes and let chill for 1–2 hours. Sprinkle with toasted slivered almonds just before serving.

coffee panna cotta with chocolate sauce

ingredients

SERVES 6

oil, for brushing

$2^1/_2$ cups heavy cream

1 vanilla bean

$^1/_3$ cup superfine sugar

2 tsp instant espresso coffee
    powder, dissolved in
    4 tbsp water

2 tsp powdered gelatin

chocolate-covered coffee
    beans, to serve

chocolate sauce

$^2/_3$ cup light cream

2 oz/55 g semisweet
    chocolate, melted

method

1 Lightly brush 6 x $^2/_3$-cup molds with oil. Place the cream in a pan. Split the vanilla bean and scrape the black seeds into the cream. Add the vanilla bean and the sugar, then heat gently until almost boiling. Strain the cream into a heatproof bowl and set aside. Place the coffee in a small heatproof bowl, sprinkle on the gelatin, and let stand for 5 minutes, or until spongy. Set the bowl over a pan of gently simmering water until the gelatin has dissolved.

2 Stir a little of the reserved cream into the gelatin mixture, then stir the gelatin mixture into the remainder of the cream. Divide the mixture among the prepared molds and let cool, then let chill in the refrigerator for 8 hours, or overnight.

3 To make the sauce, place one quarter of the cream in a bowl and stir in the melted chocolate. Gradually stir in the remaining cream, reserving 1 tablespoon. To serve the panna cotta, dip the molds briefly into hot water and turn out onto 6 dessert plates. Pour the chocolate cream around. Dot drops of the reserved cream onto the sauce and feather it with a toothpick. Decorate with chocolate-covered coffee beans and serve.

summer dessert

ingredients

SERVES 6

1 lb 8 oz/675 g mixed berries, such as blueberries, raspberries, and blackberries

3/4 cup superfine sugar

2 tbsp crème de framboise liqueur (optional)

6–8 slices day-old white bread, crusts removed

heavy cream, to serve

method

1 Pick over the berries, removing any stalks. Put the berries in a large pan with the sugar and liqueur, if using.

2 Over low heat, very slowly bring to a boil, stirring carefully to make sure that the sugar has dissolved. Cook over low heat for only 2–3 minutes, until the juices run but the berries still hold their shape.

3 Line a bowl with some of the slices of bread (cut them to shape so that the bread fits well). Spoon in the cooked fruit and juice, reserving a little of the juice for later.

4 Cover the surface with the remaining bread. Place a saucer or small plate on top. Use a large can of food or other heavy object to weight it down for at least 8 hours or overnight in the refrigerator.

5 Turn out onto a serving plate and pour over the reserved juice to color any white pieces of bread that may be showing. Serve with the cream.

chocolate brandy torte

ingredients

SERVES 12

base

scant 1/2 cup butter,
    plus extra for greasing
9 oz/250 g gingersnaps
2³/4 oz/75 g semisweet
    chocolate

filling

8 oz/225 g semisweet
    chocolate
generous 1 cup
    mascarpone cheese
2 eggs, separated
3 tbsp brandy
1¹/4 cups heavy cream
4 tbsp superfine sugar

to decorate

generous 1/3 cup heavy cream
chocolate-covered coffee
    beans

method

1 Grease the bottom and sides of a 9-inch/ 23-cm springform cake pan. Place the gingersnaps in a plastic bag and crush with a rolling pin. Transfer to a bowl. Place the chocolate and butter in a small pan and heat gently until melted, then pour over the cookie crumbs. Mix well, then press into the prepared pan. Let chill while preparing the filling.

2 To make the filling, place the chocolate in a heatproof bowl set over a pan of simmering water, and heat, stirring, until melted. Remove from the heat and beat in the mascarpone cheese, egg yolks, and brandy.

3 Whip the cream until just holding its shape. Fold in the chocolate mixture.

4 Whisk the egg whites in a spotlessly clean, grease-free bowl until soft peaks form. Add the sugar, a little at a time, and whisk until thick and glossy. Fold into the chocolate mixture, in 2 batches, until just mixed.

5 Spoon the mixture into the cake pan and let chill in the refrigerator for at least 2 hours. Carefully transfer to a serving plate. To decorate, whip the cream and pipe onto the cheesecake, add the chocolate-covered coffee beans, and serve.

irish cream cheesecake

ingredients

SERVES 12

oil, for brushing

6 oz/175 g chocolate chip
cookies

4 tbsp butter

filling

8 oz/225 g semisweet
chocolate

8 oz/225 g milk chocolate

3/4 cup superfine sugar

1 1/2 cups cream cheese

1 3/4 cups heavy cream,
whipped

3 tbsp Irish cream liqueur

whipped cream and fresh fruit,
to serve

method

1 Line the bottom of a 20-cm/8-inch springform pan with foil and brush the sides with oil. Place the cookies in a plastic bag and crush with a rolling pin. Place the butter in a pan and heat gently until just melted, then stir in the crushed cookies. Press the mixture into the bottom of the pan and chill in the refrigerator for 1 hour.

2 To make the filling, melt the semisweet and milk chocolate together, stir to combine, and let cool. Place the sugar and cream cheese in a large bowl and beat together until smooth, then fold in the whipped cream. Fold the mixture gently into the melted chocolate, then stir in the Irish cream liqueur.

3 Spoon the filling into the cake pan and smooth the surface. Cover and let chill in the refrigerator for 2 hours, or until firm. Transfer to a serving plate and cut into small slices. Serve with a spoonful of whipped cream and fresh fruit.

banana-stuffed crepes

ingredients

SERVES 4

1 1/2 cups all-purpose flour

2 tbsp light brown sugar

2 eggs

generous 1 3/4 cups milk

grated rind and juice of
     1 lemon

4 tbsp butter

3 bananas

4 tbsp corn syrup

method

1 Combine the flour and sugar and beat in the eggs and half the milk. Beat together until smooth. Gradually add the remaining milk, stirring constantly to make a smooth batter. Stir in the lemon rind.

2 Melt a little butter in an 8-inch/20-cm skillet and pour in one quarter of the batter. Tilt the skillet to coat the bottom and cook for 1–2 minutes, until set. Flip the crepe over and cook the second side. Slide out of the skillet and keep warm. Repeat to make 3 more crepes.

3 Slice the bananas and toss in the lemon juice. Pour the syrup over them and toss together. Fold each crepe in half and then in half again and fill the center with the banana mixture. Serve warm.

exotic fruit chocolate crepes

ingredients

SERVES 4

3/4 cup all-purpose flour
2 tbsp unsweetened cocoa
pinch of salt
1 egg, beaten
1¼ cups milk
oil, for frying
confectioners' sugar,
    for dusting

filling

scant ½ cup strained
    plain yogurt
generous 1 cup mascarpone
    cheese
confectioners' sugar (optional)
1 mango, peeled and diced
generous 1 cup strawberries,
    hulled and quartered
2 passion fruit

method

1 To make the filling, place the yogurt and mascarpone cheese in a bowl and sweeten with confectioners' sugar, if you like. Place the mango and strawberries in a bowl and mix together. Cut the passion fruit in half, scoop out the pulp and seeds, and add to the mango and strawberries. Stir together, then set aside.

2 To make the crepes, sift the flour, unsweetened cocoa, and salt into a bowl and make a well in the center. Add the egg and whisk with a balloon whisk. Gradually beat in the milk, drawing in the flour from the sides, to make a smooth batter. Cover and let stand for 20 minutes. Heat a small amount of oil in a 7-inch/18-cm crepe pan or skillet. Pour in just enough batter to thinly coat the bottom of the pan. Cook over medium–high heat for 1 minute, then turn and cook the other side for 30–60 seconds, or until cooked through.

3 Transfer the crepe to a plate and keep hot. Repeat with the remaining batter, stacking the cooked crepes on top of each other with parchment paper in between. Keep warm in the oven while cooking the remainder. To serve, divide the filling among the crepes, then roll up and dust with confectioners' sugar.

pears in honey syrup

ingredients

SERVES 4

4 medium-ripe pears

generous ³/₄ cup water

1 tsp sugar

1 tbsp honey

method

1 Peel each pear, leaving the stem intact. Wrap each in foil and place in a pan with the stems resting on the side of the pan. Add enough water to cover at least half of the height of the pears. Bring to a boil and simmer for 30 minutes. Remove the pears and carefully remove the foil, reserving any juices. Set aside to cool.

2 Bring the measured water to a boil. Add any pear juices, the sugar, and honey and boil for 5 minutes. Remove from the heat and let cool a little.

3 Place each pear in an individual dish. Pour a little syrup over each and serve just warm.

baked apricots with honey

ingredients

SERVES 4

butter, for greasing
4 apricots, each cut in half
    and pitted
4 tbsp slivered almonds
4 tbsp honey
pinch ground ginger or grated
    nutmeg
vanilla ice cream, to serve
    (optional)

method

1 Preheat the oven to 400°F/200°C. Lightly butter an ovenproof dish large enough to hold the apricot halves in a single layer.

2 Arrange the apricot halves in the dish, cut sides up. Sprinkle with the almonds and drizzle over the honey. Dust with the spice.

3 Bake in the preheated oven for 12–15 minutes, until the apricots are tender and the almonds golden. Remove from the oven and serve immediately, with ice cream on the side, if using.

baked stuffed peaches

ingredients

SERVES 4

4 ripe peaches

4 tbsp unsalted butter

2 tbsp light brown sugar

1 cup crushed amaretti or
  macaroons

2 tbsp amaretto liqueur

1/2 cup light cream, to serve

method

1 Preheat the oven to 350°F/180°C. Prepare the peaches by cutting them in half and removing the pits (if you want to peel them, just dip them into boiling water for 10–15 seconds and then plunge them into cold water). Place the peaches, cut-side up, in an ovenproof dish greased with 1 tablespoon of the butter.

2 In a bowl, combine the remaining butter and sugar until creamy, add the amaretti, and mix well. Stuff the peaches with the cookie filling.

3 Bake in the center of the preheated oven for 20–25 minutes, or until the peaches are soft. Pour over the liqueur and serve hot with the light cream.

broiled honeyed figs with sabayon

ingredients

SERVES 4

8 fresh figs, cut in half

4 tbsp honey

2 fresh rosemary sprigs,
   leaves removed and finely
   chopped (optional)

3 eggs

method

1 Preheat the broiler to high. Arrange the figs, cut-side up, on the broiler pan. Brush with half the honey and sprinkle over the chopped rosemary, if using. Cook under the preheated broiler for 5–6 minutes, or until just starting to caramelize.

2 Meanwhile, to make the sabayon, in a large, heatproof bowl, lightly whisk the eggs with the remaining honey, then place over a pan of simmering water. Using a hand-held electric whisk, beat the eggs and honey together for 10 minutes, or until pale and thick.

3 Put 4 fig halves on each of 4 serving plates, add a generous spoonful of the sabayon, and serve immediately.

grilled bananas

ingredients

SERVES 4

$1/2$ cup coconut cream

$2/3$ cup heavy cream

4 bananas

juice and rind of 1 lime

1 tbsp vegetable or peanut oil

scant $1/2$ cup dry unsweetened
   coconut

method

1 Put the coconut cream and heavy cream in a bowl and beat until thick but floppy. Cover and let chill in the refrigerator until ready to serve.

2 Peel the bananas and toss in the lime juice and rind. Lightly oil a preheated grill pan and cook the bananas, turning once, for 2–3 minutes, until softened and browned.

3 Toast the dry unsweetened coconut on a piece of foil under a broiler until lightly browned. Serve the bananas with the coconut cream, sprinkled with the toasted coconut.

toffee bananas

ingredients

SERVES 4

1/2 cup self-rising flour

1 egg, beaten

5 tbsp iced water

4 large, ripe bananas

3 tbsp lemon juice

2 tbsp rice flour

vegetable oil, for deep-frying

caramel

generous 1/2 cup superfine
   sugar

4 tbsp iced water, plus an
   extra bowl of iced water
   for setting

2 tbsp sesame seeds

method

1 Sift the flour into a bowl. Make a well in the center, add the egg and the iced water, and beat from the center outwards, until combined into a smooth batter.

2 Peel the bananas and cut into 2-inch/ 5-cm pieces. Gently shape them into balls with your hands. Brush with lemon juice to prevent discoloration, then roll them in rice flour until coated. Pour oil into a pan to a depth of 21/2 inches/6 cm and heat until it reaches 350–375°F/180–190°C, or until a cube of bread browns in 30 seconds. Coat the balls in the batter and cook in batches in the hot oil for about 2 minutes each, until golden. Lift them out and drain on paper towels.

3 To make the caramel, put the sugar into a small pan over low heat. Add the iced water and heat, stirring, until the sugar dissolves. Simmer for 5 minutes, remove from the heat, and stir in the sesame seeds. Toss the banana balls in the caramel, scoop them out, and drop into the bowl of iced water to set. Lift them out and divide among individual serving bowls. Serve hot.

toffee apple slices

ingredients

SERVES 4

4 apples, peeled, cored, and
each cut into thick slices
vegetable or peanut oil,
for deep-frying

batter
2/3 cup all-purpose flour
1 egg, beaten
1/2 cup cold water

toffee syrup
4 tbsp sesame oil
scant 1 1/4 cups sugar
2 tbsp sesame seeds, toasted

method

1 To prepare the batter, sift the flour and stir in the egg. Slowly add the water, beating to form a smooth and thick batter. Dip each apple slice in the batter.

2 Heat enough oil for deep-frying in a wok, deep-fat fryer, or large, heavy-bottom pan until it reaches 350–375°F/180–190°C, or until a cube of bread browns in 30 seconds. Deep-fry the apple slices until golden brown. Drain and set aside.

3 To make the toffee syrup, heat the sesame oil in a small, heavy-bottom pan and, when beginning to smoke, add the sugar, stirring constantly, until the mixture caramelizes and turns golden. Remove from the heat, then stir in the sesame seeds and pour into a large flat pan.

4 Over very low heat, place the apple slices in the syrup, turning once. When coated, dip each slice in cold water. Serve immediately.

mixed fruit salad

ingredients

SERVES 4

1 papaya, halved, peeled,
   and seeded
2 bananas, sliced thickly
1 small pineapple, peeled,
   halved, cored, and sliced
12 litchis, peeled if fresh
1 small melon, seeded and
   cut into thin wedges
2 oranges
grated rind and juice of 1 lime
2 tbsp superfine sugar

method

1 Arrange the papaya, bananas, pineapple, litchis, and melon on a serving platter. Cut off the rind and pith from the oranges. Cut the orange slices out from between the membranes and add to the fruit platter. Grate a small quantity of the discarded orange rind and add to the platter.

2 Combine the lime rind, juice, and sugar. Pour over the salad and serve.

steamed spiced exotic fruits

ingredients

SERVES 4

2 kiwi fruit, peeled and halved

4 rambutan or litchis, peeled, halved, and pitted

2 passion fruit, the flesh scooped out

8 Cape gooseberries (physalis), papery leaves removed and fruit halved

3 oz/85 g mango, cut into ¾-inch/2-cm cubes

1 sharon fruit, cut into ¾-inch/2-cm slices

3 oz/85 g fresh raspberries

2 vanilla beans, split in half lengthwise

2 cinnamon sticks, broken in half

4 star anise

4 fresh bay leaves

4 tbsp freshly squeezed orange juice

method

1 Preheat the oven to 400°F/200°C. Cut 4 x 16-inch/40-cm squares of parchment paper and 4 foil squares of the same size. Put each parchment paper square on top of a foil square and fold diagonally in half to form a triangle. Open up.

2 Divide the fruits into 4 portions and arrange each portion neatly in the center of each opened square. Add a vanilla bean half, a cinnamon stick half, a star anise, a bay leaf, and 1 tablespoon of orange juice to each triangle.

3 Close each triangle over the mixture, fold in the corners, and crumple the edges together to form airtight triangular parcels. Transfer the parcels to a cookie sheet and bake in the preheated oven for 10–12 minutes, or until they puff up with steam.

4 To serve, put each bag on a serving plate and snip open at the table.

chocolate fondue

ingredients

SERVES 6

1 pineapple

1 mango

12 Cape gooseberries

generous 1 cup fresh
     strawberries

generous 1 1/2 cups seedless
     green grapes

fondue

9 oz/250 g semisweet
     chocolate, broken into
     pieces

2/3 cup heavy cream

2 tbsp cognac

method

1 Using a sharp knife, peel and core the pineapple, then cut the flesh into cubes. Peel the mango and cut the flesh into cubes. Peel back the papery outer skin of the Cape gooseberries and twist at the top to make a "handle." Arrange all the fruit on 6 serving plates and let chill in the refrigerator.

2 To make the fondue, place the chocolate and cream in a fondue pot. Heat gently, stirring constantly, until the chocolate has melted. Stir in the cognac until thoroughly blended and the chocolate mixture is smooth.

3 Place the fondue pot over the burner to keep warm. To serve, allow each guest to dip the fruit into the sauce, using fondue forks or bamboo skewers.

chocolate temptations

ingredients

MAKES 24

12 oz/350 g bittersweet
　　chocolate
3/4 cup unsalted butter, plus
　　extra for greasing
1 tsp strong coffee
2 eggs
scant 3/4 cup light brown sugar
scant 1 1/4 cups all-purpose
　　flour
1/4 tsp baking powder
pinch of salt
2 tsp almond extract
generous 1/2 cup Brazil nuts,
　　chopped
generous 1/2 cup hazelnuts,
　　chopped
1 1/2 oz/40 g white chocolate

method

1 Preheat the oven to 350°F/180°C. Place three quarters of the bittersweet chocolate with the butter and coffee in a heatproof bowl set over a pan of gently simmering water and heat until the chocolate is almost melted.

2 Meanwhile, beat the eggs in a bowl until fluffy. Gradually whisk in the sugar until thick. Remove the chocolate from the heat and stir until smooth. Add to the egg mixture and stir until combined.

3 Sift the flour, baking powder, and salt into a bowl, then stir into the chocolate mixture. Chop three quarters of the remaining bittersweet chocolate into pieces and stir into the mixture. Stir in the almond extract and chopped nuts.

4 Put 24 tablespoonfuls of the mixture onto 1–2 large, greased cookie sheets, then transfer to the preheated oven and bake for 16 minutes. Remove from the oven and transfer to a wire rack to cool. To decorate, melt the remaining chocolate (bittersweet and white) in turn as earlier, then spoon into a pastry bag and pipe thin lines onto the cookies.

double chocolate chip cookies

ingredients

MAKES 24

$1/2$ cup unsalted butter, softened, plus extra for greasing

generous $1/4$ cup granulated sugar

generous $1/4$ cup light brown sugar

1 egg, beaten

$1/2$ tsp vanilla extract

generous $3/4$ cup all-purpose flour

2 tbsp unsweetened cocoa

$1/2$ tsp baking soda

$2/3$ cup milk chocolate chips

$1/2$ cup walnuts, coarsely chopped

method

1 Preheat the oven to 350°F/180°C, then grease 3 baking sheets. Place the butter, granulated sugar, and light brown sugar in a bowl and beat until light and fluffy. Gradually beat in the egg and vanilla extract.

2 Sift the flour, cocoa, and baking soda into the mixture and stir in carefully. Stir in the chocolate chips and walnuts. Drop dessert-spoonfuls of the mixture onto 3 prepared baking sheets, spaced well apart to allow for spreading.

3 Bake in the oven for 10–15 minutes, or until the mixture has spread and the cookies are beginning to feel firm.

4 Remove from the oven, let cool on the baking sheets for 2 minutes, then transfer to wire racks to cool completely.

oat & pecan cookies

ingredients

MAKES 15

1/2 cup unsalted butter,
    softened, plus extra for
    greasing
scant 1/2 cup light brown sugar
1 egg, beaten
1/3 cup pecans, chopped
generous 1/2 cup all-purpose
    flour
1/2 tsp baking powder
1/3 cup rolled oats

method

1 Preheat the oven to 350°F/180°C. Place the butter and sugar in a bowl and beat until light and fluffy. Gradually beat in the egg, then stir in the nuts.

2 Sift the flour and baking powder into the mixture and add the rolled oats. Stir together until well combined. Drop dessertspoonfuls of the mixture onto 2 greased cookie sheets, spaced well apart to allow for spreading.

3 Bake in the preheated oven for 15 minutes, or until pale golden. Remove from the oven and let cool on the cookie sheets for 2 minutes, then transfer to wire racks to cool completely.

gingersnaps

ingredients

MAKES 30

3 cups self-rising flour

pinch of salt

1 cup superfine sugar

1 tbsp ground ginger

1 tsp baking soda

generous 1/2 cup butter,
    plus extra for greasing

1/4 cup corn syrup

1 egg, beaten

1 tsp grated orange rind

method

1 Preheat the oven to 325°F/160°C. Sift the self-rising flour, salt, sugar, ginger, and baking soda into a large mixing bowl.

2 Melt the butter and corn syrup together in a pan over low heat. Remove the pan from the heat and let the butter and syrup mixture cool slightly, then pour it onto the dry ingredients. Add the egg and orange rind and mix thoroughly to form a dough.

3 Using your hands, carefully shape the dough into 30 even-size balls. Place the balls well apart on the prepared cookie sheets, then flatten them slightly with your fingers.

4 Bake in the preheated oven for 15–20 minutes, until golden. Carefully transfer the cookies to a wire rack to cool.

butter cookies

ingredients

MAKES ABOUT 36

3/4 cup butter

3/4 cup superfine sugar

1 egg

2 cups self-rising flour

finely grated rind of 1 lemon

3 tbsp slivered almonds
    (optional)

method

1 Preheat the oven to 350°F/180°C. Put the butter and sugar in a bowl and whisk until light and fluffy. Whisk in the egg, then fold in the flour and lemon rind.

2 Turn out the dough onto a lightly floured surface and knead gently until smooth. Form the mixture into rolls the thickness of a finger, then cut into 4-inch/10-cm lengths. Shape each roll into an S shape and place on baking sheets, allowing room for spreading. If using, stud with a few slivered almonds.

3 Bake the cookies in the preheated oven for about 15 minutes, until lightly browned. Cool on a wire rack. Store the cookies in an airtight tin.

almond biscotti

ingredients

MAKES 20–24

1³/₄ cups all-purpose flour,
    plus extra for dusting
1 tsp baking powder
pinch of salt
³/₄ cup superfine sugar
2 eggs, beaten
finely grated rind of 1 unwaxed
    orange
²/₃ cup whole blanched
    almonds, lightly toasted

method

1 Preheat the oven to 350°F/180°C, then lightly dust a cookie sheet with flour. Sift the flour, baking powder, and salt into a bowl. Add the sugar, eggs, and orange rind and mix to a dough, then knead in the toasted almonds.

2 Using your hands, roll the dough into a ball, cut in half, and roll each portion into a log about 1¹/₂ inches/4 cm in diameter. Place on the floured cookie sheet and bake in the oven for 10 minutes. Remove from the oven and let cool for 5 minutes.

3 Using a serrated knife, cut the logs into ¹/₂ inch/1 cm thick diagonal slices. Arrange the slices on the cookie sheet and return to the oven for 15 minutes, or until slightly golden. Transfer to a wire rack to cool and crispen.

cherry & golden raisin rockies

ingredients

MAKES 10

1³/₄ cups self-rising flour

1 tsp ground allspice

6 tbsp butter, plus extra for
　greasing

scant 1¹/₂ cup superfine sugar

¹/₄ cup candied cherries,
　quartered

¹/₃ cup golden raisins

1 egg

2 tbsp milk

raw sugar, for sprinkling

method

1 Preheat the oven to 400°F/200°C, then grease a cookie sheet. Sift the flour and allspice into a bowl. Add the butter and rub it in until the mixture resembles bread crumbs. Stir in the sugar, cherries, and golden raisins.

2 Break the egg into a bowl and whisk in the milk. Pour most of the egg mixture into the dry ingredients and mix with a fork to make a stiff, coarse dough, adding the rest of the egg and milk, if necessary.

3 Using 2 forks, pile the mixture into 10 rocky heaps on the prepared cookie sheet. Sprinkle with raw sugar. Bake in the oven for 10–15 minutes, or until golden and firm to the touch. Let cool on the cookie sheet for 2 minutes, then transfer to a wire rack to cool completely.

hazelnut chocolate crunch

ingredients

MAKES 12

1/2 cup unsalted butter,
    plus extra for greasing
generous 2 cups rolled oats
1/3 cup hazelnuts, lightly
    toasted and chopped
generous 1/3 cup all-purpose
    flour
scant 1/2 cup light brown sugar
2 tbsp corn syrup
1/3 cup bittersweet chocolate
    chips

method

1 Preheat the oven to 350°F/180°C. Mix the oats, nuts, and flour in a large bowl.

2 Place the butter, sugar, and syrup in a large pan and heat gently until the sugar has dissolved. Pour in the dry ingredients and mix well. Stir in the chocolate chips.

3 Turn the mixture into a greased 9-inch/23-cm shallow, square baking pan and bake in the preheated oven for 20–25 minutes, or until golden brown and firm to the touch. Using a knife, mark into 12 rectangles and let cool in the pan. Cut the hazelnut chocolate crunch bars with a sharp knife before carefully removing them from the pan.

caramel chocolate shortbread

ingredients

MAKES 12

¹/₂ cup unsalted butter,
    plus extra for greasing
scant 1¹/₄ cups all-purpose
    flour
¹/₄ cup superfine sugar

filling and topping
scant 1 cup butter
generous ¹/₂ cup superfine
    sugar
3 tbsp corn syrup
14 oz/400 g canned
    condensed milk
7 oz/200 g bittersweet
    chocolate, broken into
    pieces

method

1 Preheat the oven to 350°F/180°C. Place the butter, flour, and sugar in a food processor and process until they begin to bind together. Press the mixture into a greased 9-inch/ 23-cm shallow square cake pan lined with parchment paper and smooth the top. Bake in the preheated oven for 20–25 minutes, or until golden.

2 Meanwhile, make the filling. Place the butter, sugar, syrup, and condensed milk in a pan and heat gently until the sugar has dissolved. Bring to a boil and simmer for 6–8 minutes, stirring constantly, until the mixture becomes very thick. Remove the shortbread from the oven, then pour over the filling and chill in the refrigerator until firm.

3 To make the topping, melt the chocolate in a heatproof bowl set over a pan of gently simmering water. Remove from the heat and let cool slightly, then spread over the caramel. Chill in the refrigerator until set. Cut into 12 pieces with a sharp knife and serve.

chocolate coconut layers

ingredients

MAKES 9

8 oz/225 g chocolate graham
   crackers
6 tbsp unsalted butter or
   margarine, plus extra for
   greasing
scant 1 cup canned
   evaporated milk
1 egg, beaten
1 tsp vanilla extract
2 tbsp superfine sugar
scant 1/3 cup self-rising flour,
   sifted
scant 1 1/3 cups dry
   unsweetened coconut
1 3/4 oz/50 g semisweet
   chocolate (optional)

method

1 Preheat the oven to 375°F/190°C. Grease a shallow 20-cm/8-inch square cake pan and line the bottom with parchment paper.

2 Crush the crackers in a plastic bag with a rolling pin or process them in a food processor. Melt the butter in a pan and stir in the crushed crackers thoroughly. Remove from the heat and press the mixture into the bottom of the prepared cake pan.

3 In a separate bowl, beat together the evaporated milk, egg, vanilla, and sugar until smooth. Stir in the flour and coconut. Pour over the cracker layer and use a spatula to smooth the top.

4 Bake in the preheated oven for 30 minutes, or until the coconut topping has become firm and just golden. Remove from the oven and let cool in the cake pan for about 5 minutes, then cut into squares. Let cool completely in the pan.

5 Carefully remove the squares from the pan and place them on a cutting board. Melt the semisweet chocolate, if using, and drizzle it over the squares to decorate them. Let the chocolate set before serving.

pecan brownies

ingredients

MAKES 20

2¹/₂ oz/70 g bittersweet
    chocolate

scant 1 cup all-purpose flour

³/₄ tsp baking soda

¹/₄ tsp baking powder

¹/₃ cup pecans

1 cup unsalted butter,
    plus extra for greasing

¹/₂ cup raw sugar

¹/₂ tsp almond extract

1 egg

1 tsp milk

method

1 Preheat the oven to 350°F/180°C. Grease a large baking dish and line it with parchment paper.

2 Put the chocolate in a heatproof bowl set over a pan of gently simmering water and heat until it is melted. Meanwhile, sift together the flour, baking soda, and baking powder into a large bowl.

3 Finely chop the pecans and set aside. In a separate bowl, beat together the butter and sugar, then mix in the almond extract and the egg. Remove the chocolate from the heat and stir into the butter mixture. Add the flour mixture, milk, and chopped nuts to the bowl and stir until well combined.

4 Spoon the mixture into the prepared baking dish and smooth it. Transfer to the preheated oven and cook for 30 minutes, or until firm to the touch (it should still be a little soft in the center). Remove from the oven and let cool completely. Cut into 20 squares and serve.

carrot bars

ingredients

MAKES 14–16

corn oil, for oiling

3/4 cup unsalted butter

1/2 cup brown sugar

2 eggs, beaten

scant 1/2 cup self-rising
     whole wheat flour, sifted

1 tsp baking powder, sifted

1 tsp ground cinnamon, sifted

generous 1 1/8 cups ground
     almonds

4 oz/115 g carrot, coarsely
     grated

1/2 cup golden raisins

1/2 cup plumped dried
     apricots, finely chopped

1/3 cup toasted chopped
     hazelnuts

1 tbsp slivered almonds

method

1 Preheat the oven to 350°F/180°C. Lightly oil and line a 10 x 8-inch/25 x 20-cm shallow, rectangular baking pan with nonstick parchment paper.

2 Cream the butter and sugar together in a bowl until light and fluffy, then gradually beat in the eggs, adding a little flour after each addition.

3 Add all the remaining ingredients, except the slivered almonds. Spoon the mixture into the prepared pan and smooth the top. Sprinkle with the slivered almonds.

4 Bake in the preheated oven for 40 minutes, or until the mixture is cooked and a skewer inserted into the center comes out clean.

5 Remove from the oven and let cool in the pan. Remove from the pan, discard the lining paper, and cut into bars.

apple & cinnamon muffins

ingredients

MAKES 6

scant 2/3 cup all-purpose
   whole wheat flour
1/2 cup all-purpose white flour
1 1/2 tsp baking powder
pinch of salt
1 tsp ground cinnamon
scant 1/4 cup superfine sugar
2 small apples, peeled, cored,
   and finely chopped
1/2 cup milk
1 egg, beaten
4 tbsp butter, melted

topping

12 brown sugar lumps,
   coarsely crushed
1/2 tsp ground cinnamon

method

1 Preheat the oven to 400°F/200°C. Place 6 muffin paper liners in a muffin pan.

2 Sift both flours, baking powder, salt, and cinnamon together into a large bowl and stir in the sugar and chopped apples. Place the milk, egg, and butter in a separate bowl and mix. Add the wet ingredients to the dry ingredients and gently stir until just combined.

3 Divide the batter evenly among the paper liners. To make the topping, mix the crushed sugar lumps and cinnamon together and sprinkle over the muffins. Bake in the oven for 20–25 minutes, or until risen and golden. Remove the muffins from the oven and serve warm or place them on a cooling rack and let cool.

banana pecan muffins

ingredients

MAKES 8

generous 1 cup all-purpose
    flour
1¹/₂ tsp baking powder
pinch of salt
¹/₃ cup superfine sugar
1 cup shelled pecans, coarsely
    chopped
2 large ripe bananas, mashed
5 tbsp milk
2 tbsp butter, melted
1 large egg, beaten
¹/₂ tsp vanilla extract

method

1 Preheat the oven to 375°F/190°C. Place 8 muffin paper liners in a muffin pan. Sift the flour, baking powder, and salt into a bowl, add the sugar and pecans, and stir to combine.

2 Place the mashed bananas, milk, butter, egg, and vanilla extract in a separate bowl and mix together. Add the wet ingredients to the dry ingredients and gently stir until just combined.

3 Divide the batter evenly among the paper liners and bake in the oven for 20–25 minutes, until risen and golden. Remove the muffins from the oven, place them on a cooling rack, and let cool.

doughnut muffins

ingredients

MAKES 12

3/4 cup butter, softened,
   plus extra for greasing
1 cup superfine sugar
2 large eggs, lightly beaten
generous 2 1/2 cups all-purpose
   flour
3/4 tbsp baking powder
1/4 tsp baking soda
pinch of salt
1/2 tsp freshly grated nutmeg
generous 1 cup milk

topping
1/2 cup superfine sugar
1 tsp ground cinnamon
2 tbsp butter, melted

method

1 Preheat the oven to 350°F/180°C. Grease a deep 12-cup muffin pan. In a large bowl, beat the butter and sugar together until light and creamy. Add the eggs, a little at a time, beating well between additions.

2 Sift the flour, baking powder, baking soda, salt, and nutmeg together. Add half to the creamed mixture with half of the milk. Gently fold the ingredients together before incorporating the remaining flour and milk. Spoon the mixture into the prepared muffin pan, filling each hole to about two-thirds full. Bake for 15–20 minutes, or until the muffins are lightly brown and firm to the touch.

3 For the topping, mix the sugar and cinnamon together. While the muffins are still warm from the oven, brush lightly with melted butter and sprinkle over the cinnamon and sugar mixture. Eat warm or cold.

fudge nut muffins

ingredients

MAKES 12

generous 1¾ cups all-purpose
   flour
4 tsp baking powder
½ cup superfine sugar
6 tbsp crunchy peanut butter
1 large egg, beaten
4 tbsp butter, melted
¾ cup milk
5½ oz/150 g vanilla fudge,
   cut into small pieces
3 tbsp coarsely chopped
   unsalted peanuts

method

1 Preheat the oven to 400°F/200°C. Line a 12-cup muffin pan with double muffin paper liners. Sift the flour and baking powder into a bowl. Stir in the superfine sugar. Add the peanut butter and stir until the mixture resembles bread crumbs.

2 Place the egg, butter, and milk in a separate bowl and beat until blended, then stir into the dry ingredients until just blended. Lightly stir in the fudge pieces. Divide the batter evenly among the muffin liners.

3 Sprinkle the chopped peanuts on top and bake in the oven for 20–25 minutes, until well risen and firm to the touch. Remove the muffins from the oven and let cool for 2 minutes, then place them on a cooling rack to cool completely.

chocolate chip muffins

ingredients

MAKES 12

3 tbsp soft margarine

1 cup superfine sugar

2 large eggs

$2/3$ cup plain yogurt

5 tbsp milk

2 cups all-purpose flour

1 tsp baking soda

1 cup semisweet chocolate
  chips

method

1 Preheat the oven to 400°F/200°C. Line a 12-cup muffin pan with muffin paper liners.

2 Place the margarine and sugar in a mixing bowl and beat with a wooden spoon until light and fluffy. Beat in the eggs, yogurt, and milk until combined.

3 Sift the flour and baking soda into the batter. Stir until just blended.

4 Stir in the chocolate chips, then divide the batter evenly among the paper liners and bake in the oven for 25 minutes, or until risen and golden. Remove the muffins from the oven and let cool in the pan for 5 minutes, then place them on a cooling rack to cool completely.

moist walnut cupcakes

ingredients

MAKES 12

3/4 cup walnuts
4 tbsp butter, softened
1/2 cup superfine sugar
grated rind of 1/2 lemon
1/2 cup self-rising flour
2 eggs
12 walnut halves, to decorate

frosting

4 tbsp butter, softened
3/4 cup confectioners' sugar
grated rind of 1/2 lemon
1 tsp lemon juice

method

1 Preheat the oven to 375°F/190°C. Put 12 muffin paper liners in a muffin pan, or put 12 double-layer muffin paper liners on a baking sheet.

2 Put the walnuts in a food processor and, using a pulsating action, blend until finely ground, being careful not to overgrind, which will turn them to oil. Add the butter, cut into small pieces, along with the sugar, lemon rind, flour, and eggs, then blend until evenly mixed. Spoon the batter into the paper liners.

3 Bake the cupcakes in the preheated oven for 20 minutes, or until well risen and golden brown. Transfer to a wire rack and let cool.

4 To make the frosting, put the butter in a bowl and beat until fluffy. Sift in the confectioners' sugar, add the lemon rind and juice, and mix well together.

5 When the cupcakes are cold, spread the frosting on top of each cupcake and top with a walnut half to decorate.

frosted peanut butter cupcakes

ingredients

MAKES 16

4 tbsp butter, softened,
    or soft margarine
generous 1 1/8 cups light
    brown sugar
generous 1/3 cup crunchy
    peanut butter
2 eggs, lightly beaten
1 tsp vanilla extract
generous 1 1/2 cups all-purpose
    flour
2 tsp baking powder
generous 1/3 cup milk

frosting

scant 1 cup cream cheese
2 tbsp butter, softened
2 cups confectioners' sugar

method

1 Preheat the oven to 350°F/180°C. Put 16 muffin paper liners in a muffin pan.

2 Put the butter, sugar, and peanut butter in a bowl and beat together for 1–2 minutes, or until well mixed. Gradually add the eggs, beating well after each addition, then add the vanilla extract. Sift in the flour and baking powder and then, using a metal spoon, fold them into the mixture, alternating with the milk. Spoon the batter into the paper liners.

3 Bake the cupcakes in the preheated oven for 25 minutes, or until well risen and golden brown. Transfer to a wire rack and let cool.

4 To make the frosting, put the cream cheese and butter in a large bowl and, using an electric hand whisk, beat together until smooth. Sift the confectioners' sugar into the mixture, then beat together until well mixed.

5 When the cupcakes are cold, spread the frosting on top of each cupcake, swirling it with a round-bladed knife. Store the cupcakes in the refrigerator until ready to serve.

chocolate butterfly cakes

ingredients

MAKES 12

8 tbsp soft margarine

1/2 cup superfine sugar

generous 1 1/2 cups self-rising
flour

2 large eggs

2 tbsp unsweetened cocoa

1 oz/25 g semisweet
chocolate, melted

confectioners' sugar,
for dusting

filling

6 tbsp butter, softened

1 1/2 cups confectioners' sugar

1 oz/25 g semisweet
chocolate, melted

method

1 Preheat the oven to 350°F/180°C. Put
12 muffin paper liners in a muffin pan,
or put 12 double-layer paper liners on a
baking sheet.

2 Put the margarine, sugar, flour, eggs, and
cocoa in a large bowl and, using an electric
hand whisk, beat together until just smooth.
Beat in the melted chocolate. Spoon the
batter into the paper liners, filling them
three-quarters full.

3 Bake the cupcakes in the preheated oven
for 15 minutes, or until springy to the touch.
Transfer to a wire rack and let cool.

4 To make the filling, put the butter in a bowl
and beat until fluffy. Sift in the confectioners'
sugar and beat together until smooth. Add
the melted chocolate and beat together until
well mixed.

5 When the cupcakes are cold, use a serrated
knife to cut a circle from the top of each cake
and then cut each circle in half. Spread or
pipe a little of the filling into the center of
each cupcake and press the 2 semicircular
halves into it at an angle to resemble butterfly
wings. Dust with sifted confectioners' sugar
before serving.

marbled chocolate cupcakes

ingredients

MAKES 21

3/4 cup soft margarine

generous 3/4 cup superfine
   sugar

3 eggs

scant 1 1/4 cups self-rising flour

2 tbsp milk

2 oz/55 g semisweet
   chocolate, melted

method

1 Preheat the oven to 350°F/180°C. Put 21 muffin paper liners in a muffin pan, or put 21 double-layer paper liners on a baking sheet.

2 Put the margarine, sugar, eggs, flour, and milk in a large bowl and, using an electric hand whisk, beat together until just smooth.

3 Divide the batter between 2 bowls. Add the melted chocolate to one bowl and stir together until well mixed. Using a teaspoon, and alternating the chocolate batter with the plain batter, put 4 half-teaspoons into each paper liner.

4 Bake the cupcakes in the preheated oven for 20 minutes, or until well risen and springy to the touch. Transfer to a wire rack and let cool.

anchovies
linguine with anchovies, olives &
capers 390
linguine with bacon & olives 324
salad Niçoise 88
spaghetti with tuna & parlsey 388
tapenade 126
apples
apple & blackberry crumble 616
apple & cinnamon muffins 698
mackerel & potato salad 94
paper-thin fruit pies 620
toffee apple slices 666
apricots
baked apricots with honey 656
carrot bars 696
chicken tagine 234
artichoke paella 588
asparagus
pasta with green vegetables 568
risotto primavera 572
shrimp & asparagus risotto 460
stir-fried rice with green vegetables 494
tagliatelle with asparagus & Gorgonzola
sauce 552
avocados
avocado salad with lime dressing 56
chicken tacos from puebla 230
chile bean cakes with avocado salsa 114
guacamole 122
salmon & avocado salad 92

bacon
bacon-wrapped chicken burgers 232
linguine with bacon & olives 324
spaghetti alla carbonara 322
bamboo shoots
beef chop suey 258
beef stir-fry 264
Chinese vegetables & bean sprouts with
noodles 492
crispy spring rolls 110
ginger chicken with noodles 168
shrimp laksa 46
sweet-&-sour noodles with chicken 170
bananas
banana pecan muffins 700
banana-stuffed crepes 650
grilled bananas 662
mixed fruit salad 668
toffee bananas 664
bean sprouts
beef chow mein 268
beef stir-fry 264
chicken chow mein 152
Chinese vegetables & bean sprouts with
noodles 492
classic stir-fried vegetables 496
crispy spring rolls 110
egg fu yung 592
five-spice chicken with vegetables 160
Indonesian chicken salad 78
pad thai 338
pork lo mein 334
rice noodles with chicken, shrimp &
tofu 172
stir-fried beef with bean sprouts 272
stir-fried pork with vegetables 342
yaki soba 154

beans
chicken tacos from puebla 230
chile bean cakes with avocado salsa 114
falafel with tahini sauce 108
vegetarian paella 586
see also kidney beans
beef
beef chop suey 258
beef chow mein 268
beef skewers with orange & garlic 284
beef stir-fry 264
beef with fresh noodles 266
beef with onions & broccoli 270
broiled beef salad 80
egg-fried rice with seven-spice beef 280
Greek-style beef kebabs 282
grilled steak with tomatoes & garlic 256
hot beef & coconut curry 278
hot sesame beef 260
moussaka 298
mussaman curry 276
peppered beef salad 82
rice sticks with beef in black bean
sauce 262
spaghetti with meatballs 252
spicy beef & noodle soup 42
spicy beef with potato 274
stir-fried beef with bean sprouts 272
tagliatelle with a rich meat sauce 254
beets: Cajun chicken salad 74
bell peppers
Basque-style cod 404
beef stir-fry 264
broiled tuna & vegetable kebabs 384
charbroiled pepper salad 54
chicken fajitas 228
chile pork with tagliatelle 328
farfalle with chicken, broccoli & roasted
red bell peppers 136
jambalaya 242
linguine with lamb & bell pepper sauce 314
macaroni with sausage, pepperoncini &
olives 330
marinated lamb & vegetable kebabs 294
paella with pork & chorizo 358
pasta salad with charbroiled bell
peppers 64
penne with pepper & goat cheese
sauce 562
peppered beef salad 82
pepperoni pasta 326
provolone cheese & vegetable kebabs 540
red curry pork with bell peppers 336
rice sticks with beef in black bean
sauce 262
roasted monkfish 400
roasted red bell peppers 534
roasted summer vegetables 532
sausages with lentils 360
spaghetti with roasted garlic & bell pepper
sauce 564
Spanish swordfish stew 398
spicy Szechuan pork 346
sweet potato & mozzarella salad 68
Szechuan-style pork with bell pepper 348
vegetarian paella 586
blackberries
apple & blackberry crumble 616
summer dessert 644
warm fruit nests 622

bok choy
chicken with bok choy 164
chicken with vegetables & cilantro rice 246
sweet-&-sour vegetables with cashews 488
broccoli
beef chop suey 258
beef with onions & broccoli 270
chicken & broccoli soup 38
chicken with bok choy 164
chile broccoli pasta 554
classic stir-fried vegetables 496
farfalle with chicken, broccoli & roasted red
bell peppers 136
fusilli with monkfish & broccoli 402
hot sesame beef 260
pasta with green vegetables 568
spicy tofu 504
stir-fried pork with vegetables 342
sweet-&-sour vegetables with cashews 488
vegetable & noodle soup 32
butter cookies 682

capers
linguine with anchovies, olives &
capers 390
salmon steaks with green sauce 374
skate in mustard & caper sauce 418
swordfish with olives & capers 396
tapenade 126
carrots
carrot & pumpkin curry 522
carrot bars 696
vegetable rösti 106
cashew nuts
broiled beef salad 80
cauliflower & beans with cashews 508
chicken, mushroom & cashew risotto 238
chicken with cashew nuts 148
shrimp, snow peas & cashew nuts 454
sweet-&-sour vegetables with cashews 488
cauliflower & beans with cashews 508
celeriac, chestnut, spinach & feta filo pies 528
cheese
bacon-wrapped chicken burgers 232
chicken pinwheels with bleu cheese &
herbs 196
chicken rolls with cheese & pine nuts 198
corn, potato & cheese soup 30
crunchy walnut risotto 580
fusilli with monkfish & broccoli 402
pasta salad with nuts & Gorgonzola 70
pesto & ricotta chicken with tomato
vinaigrette 204
pork tenderloin with fennel 320
provolone cheese & vegetable kebabs 540
risotto with four cheeses 578
roasted red bell peppers 534
stuffed portobello mushrooms 538
tagliatelle with asparagus & Gorgonzola
sauce 552
see also feta cheese; goat cheese;
mascarpone cheese; mozzarella;
Parmesan cheese
cherry & golden raisin rockies 686
**chestnuts: celeriac, chestnut, spinach &
feta filo pies 528**
chicken
bacon-wrapped chicken burgers 232
balti chicken 174
Cajun chicken salad 74

chicken & broccoli soup 38
chicken & duck paella with orange 240
chicken & ginger stir-fry 162
chicken & pasta broth 36
chicken & peanut curry 184
chicken & tarragon soup 40
chicken chow mein 152
chicken fajitas 228
chicken fried rice 150
chicken kebabs with yogurt sauce 220
chicken Kiev 200
chicken, mushroom & cashew risotto 238
chicken pasanda 176
chicken pinwheels with bleu cheese &
    herbs 196
chicken risotto with saffron 236
chicken rolls with cheese & pine nuts 198
chicken satay 222
chicken tacos from puebla 230
chicken tagine 234
chicken with basil & pine nut pesto 134
chicken with bok choy 164
chicken with cashew nuts 148
chicken with garlic 216
chicken with goat cheese & basil 210
chicken with saffron mash 206
chicken with vegetables & cilantro rice 246
chicken with walnut sauce 212
chicken with yellow curry sauce 166
creamy chicken curry with lemon rice 182
egg-fried rice with chicken 244
farfalle with chicken, broccoli & roasted red
    bell peppers 136
fettuccine with chicken & onion cream
    sauce 138
five-spice chicken with vegetables 160
fruity chicken fusilli 144
ginger chicken with noodles 168
gingered chicken kebabs 224
gong bau chicken 156
green chicken curry 186
grilled chicken with lemon 192
Indonesian chicken salad 78
jambalaya 242
lemongrass chicken skewers 218
lime chicken with mint 190
Moroccan chicken 226
paella with pork & chorizo 358
paprika chicken on a bed of onions &
    ham 214
pasta with chicken & feta 142
pesto & ricotta chicken with tomato
    vinaigrette 204
red hot chili chicken 180
rice noodles with chicken, shrimp &
    tofu 172
roasted chicken with sun-blush tomato
    pesto 202
shredded chicken & mixed mushrooms 158
spaghetti with parsley chicken 140
spiced cilantro chicken 188
spicy chicken salad 76
sticky lime chicken 194
sweet-&-sour chicken 146
sweet-&-sour noodles with chicken 170
tarragon chicken 208
Thai red chicken curry 178
yaki soba 154
chicken livers: tagliatelle with a rich meat
    sauce 254

chickpeas
    chicken tagine 234
    chickpea curry 516
    falafel with tahini sauce 108
    lamb stew with chickpeas 306
    spinach with chickpeas 514
chiles
    balti chicken 174
    chicken & ginger stir-fry 162
    chicken pasanda 176
    chile bean cakes with avocado salsa 114
    chile broccoli pasta 554
    chile pork with tagliatelle 328
    chiles stuffed with fish paste 424
    creamy chicken curry with lemon rice 182
    gong bau chicken 156
    guacamole 122
    hot pepper lamb in red wine risotto 312
    peppered beef salad 82
    red hot chili chicken 180
    Sicilian tuna 382
    spiced steamed fish 428
    spicy scallops with lime & chile 472
    sweet chile squid 478
    Thai red chicken curry 178
    Thai tofu cakes with chile dip 112
Chinese cabbage
    Chinese vegetables & bean sprouts with
        noodles 492
    crisp noodle & vegetable stir-fry 490
chocolate
    cappuccino soufflés 606
    caramel chocolate shortbread 690
    chocolate brandy torte 646
    chocolate butterfly cakes 712
    chocolate chip muffins 706
    chocolate coconut layers 692
    chocolate fondue 672
    chocolate mousse 634
    chocolate tartlets 626
    chocolate temptations 674
    chocolate trifle 636
    coffee panna cotta with chocolate
        sauce 642
    double chocolate chip cookies 676
    exotic fruit chocolate crepes 652
    hazelnut chocolate crunch 688
    individual molten chocolate cakes 610
    Irish cream cheesecake 648
    marbled chocolate cupcakes 714
    tiramisu 638
    white chocolate mousse 632
clams
    Catalan fish stew 434
    quick clam chowder 50
    spaghetti with clams 462
coconut
    beef with onions & broccoli 270
    chicken & peanut curry 184
    chicken with vegetables & cilantro rice 246
    chocolate coconut layers 692
    corn & crab soup 48
    creamy chicken curry with lemon rice 182
    egg-fried rice with chicken 244
    fish curry with rice noodles 436
    fish in coconut 438
    green chicken curry 186
    hot beef & coconut curry 278
    lamb with lime leaves 288
    mussaman curry 276

red curry pork with bell peppers 336
red lamb curry 286
shrimp laksa 46
spiced cilantro chicken 188
Thai red chicken curry 178
vegetable & coconut curry 512
vegetable & noodle soup 32
cod
    Basque-style cod 404
    cod with catalan spinach 406
    fish curry with rice noodles 436
    Italian fish 408
    seafood paella with lemon & herbs 440
coffee
    cappuccino soufflés 606
    coffee panna cotta with chocolate
        sauce 642
    sticky coffee & walnut sponges 608
    tiramisu 638
corn
    baby corn with dal 524
    chicken fried rice 150
    chicken with bok choy 164
    chicken with yellow curry sauce 166
    classic stir-fried vegetables 496
    corn & crab soup 48
    corn, potato & cheese soup 30
    jambalaya 242
    mixed vegetables with quick-fried basil 506
    sour & spicy pork 354
    stir-fried lamb with mint 290
    stir-fried pork with vegetables 342
crabmeat: corn & crab soup 48

doughnut muffins 702

duck: chicken & duck paella with orange 240

eggplants
    chicken tagine 234
    eggplant & bean curry 510
    eggplant dip 124
    eggplant gratin 530
    gingered chicken kebabs 224
    lamb with eggplant & black olive sauce 302
    moussaka 298
    roasted monkfish 400
    roasted summer vegetables 532
    sweet potato & mozzarella salad 68
    Thai red chicken curry 178
    vegetarian paella 586
eggs
    deviled eggs 116
    egg-fried rice with chicken 244
    egg-fried rice with peas 594
    egg-fried rice with seven-spice beef 280
    egg-fried rice with vegetables & crispy
        onions 596
    egg fu yung 592
    five-spice crispy pork with egg-fried
        rice 350
    salad Niçoise 88
    seafood omelet 448
    spaghetti alla carbonara 322
    spinach & mushroom tortilla 600
    zabaglione 612

fava beans
    eggplant & bean curry 510
    fava bean & mint soup 26
    Moorish fava bean dip 128

pork with mixed green beans 344
vegetable & bean soup 16
fennel
orange & fennel salad 58
pork tenderloin with fennel 320
pork with fennel & juniper 318
roast sea bream with fennel 422
roasted summer vegetables 532
Sicilian tuna 382
stuffed portobello mushrooms 538
feta cheese
celeriac, chestnut, spinach & feta filo
pies 528
Greek salad 60
green bean salad with feta cheese 52
pasta with chicken & feta 142
stuffed zucchini with walnuts & feta 536
sweet potato, mint & feta rösti 104
zucchini fritters with yogurt dip 102
figs
broiled honeyed figs with sabayon 660
mixed antipasto meat platter 84
Parma ham & figs 86
fish & seafood
broiled red snapper with garlic 426
Catalan fish stew 434
chiles stuffed with fish paste 424
fish curry with rice noodles 436
fish in coconut 438
fish parcels with fresh herbs 412
fishermen's soup 44
hake in white wine 414
mackerel & potato salad 94
Marseilles-style fish stew 432
nut-crusted halibut 410
rice with seafood & squid 442
roast sea bream with fennel 422
seafood paella with lemon & herbs 440
skate in mustard & caper sauce 418
sole à la meunière 416
spiced steamed fish 428
sweet-&-sour sea bass 420
trout in lemon & red wine sauce 430
see also clams; cod; monkfish; mussels;
salmon; sardines; scallops; shrimp;
squid; swordfish; tuna

ginger
chicken & ginger stir-fry 162
ginger chicken with noodles 168
ginger shrimp with oyster mushrooms 452
gingered chicken kebabs 224
gingersnaps 680
peach & preserved ginger tarte tatin 618
tuna & tomato salad with ginger
dressing 90
goat cheese
chicken with goat cheese & basil 210
penne with pepper & goat cheese
sauce 562
warm red lentil salad with goat cheese 72
green beans
cauliflower & beans with cashews 508
crisp noodle & vegetable stir-fry 490
eggplant & bean curry 510
green bean salad with feta cheese 52
pork hash 364
pork with mixed green beans 344
risotto primavera 572

salad Niçoise 88
vegetable & bean soup 16
hake in white wine 414
ham
mixed antipasto meat platter 84
pan-fried pork with mozzarella 316
paprika chicken on a bed of onions &
ham 214
Parma ham & figs 86
rigatoni with ham, tomato & chile
sauce 332
honey
baked apricots with honey 656
pears in honey syrup 654
walnut pastries 624

kidney beans
baked portobello mushrooms 598
chicken & duck paella with orange 240
kidney bean risotto 582

lamb
Grecian meatballs 296
hot pepper lamb in red wine risotto 312
lamb skewers with lemon 292
lamb stew with chickpeas 306
lamb with balsamic & rosemary
marinade 300
lamb with eggplant & black olive sauce 302
lamb with lime leaves 288
lamb with zucchini & tomatoes 304
linguine with lamb & yellow pepper
sauce 314
marinated lamb & vegetable kebabs 294
red lamb curry 286
stir-fried lamb with mint 290
Xinjiang lamb casserole 310
Xinjiang rice pot with lamb 308
leek & potato soup 22
lemons
broiled sardines with lemon sauce 392
creamy chicken curry with lemon rice 182
fish parcels with fresh herbs 412
fresh sardines baked with lemon &
oregano 394
grilled chicken with lemon 192
lamb skewers with lemon 292
saffron & lemon risotto with scallops 468
Sicilian tuna 382
sole à la meunière 416
lentils
baby corn with dal 524
brown lentil & pasta soup 18
brown rice vegetable pilaf 590
lentil & rice casserole 526
lentil bolognese 542
sausages with lentils 360
sweet potato curry with lentils 518
warm red lentil salad with goat cheese 72
limes
avocado salad with lime dressing 56
lime chicken with mint 190
lime-drizzled shrimp 118
spicy scallops with lime & chile 472
sticky lime chicken 194

mackerel & potato salad 94
mangoes
Cajun chicken salad 74
chocolate fondue 672

creamy mango brûlée 628
exotic fruit chocolate crepes 652
fruity chicken fusilli 144
steamed spiced exotic fruits 670
mascarpone cheese
chocolate brandy torte 646
creamy mango brûlée 628
exotic fruit chocolate crepes 652
mascarpone creams 640
tiramisu 638
melon
mixed antipasto meat platter 84
mixed fruit salad 668
mint
fava bean & mint soup 26
lime chicken with mint 190
minted green risotto 576
Moorish fava bean dip 128
stir-fried lamb with mint 290
sweet potato, mint & feta rösti 104
monkfish
fish curry with rice noodles 436
fusilli with monkfish & broccoli 402
roasted monkfish 400
mozzarella
eggplant gratin 530
pan-fried pork with mozzarella 316
sweet potato & mozzarella salad 68
three-color salad 66
mushrooms
baked portobello mushrooms 598
beef chop suey 258
beef with fresh noodles 266
chicken chow mein 152
chicken, mushroom & cashew risotto 238
classic stir-fried vegetables 496
creamy spinach & mushroom pasta 558
curried noodles with shrimp & straw
mushrooms 456
fettuccine with scallops & porcini 466
ginger shrimp with oyster mushrooms 452
hot-&-sour soup 34
kidney bean risotto 582
linguine with bacon & olives 324
mushroom stroganoff 544
oyster mushrooms & vegetables with
peanut chile sauce 498
penne in a creamy mushroom sauce 560
pork lo mein 334
provolone cheese & vegetable kebabs 540
sautéed garlic mushrooms 100
shredded chicken & mixed mushrooms 158
spinach & mushroom tortilla 600
stuffed portobello mushrooms 538
sweet-&-sour sea bass 420
wild mushroom risotto 574
mussels
Catalan fish stew 434
tagliatelle & mussels with white wine, garlic
& parsley 464

noodles
beef chow mein 268
beef with fresh noodles 266
chicken chow mein 152
Chinese vegetables & bean sprouts with
noodles 492
crisp noodle & vegetable stir-fry 490
curried noodles with shrimp & straw
mushrooms 456

fish curry with rice noodles 435
ginger chicken with noodles 168
hoisin pork with garlic noodles 352
hot-&-sour soup 34
pad thai 338
pork lo mein 334
rice noodles with chicken, shrimp & tofu 172
sour & spicy pork 354
spicy beef & noodle soup 42
sweet-&-sour noodles with chicken 170
vegetable & noodle soup 32
yaki soba 154
nuts
    almond biscotti 684
    banana pecan muffins 700
    carrot bars 696
    chocolate temptations 674
    hazelnut chocolate crunch 688
    nut-crusted halibut 410
    oat & pecan cookies 678
    pecan brownies 694
    see also cashew nuts; peanuts; walnuts

oats
    hazelnut chocolate crunch 688
    oat & pecan cookies 678
olives
    deviled eggs 116
    Greek salad 60
    lamb with eggplant & black olive sauce 302
    linguine with anchovies, olives & capers 390
    linguine with bacon & olives 324
    macaroni with sausage, pepperoncini & olives 330
    swordfish with olives & capers 396
    tapenade 126
oranges
    beef skewers with orange & garlic 284
    chicken & duck paella with orange 240
    mixed fruit salad 668
    orange & fennel salad 58
    pork with fennel & juniper 318

papaya
    mixed fruit salad 668
    shrimp & papaya salad 96
Parmesan cheese
    chicken Kiev 200
    eggplant gratin 530
    fettuccine alfredo 548
    spaghetti alla carbonara 322
pasta
    brown lentil & pasta soup 18
    chicken & pasta broth 36
    chicken with basil & pine nut pesto 134
    chile broccoli pasta 554
    chile pork with tagliatelle 328
    creamy spinach & mushroom pasta 558
    farfalle with chicken, broccoli & roasted red bell peppers 136
    fettuccine alfredo 548
    fettuccine with chicken & onion cream sauce 138
    fettuccine with scallops & porcini 466
    fruity chicken fusilli 144
    fusilli with hot Cajun seafood sauce 446
    fusilli with monkfish & broccoli 402
    fusilli with zucchini, lemon & rosemary 566

linguine with anchovies, olives & capers 390
linguine with bacon & olives 324
linguine with lamb & bell pepper sauce 314
linguine with smoked salmon & arugula 378
macaroni with sausage, pepperoncini & olives 330
pasta salad with charbroiled bell peppers 64
pasta salad with nuts & gorgonzola 70
pasta with chicken & feta 142
pasta with green vegetables 568
pasta with pesto 556
penne in a creamy mushroom sauce 560
penne with pepper & goat cheese sauce 562
penne with squid & tomatoes 476
pepperoni pasta 326
rigatoni with ham, tomato & chile sauce 332
spaghetti alla carbonara 322
spaghetti olio e aglio 546
spaghetti with clams 462
spaghetti with meatballs 252
spaghetti with parsley chicken 140
spaghetti with roasted garlic & bell pepper sauce 564
spaghetti with shrimp 444
spaghetti with tomato, garlic & basil sauce 550
spaghetti with tuna & parsley 388
tagliatelle & mussels with white wine, garlic & parsley 464
tagliatelle with a rich meat sauce 254
tagliatelle with asparagus & Gorgonzola sauce 552
peaches
    baked stuffed peaches 658
    peach & preserved ginger tarte tatin 618
    peach cobbler 614
peanuts
    chicken & peanut curry 184
    chicken satay 222
    chile pork with tagliatelle 328
    frosted peanut butter cupcakes 710
    fudge nut muffins 704
    gong bau chicken 156
    Indonesian chicken salad 78
    mussaman curry 276
    oyster mushrooms & vegetables with peanut chile sauce 498
    pad thai 338
    pork with mixed green beans 344
    rice noodles with chicken, shrimp & tofu 172
    stir-fried beef with bean sprouts 272
    Thai red chicken curry 178
pears in honey syrup 654
peas
    chicken fried rice 150
    egg-fried rice with peas 594
    jambalaya 242
    minted green risotto 576
    pasta with green vegetables 568
    risotto primavera 572
pesto
    chicken with basil & pine nut pesto 134
    pasta with pesto 556
    pesto & ricotta chicken with tomato vinaigrette 204
    potato & pesto soup 24
    roasted chicken with sun-blush tomato pesto 202

pine nuts
    chicken rolls with cheese & pine nuts 198
    chicken with basil & pine nut pesto 134
    risotto with tuna & pine nuts 386
pineapple
    chicken & peanut curry 184
    chocolate fondue 672
    Indonesian chicken salad 78
    mixed fruit salad 668
    spareribs in a sweet-&-sour sauce 356
    spiced tuna in sweet-&-sour sauce 380
pork
    chile pork with tagliatelle 328
    five-spice crispy pork with egg-fried rice 350
    hoisin pork with garlic noodles 352
    pad thai 338
    paella with pork & chorizo 358
    pan-fried pork with mozzarella 316
    pork hash 364
    pork lo mein 334
    pork tenderloin with fennel 320
    pork with fennel & juniper 318
    pork with mixed green beans 344
    red curry pork with bell peppers 336
    sour & spicy pork 354
    spareribs in a sweet-&-sour sauce 356
    spicy fried ground pork 340
    spicy Szechuan pork 346
    stir-fried pork with vegetables 342
    Szechuan-style pork with bell pepper 348
potatoes
    chicken with saffron mash 206
    corn, potato & cheese soup 30
    herby potato salad 62
    Indonesian chicken salad 78
    leek & potato soup 22
    mackerel & potato salad 94
    potato & pesto soup 24
    potato & spinach gnocchi 570
    potato & spinach yellow curry 520
    salmon & avocado salad 92
    spicy beef with potato 274
    spicy chicken salad 76
    Thai potato stir-fry 500
pumpkin: carrot & pumpkin curry 522

raspberries
    steamed spiced exotic fruits 670
    summer dessert 644
    warm fruit nests 622
rice
    artichoke paella 588
    black rice 482
    brown rice vegetable pilaf 590
    chicken & duck paella with orange 240
    chicken fried rice 150
    chicken, mushroom & cashew risotto 238
    chicken risotto with saffron 236
    chicken with vegetables & cilantro rice 246
    creamy chicken curry with lemon rice 182
    crunchy walnut risotto 580
    egg-fried rice with chicken 244
    egg-fried rice with peas 594
    egg-fried rice with seven-spice beef 280
    egg-fried rice with vegetables & crispy onions 596
    egg fu yung 592
    five-spice crispy pork with egg-fried rice 350

hot pepper lamb in red wine risotto 312
jambalaya 242
kidney bean risotto 582
lentil & rice casserole 526
minted green risotto 576
paella with pork & chorizo 358
pork hash 364
red wine, herb & sun-dried tomato
    risotto 584
rice with seafood & squid 442
risotto primavera 572
risotto with four cheeses 578
risotto with tuna & pine nuts 386
saffron & lemon risotto with scallops 468
sausage & rosemary risotto 362
seafood paella with lemon & herbs 440
shrimp & asparagus risotto 460
shrimp pilaf 458
Spanish-style rice pudding 630
stir-fried rice with green vegetables 494
vegetarian paella 586
wild mushroom risotto 574
Xinjiang rice pot with lamb 308
rice sticks with beef in black bean sauce 262

saffron
chicken risotto with saffron 236
chicken with saffron mash 206
saffron & lemon risotto with scallops 468
salmon
fish curry with rice noodles 436
linguine with smoked salmon &
    arugula 378
pan-fried spiced salmon 372
rice with seafood & squid 442
roast salmon with lemon & herbs 370
salmon & avocado salad 92
salmon steaks with green sauce 374
salmon with red curry in banana leaves 376
sardines
broiled sardines with lemon sauce 392
fresh sardines baked with lemon &
    oregano 394
sausages
lamb stew with chickpeas 306
macaroni with sausage, pepperoncini &
    olives 330
paella with pork & chorizo 358
pepperoni pasta 326
sausage & rosemary risotto 362
sausages with lentils 360
scallops
fettuccine with scallops & porcini 466
fusilli with hot Cajun seafood sauce 446
saffron & lemon risotto with scallops 468
scallops with bread crumbs & parsley 474
simple stir-fried scallops 470
spicy scallops with lime & chile 472
shrimp
black rice 482
Catalan fish stew 434
curried noodles with shrimp & straw
    mushrooms 456
fish in coconut 438
fusilli with hot Cajun seafood sauce 446
ginger shrimp with oyster mushrooms 452
lime-drizzled shrimp 118
Marseilles-style fish stew 432
pad thai 338
paella with pork & chorizo 358

paprika shrimp 450
rice noodles with chicken, shrimp &
    tofu 172
seafood omelet 448
seafood paella with lemon & herbs 440
shrimp & asparagus risotto 460
shrimp & papaya salad 96
shrimp cocktail 98
shrimp laksa 46
shrimp pilaf 458
shrimp, snow peas & cashew nuts 454
spaghetti with shrimp 444
yaki soba 154
skate in mustard & caper sauce 418
snow peas
beef chop suey 258
pasta with green vegetables 568
rice noodles with chicken, shrimp &
    tofu 172
shrimp, snow peas & cashew nuts 454
sole à la meunière 416
spinach
celeriac, chestnut, spinach & feta filo
    pies 528
cod with catalan spinach 406
creamy spinach & mushroom pasta 558
minted green risotto 576
potato & spinach gnocchi 570
potato & spinach yellow curry 520
spicy beef with potato 274
spinach & mushroom tortilla 600
spinach with chickpeas 514
squid
black rice 482
calamares 120
fish in coconut 438
Marseilles-style fish stew 432
penne with squid & tomatoes 476
rice with seafood & squid 442
seafood paella with lemon & herbs 440
stir-fried squid with hot black bean
    sauce 480
sweet chile squid 478
strawberries
chocolate fondue 672
exotic fruit chocolate crepes 652
sweet potatoes
sweet potato & mozzarella salad 68
sweet potato curry with lentils 518
sweet potato, mint & feta rösti 104
vegetable rösti 106
swordfish
Spanish swordfish stew 398
swordfish with olives & capers 396

tofu
rice noodles with chicken, shrimp &
    tofu 172
spicy tofu 504
Thai tofu cakes with chile dip 112
tofu & green vegetable curry 502
tomatoes
broiled tuna & vegetable kebabs 384
Greek salad 60
grilled steak with tomatoes & garlic 256
herby potato salad 62
hot pepper lamb in red wine risotto 312
jambalaya 242
lamb with zucchini & tomatoes 304
lentil & rice casserole 526

lentil bolognese 542
linguine with anchovies, olives &
    capers 390
penne with squid & tomatoes 476
pepperoni pasta 326
pesto & ricotta chicken with tomato
    vinaigrette 204
pork hash 364
red wine, herb & sun-dried tomato
    risotto 584
rigatoni with ham, tomato & chile
    sauce 332
roasted chicken with sun-blush tomato
    pesto 202
spaghetti with tomato, garlic & basil
    sauce 550
three-color salad 66
tuna & tomato salad with ginger
    dressing 90
vegetarian paella 586
yogurt & tomato soup 28
tuna
broiled tuna & vegetable kebabs 384
risotto with tuna & pine nuts 386
salad Niçoise 88
seafood omelet 448
Sicilian tuna 382
spaghetti with tuna & parsley 388
spiced tuna in sweet-&-sour sauce 380
tuna & tomato salad with ginger
    dressing 90

walnuts
chicken with walnut sauce 212
crunchy walnut risotto 580
double chocolate chip cookies 676
moist walnut cupcakes 708
pasta salad with nuts & gorgonzola 70
sticky coffee & walnut sponges 608
stuffed zucchini with walnuts & feta 536
walnut pastries 624
water chestnuts
beef chop suey 258
Chinese vegetables & bean sprouts with
    noodles 492
classic stir-fried vegetables 496
hot-&-sour soup 34
mixed vegetables with quick-fried basil 506
red lamb curry 286
watercress soup 20

yogurt
chicken kebabs with yogurt sauce 220
yogurt & tomato soup 28
zucchini fritters with yogurt dip 102

zucchini
crisp noodle & vegetable stir-fry 490
fusilli with zucchini, lemon & rosemary 566
gingered chicken kebabs 224
lamb with zucchini & tomatoes 304
marinated lamb & vegetable kebabs 294
pasta with green vegetables 568
provolone cheese & vegetable kebabs 540
risotto primavera 572
roasted summer vegetables 532
stuffed zucchini with walnuts & feta 536
vegetable & bean soup 16
vegetable rösti 106
zucchini fritters with yogurt dip 102